IN DEFENSE OF SKA

AARON CARNES

CL◢SH

Copyright © 2021 by Aaron Carnes

Cover design by Matthew Revert

Cover photo by Cam Evans; Artwork by Ken Davis; Concept by Aaron Carnes, Amy Bee and Adam Davis

ISBN: 978-1-944866-78-5

CLASH Books

Troy, NY

clashbooks.com

This book is dedicated to Alex, Mike, Rudy, Geoff and Seth.
Let's go out and eat a boneyard.

CONTENTS

FOREWORD BY JEFF ROSENSTOCK

First things first. The argument that "ska is bad" is boring. Taking a cheap shot at an easy target is wack as fuck and generalizing a multigenerational globe-spanning movement is a pretty antiquated way to be, bud. So kindly shut the hell up with that immediately, thanks. Sorry. Sorry to come out of the gate bitter in the *forward* of a book that has no shortage of its own vengeful clapbacks at the doubters of ska.

Okay. You got me. "The doubters of ska" is a pretty ridiculous way to frame it. But come on, it's also pretty ridiculous for the entirety of ska to have been declared **NO GOOD** by cultural gatekeepers and tastemakers across the board. For decades they have actively shit on a genre that has its roots in working-class rebellion and racial unity and evolved to create space for anxious outcasts who feel better when they slap on a dinosaur costume and play music with their friends, as a crowd of their peers toss around an inflatable pool toy and sing along to songs about tacos or some shit. The best of ska music has always been held fast to the ethos that everyone is included.

In this book, Aaron Carnes traverses the many eras of ska and punk/ska across the world. As a fan, I was excited to read about bands I grew up loving, driving their vans to shows in bumfuck towns, sleeping on floors, and waking up to do it again the next day. Reading this also introduced me to a bunch of bands I had never heard of, which surprised me 'cause I feel like I'm pretty well-versed. It's deep-ass lore, jumbo-sized bands meeting other jumbo-sized bands in sister cities, forming a familial bond through the power of music. This was the book I never knew I was waiting for. It's like no other music history retrospective I've ever read. It holds nothing but ska—the most disregarded genre of music—in regard. And it doesn't hold back any punches.

However, my personal touchstones of punk/ska feel like they were mostly left out.

In 1997, probably, my friends and I saw Minneapolis band Animal Chin play a show at the Deja One catering hall in Long Island, and our lives were forever changed. I can't articulate how captivating Animal Chin were on stage. I assumed they were a huge band, but their CDs weren't available at Nobody Beats The Wiz like the other ska bands I knew. I listened to *All The Kids Agree* endlessly. Our small circle of friends continued to find local punk/ska bands in a five-hour radius that blew us away with their maxed-out live energy. In Long Island, there were several eight-band bills every weekend, and everyone showed up early to hang out and dance all day. Pretty sick if you're a teen whose idea of fun isn't drinking Bud Lights in the bowling alley parking lot.

Fellow north-easterners Big D and the Kids Table, Kicked in the Head, Catch 22, and Day 19 would play these shows where sweat was dripping from the VFW hall ceiling at the end of the night. When I started touring, my band met up Jackmove, Murphy's Kids and Neighborhood Friendly from Virginia, or The Know How and Bum Ruckus from Florida. All of them were rocking the fuck out in any room that would have them. In Lafayette, Louisiana—a city I had never even heard of—Odd Arnie were playing bars and people were cutting fucking loose. From a fan's perspective, I want 1,000 words devoted to Against All Authority! The fact that these bands are mostly absent from this book isn't really an oversight; it's more of a testament to the enormity of the ska scene. There's not enough time to get to it all and there's always more to discover. Shit, there's a chapter in here about my band and I feel like we didn't even get half the members in—shout out to Chris Valentino, Steve Connolly, Eric Buccello, and that guy Dan who played bari sax with us one time. The community is just huge.

So, OF FUCKING COURSE a grand musical environment anchored in acceptance, DIY-ethics, and uncontrollable chaos was never really going to get a gold star from label execs or pretentious pundits. It's a lot easier to sell a good-lookin', well-dressed singer who carefully sticks to a plan than seven overweight kids in Hawaiian shirts who love to goof real hard. Dissing ska also helps add to the problematic (and profitable!) power dynamics of rock star celebrity musicians as idols and heroes. Ska invites even the lamest lamer to participate and often aims to take down the barrier between the audience and performer. Lyrically, it regularly speaks to depression and the idea that the systems you are raised to believe in are actually holding you down. You can't make money on all that!!!

Yet, ska keeps going, cowardly music press, too-cool punx, and shaming from the industry aside. Ska continues to provide a home for the weirdos of the world, as you will find throughout the pages of this book. It doesn't get love from elitist critics which, in my opinion, makes ska actual outsider art. And by outsider art, I don't mean think pieces that either drive you to repulsion, confusion, or boredom— ya know, the kind of "outsider" art that mainstream critics love to look at and say "hmmm... now that's art." I'm talking about art made by outsiders of the social ruling class, which doesn't preclude it from being danceable, catchy, and, on occasion, smart. No one is feigning an understanding of what's going on at a ska show. Everybody knows what's going on. It fucking rocks.

So huck yer lil' negative connotations of ska into the fuckin' trash where they belong, take a deep breath, and allow yourself to reapproach the genre as the underdog that gets kicked while it's down on the ground but keeps on getting back up.

Or don't. Ska don't care.

FIRST THINGS FIRST...

I love ska. Unabashedly.

I've written about music in one form or another for the last ten years. I rarely write about ska. Magazines and newspapers aren't interested. Sure, Hard Times likes a sorry/not sorry satirical ska skewer every now and again. But *serious* outlets say no thank you, probably to keep their own secret ska lives safely hidden from judgmental eyes.

Other subgenres don't suffer this degree of abandonment from the industry. Some of the most obscure sub-sub-genres of music have been discovered, dusted off, and refurbished with a nice new sheen of esteem and a heavy layer of nostalgia. I once flipped through a book where the author wrote gorgeous prose about the lawless, violent, bloody shows of bay area thrash in the '80s, and thought, "*This* is more respected than ska?"

Every ska fan has *the* moment. They're bopping along, listening to R.E.M. or Death Grips, just having a nice orderly life. Their musical proclivities are safe and predictable. *Pitchfork* certified. Then they meet a horn player who takes them to a show. A *ska* show. And just like that: ska fan for life. For me, the moment was in 1992 and the show was Skankin' Pickle. Later I started my own ska band, Flat Planet. We toured, we released music, we had the time of our lives. And now I return the favor by writing everything I ever wanted to say about ska that was unsuited for mainstream tastes.

Flat Planet Practice Room

This is not by any means a complete history of ska. I make no claim to give every key ska musician a voice or to tell a complete story of ska's evolution over a specific time frame. This book explores what it means to love ska—the most maligned genre of music that everyone else hates with a passion. Ska fans deserve a seat at the big kids table alongside punk, metal, jazz, hip-hop and alternative rock.

Hopefully, this book will challenge your pre-conceived stereotypes about ska. If nothing else, I hope you can read it with an open mind and realize that you don't know jack about the genre you confidently hate. Maybe you'll even learn a few things in the process. Who knows, maybe you'll even give ska a chance. My editor did after the final edit of this book.

With that, I present to you my defense of ska.

Yours truly

A VERY BRIEF HISTORY OF SKA

Ska originated in the ghettos of West Kingston, Jamaica in the '50s; a bouncy, horn-driven dance music that mixed elements of jazz, the grittiest American rhythm and blues tracks, and traditional Jamaican folk music of the time known as mento. Its exact origins are unknown— even how it became known as "ska." If you asked ten Jamaican musicians from this era who invented ska, you'll hear ten different stories.

Ska music evolved alongside Jamaica's independence and growing national identity in the early '60s. Those early ska tracks are lo-fi, wonky and performed on often out-of-tune instruments. They're also some of the best, most danceable songs ever recorded. Several artists from this time period were unsung musical geniuses—like trombonist Don Drummond—and deserve the respect and reverence we give American jazz pioneers like Miles Davis and Dizzy Gillespie.

Over time ska evolved into rocksteady, and then reggae, which branched into the spiritual and politically-fervent roots reggae, with a slowed down tempo and deep bass. In this era, Jamaican music gained international traction and caught the ears of hippies, punks, and counterculture music lovers. But in late '70s England, ska resurfaced. Punks, skinheads, mods, and Caribbean immigrants revived the genre into a new, politically charged, punked-up form of the music we now refer to as 2 Tone ska. These bands (The Specials, The Selecter, English Beat, Madness) were mostly mixed with white and black

1

members, with short hair, and snappy suits, modeling their fashion after '60s Jamaican rude boy attire. England went full on 2 Tone fever in the spring of 1979 when the Specials released their debut single "Gangsters." 2 Tone bands surprisingly took over the British charts for almost two years.

The Selecter being interviewed backstage at the Lanchester Polytechnic in Coventry, UK, 1980

It was a season of pop music unlike any before or since. A handful of bands played a retro, punky, dance music, with very specific political messages aimed at the oppressive Thatcher government in England, and gave a big middle finger to the racist, right-wing fascist National Front party that was openly campaigning to remove immigrants from the country. And these bands were top 40! Pop has never been as exciting and poignant as it was in the 2 Tone years.

The Specials' Lynval Golding on the 2 Tone tour at the Top Rank Club in Sheffield, 1979

Over time the music spread globally. In the states, 2 Tone only managed to find a cult fanbase. But enough kids fell head over heels with the music that nearly every major city would have their own ska band by the late-80s. These bands drew massive crowds despite being completely off the radar. By the mid-90s, after a long decade and a half period in the underground, ska had a brief moment in the US pop culture machine, in-between grunge and the swing revival. This interval is often referred to as "third wave." Not a particularly great descriptor, as ska had a loyal and consistent audience since the 2 Tone bands revived it, complete with record labels, zines, and a well-established touring circuit. "Third wave" suggests a few bands in 1996 suddenly took a fancy to 'ol timey ska music, kind of like the swing revival.

Post-mainstream, ska became the most mocked, and humiliating music to affiliate with. But the music bullies did little to diminish its rabid cult fandom. Globally, its popularity has only grown. Not only did several countries develop ska scenes off of 2 Tone's popularity in the '80s; a lot of new countries came to embrace it years down the road. In Mexico, there are now several, large all-ska festivals that draw 25,000 people a pop, sometimes more.

The internet has helped ska grow once again by connecting all these disparate fans together and showing them that ska was never a trend. It's a way of life.

CHECKERED PAST

Brandon Flowers, lead singer of '80s-throwback alt-rock superstars The Killers, was thoroughly annoyed by The Bravery in 2005 when they were getting tons of acclaim for their dance-punk hit "An Honest Mistake." As far as he was concerned, The Bravery was nothing but a bunch of insincere Killers wannabes. This hostility quickly turned into a public beef between the two. But in their mudslinging, Flowers crossed a line: He outed The Bravery as ex-ska musicians.

Sam Endicott, The Bravery's lead singer, was so taken back by this sinister low blow, all he could do in response was sling the stupidest insults that popped into his head and refer to Flowers as a "little girl," and insist that the mere act of retaliating was like "picking on a kid in a wheelchair."

Music lovers everywhere were shocked to learn the coolest band on the planet had such a treacherous past, playing literally the worst music ever invented. Flower's revelation got music pundits thinking. *What OTHER popular artists might have once been ska musicians?* It was a life-shattering exposé waiting to be penned. In no time, ska-shaming articles, topped with belabored punny headlines, rolled out. *Spin* magazine went with the obvious "Ska-letons in the Closet," stating in the article that "there's nothing *uncooler* than a past spent skanking." While *Entertainment Weekly* chose the nonsensical

"Reaching for The Ska." What exactly did these inquisitive journalists uncover?

It turns out The Bravery's ska past is worse than previously imagined. A white guy dreadlock-sporting Endicott and future Bravery keyboardist John Conway were in a band called Skabba The Hut. They weren't half bad despite the overall frat-guy vibe (it worked for Sublime!) and the overtly tacky band motto, "Bust a nut with Skabba The Hut." Also, why did they have a band motto? Skabba eventually changed their name to The Conquistadors in 1999, adopting a New Wave sound and scoring the "house band" gig for the third season of Comedy Central's *Premium Blend*. In the ashes of The Conquistadors in 2003, Endicott and Conway, in spite of their overwhelming love for ska, formed the Bravery with a few other guys.

These articles revealed many former ska musicians hidden as hipsters in plain sight. Indie darlings, The Walkmen, who scored a 9.2 from *Pitchfork* for their moody *Bows and Arrows* in 2004, were revealed to have three members from former DC ska band Ignobles. Franz Ferdinand's lead singer Alex Kapranos, who enjoyed significant success with the critically acclaimed "Take Me Out," once played guitar, drums and keys for the brilliantly named ska group The Amphetameanies, alongside Belle and Sebastian trumpet player Mick Cooke. And all four members of the band The Stills, who AllMusic once described as having "brooding post-punk soundscapes and art-rock swagger," were in the ska band The Undercovers who *Spin* revealed as "a bunch of wife-beater-wearing rink rats who gelled their hair to epic heights."

But, get this. It turns out The Killers had one of those ska people lurking in their band. Drummer Ronnie Vannucci once played in Attaboy Skip, a band that played ska-covers aplenty, including the *Ghostbusters* theme song and some ironic ska'd up Twisted Sister hits. Plus, they had two "sax-a-mo-fone" players in the group. Flowers, I'm assuming, learned of Vannucci's former ska predilections when these articles came out, and punched the nearest wall with all his strength and frustration, but, in a moment of compassion, allowed him to stay in the Killers.

Obviously, being outed as a ska musician in the ska-hating mid-2000s was a humiliating affair, but it continues today. Maybe you've seen one of the many interviews of actor Oscar Isaac getting grilled on his brief and unremarkable ska past. He played in Florida bands The

Worms and the Blinking Underdogs. Go dig up a YouTube clip of the Blinking Underdogs and tell me MU330's Dan Potthast didn't influence Isaac's dynamic melody structure and New Wave-y songwriting style.

Isaac's ska past was but a blip in his life as a young adult. I asked Less Than Jakes's lead singer/guitarist Chris DeMakes if he remembers playing with either of Isaac's bands in the '90s Florida scene, and he drew a blank. These weren't bands that got far.

But the media is in love with the idea of Isaac as a once lowly ska guy that managed to ascend to non-ska heights. In 2015, when Isaac was out promoting *Star Wars: The Force Awakens*, *Business Insider* actually ran this headline: "How Oscar Isaac went from being a ska musician in Florida to a lead in the next 'Star Wars' movie," as though some dumb bands he played in as a teenager had anything to do with his acting career as an adult. In late 2020, when a new photo of Blinking Underdogs emerged on Twitter, every publication rewrote their "Oscar Isaac was in a 90s ska band" article, as though we didn't already go through this five-years earlier. But it's ska, and for some reason, that fascinates people. *You* were in a ska band? That's impossible! But...but...You're *so* cool now.

Can you imagine the same headline if Isaac was a former grind-core vocalist? No, because it's not embarrassing to have a grindcore past. Maybe a little scary. At this point, so many people have involved themselves with ska one way or another. So why is everyone eager to out former ska musicians?

Roosters, Dolphins and Ninjas

Indie-electronic artist Dan Deacon remembers when *Stereogum* exposed his ska-past. It was in 2009, just a couple years after he released his 2007 breakthrough *Spiderman of the Rings*. The album launched Deacon from an obscure, super cool underground noise musician to suddenly having his name pop up in all the hip music publications. His song "The Crystal Cat" was a top pick on *Rolling Stone*'s best songs of 2007 and *Pitchfork*'s top tracks of the 2000s.

The *Stereogum* article linked to an archive website of his old Long Island ska band Channel 59. Clicking revealed a bunch of goofy high school pictures. Several showed Deacon happily skanking both on stage and in the crowd, wearing an assortment of Hawaiian shirts and pork pie hats, and hugging inflatable dinosaurs. Having those pictures out there for everyone to see, and judge, was embarrassing.

"I think they were like, 'Ha Ha! We're going to ruin this guy's career and talk about his ridiculous ska band.' It was a gotcha piece. *He was in a ska band! Who's next?*" Deacon tells me over the phone while busy recording his newest non-ska album. "It frightened me. Ska was so ridiculed for such a long period of time. For many people, it was the worst music that has ever existed. I was worried about not being taken seriously."

The question then became, how much damage control should he do? Deacon ignored it at first. He didn't really like music pundits anyway. They already wrote articles making fun of him for being a balding, nerdy, electronic guy. But no longer would he pass for cool-nerd. He was ska-nerd now.

Deacon soon realized his ska ties weren't hurting him. His fans already viewed him favorably as a goofy outsider. So, he simply continued on, releasing oddball music and crazy videos and making his live shows fun. "I think if it was Portishead, and it came out that they used to be called the Skavangelists or something, they might have a hard time maintaining their intense persona. I'm not Portishead," Deacon says.

Could it be that a ska past isn't as big a deal as it's treated by the ska haters working for hipster outlets? It might even be an asset. Look at Deacon's live show. He's not one of those DJs standing behind their laptops on stage, sipping craft beer, scrolling through Twitter. He directly engages with the audience, often from within the crowd, encouraging people to melt their inhabitations and participate with the music on a vulnerable level. The goal is to blur the line between performer and audience.

"You can go to a game and say *we* won, or *we* lost. No one says, 'Oh I went to see Built to Spill, and *we* were awesome. *We* played all of my favorite songs," Deacon says. "I try to create situations where people would describe it as *we*."

Anyone who's been to a ska show knows the important role the audience plays. It's a circle of energy that everyone participates in. Deacon has garnered critical praise for tearing down the fourth wall and engaging people that are used to hiding their face in their phones. This instinct took root during his ska years.

Unlike Isaac and his insignificant ska past, Deacon's band Channel 59 was a huge part of his early music life. They formed in the mid-90s while Deacon and his friends were still in high school and lasted four years, till they went off to college.

The original incarnation was a Boredoms-esque drum-free noise project. Deacon played the tuba. The band didn't play shows, but they did do plenty of photo shoots, which were as artistically adventurous as their rhythmically-liberated noise jams. Eventually, they enlisted a drummer. The lead singer quit because 'drums' meant 'selling out.' From that moment on, Deacon dropped the tuba and assumed lead singer duties. Their interests shifted to Moon Records-style ska bands like The Scofflaws, and Skavoovie and the Epitones, which they modeled themselves after with the best of their abilities. But they played their songs so fast they were no longer danceable.

Channel 59's first gig, amazingly, was with The Scofflaws. They got the show because they called the phone number on a Scofflaws flyer they found on a telephone pole and promised the promoter they'd draw a bunch of kids. And the kids came. Their next show was opening for Edna's Goldfish at Deja One, a venue that was ground zero for Long Island's '90s ska scene. They ended up playing second on the bill because the much more experienced Chimichanga needed to leave early. Not playing as opener was a major plus. People were ready to dance by the second band, and they went nuts for Channel 59. After that show, Channel 59 was a legitimate force within the Long Island ska scene.

The group ballooned to fourteen members, big even for a ska band. "We had a problem telling anyone they couldn't be in the band," Deacon says. The big size added to the wild stage energy. They were wacky when it came to lyrics and performance. Song topics ranged from roosters to dolphins to ninjas and included one traditional Jamaican style ska song; mostly instrumental with single phrases shouted between horn lines. But rather than something cool Prince Buster would call out, like, "Al Capone's guns don't argue" Deacon shouted names of John Leguizamo movies. One of Deacon's more peculiar antics was reciting word for word the in-between stage banter from the Pietasters *Strapped Live!* album. When people asked him why, he shrugged.

Shows were over-the-top fun with props and huge audience participation. They once opened for Less Than Jake at the Vanderbilt and ran to the pool supply store to buy all the pool noodles and inflatable octopuses they could afford, hoping to make such a big impression —negative, positive, either way—that Less Than Jake would beg Channel 59 to join them on tour. In hindsight, Deacon realizes this likely had the exact opposite effect he was going for. "Let's do the dumbest shit we possibly can. Let's prove to these people that they would never want to take us on tour," Deacon says. "That was kind of our thing."

Near the end of the band's run, the electronic weirdo genius Deacon was becoming showed itself as Channel 59 teetered into performance art territory. The most famous example was the single-chord rock song, "All Night Party" that they'd play way too long, repeating one line: *All-night party/all-night party/all-night party/how long is the party?/All night!* Sometimes it lasted for the entire 30-minute set. The audience loved it, then hated it, and then eventually loved it again. And that's when Channel 59 ended the song. They never wanted to lose the audience completely.

It's easy to get caught up in shameful feelings about ska when the mainstream narrative is so consistently dismissive and mocking. It's also easy to believe fun or silly songs are somehow less meaningful, or have less purpose than moody, serious music. But Deacon recalls his ska years as important, especially because his mother was ill with cancer at the time.

"Ska was a way for me to escape into this happy, weird, 'everything's fun, but nothing's important' place," Deacon says. "Listening to ska transports me immediately back to this mindset that music is fun. And people get together to have fun."

To some people, this kind of wackiness is an afront to music, and is exactly why a lot of people have a hard time even considering ska a genre of music worth serious consideration. "You got a band with a clarinet and a guy with one of those store-bought horse masks, and they're up there having the time of their lives. That kind of takes away from the sanctity for somebody that puts music on that pedestal," Deacon says. "People don't understand how people who like ska can interact with it that way. They see it as insincere or mocking when it's not. People take everything way too fucking seriously. I think ska doesn't feed into that."

IN DEFENSE OF SKA

Whatever initial reservations Deacon may have had about his indie cred tainted by his ska past is over. He continues to invigorate his crowd to embrace the beauty and silliness in music.

Elvis Should Play Ska

A lot of old bands assumed they'd escaped getting outed for their young ska days. Tears for Fears went through their entire run in the '80s and '90s without Kurt Loder demanding the details on their early '80s ska band, Graduate. The internet changed that. Now anyone can scrounge up old ska clips of the Tears for Fears guys bouncing around in suits and blast the evidence on Instagram.

I requested an interview with Tears for Fears' Roland Orzabal and Curt Smith but never heard back. (I guess they didn't want me to out them for their ska past. Too late!) I did track down bandmate John Baker, who played guitar in Graduate, and he gave me the full story. Turns out Graduate only had one ska song, and it was a doozy: "Elvis Should Play Ska."

I listened to Graduate's full-length album *Acting My Age*. "Elvis Should Play Ska," their "embarrassing" song, is the best tune on the record. It's catchy, has a sharp wit, and intricate lead guitar work. It's the song where you can start to hear Orzabal's future Tears For Fears songwriting chops blossom. Was it such a bad thing that he was dabbling in ska?

Graduate demoed their initial batch of songs in 1979. They were New Wave, mod guitar-driven pop, but, at the time, 2 Tone burst on the scene and captured Orzabal's fancy. In the heat of his ska obsession, he read an interview in a local newspaper where Elvis Costello complained that 2 Tone bands had no longevity, and that it would disappear from sight in no time. Orzabal wrote "Elvis Should Play Ska" as a defense of the genre.

"He [Orzabal] was just having a little bit of fun. The whole thing was tongue-in-cheek," Baker says. Orzabal's jab was perfectly timed, as Costello coincidentally recorded a couple of ska songs for *Get Happy* in 1980. Did Orzabal's directive influence Costello to play ska? All signs point to maybe.

Graduate press photo at Kingswood school in Bath, UK, 1979

Graduate was signed in January of 1980 by Pye Records, a label once thriving in the '60s and '70s. When the label listened to the band's demos, "Elvis Should Play Ska" stood out as the potential single. "We weren't convinced it was the right song to put out because we weren't a ska band," Baker says. "They convinced us it would sound good on radio, which it did. They got that bit right."

Given the go ahead, Pye released "Elvis" in April of 1980. The song went to top ten in Spain. In England, it hovered just below top 75. The goal was to get on the British music chart TV show *Top of the Pops*, which showcased hits by the latest pop bands. Careers in England have been made by a good *Top of the Pops* performance. If a single made it into the top 75, hitting *Top of the Pops* was more likely. Graduate just missed out. Had the song been a hit, it would've been an unusual addition to the British ska movement of 1980, since Graduate had nothing to do with 2 Tone besides an appreciation for what those bands started.

"We weren't trying to be authentic. It doesn't sound like 2 Tone. It nowhere near sounds like traditional ska. It's got an amazing presence when you hear it on the radio. We were quite pleased with the sound of it," Baker says.

"great little pop band"

Graduate had material ready to go for a second album but ended up getting dropped by the label. "I think Pye signed us because we looked like a great little pop band," Baker says. "Once those couple of singles had not made it, they didn't know what to do. They didn't bother." Orzabal and Smith then formed Tears For Fears, a band so serious and intense, scream therapy was one of its influences. They left their brush with ska behind for good. But the wit on "Elvis Should Play Ska" carried over into the entire Tears For Fears catalog.

What did Costello think of the song? I was dying to know. Nowhere in his 674-page autobiography did it mention what I consider to be the most interesting moment of his career: getting called out by a band for *not* playing ska.

I emailed his manager and was surprised to get a reply. But, no surprise, Costello didn't want to comment on the subject.

The Cat With 2 Heads

It seems fitting to conclude this chapter by outing someone whose ska past is virtually unknown, and for some reason hasn't yet been dug up by music bloggers. The perpetrator is Barry Johnson of the indie-punk band, Joyce Manor.

The band is kind of a big deal. Music writers fall in love with them for their eclectic approach to punk that incorporates emo, jangle-pop, slow alt-rock riffs, and tearful post-punk melodies. Ska also happens to be a significant influence, but pundits haven't outed them, choosing to keep the band's ska roots under wrap so as to protect themselves from a potential internet shaming.

Disclaimer: I'm not the first to out Johnson for his ska past. My friend, Bob Vielma, did so on his blog *Phat 'n' Phunky*. So, it's his fault.

Don't worry. Johnson isn't embarrassed by ska. He was eager to talk to me; ready to go deep with anyone willing to chat about lesser-known '90s ska bands like the Impossibles and Siren Six. He also wanted to stand up and make it clear what a significant impact his ska past had on his success as an indie-punk *Pitchfork* darling.

There's a rude boy hidden under that Hawaiian shirt

Pre-Joyce Manor, Johnson's dealt with plenty of people trying to ska shame him. In high school, when all his peers were over and done with ska, Johnson still proudly went to bat for the genre and was ruthlessly teased for it. He walked around in a Mustard Plug shirt, and kids mocked him by skanking and mimicking air trumpets in his face, as people tend to do to ska fans.

"It made me dig my heels in. It was like, 'No, you guys don't know shit about basslines and counter-melodies.' Everyone that went to the shows was proud to be ska, proud to be the weird mega nerds and stuff. I held on to that for a long time," Johnson tells me.

He found ska in junior high in '97 when it was on MTV, but soon lost interest. Then he met a darkly dressed morose-looking guy in high school. Johnson was on the prowl for some depressing music and figured this guy would have the scoop on some super downer recommendations. But the guy wasn't an emo dude; he was a Star Wars fan who liked to dress like Luke Skywalker. And he loved ska.

Skywalker Guy introduced Johnson to a full range of ska bands, not just the stuff on MTV, but bands like Let's Go Bowling and The Toasters. The two walked around school singing Aquabats songs. Skywalker did an amazing "The Cat With 2 Heads," and when Johnson downloaded the real version, he was shocked to hear just how accurately his friend conveyed the vibe.

Johnson was also really into indie rock. Stuff like Magnetic Fields, Guided By Voices, as well as punk and alt-rock bands like The Smiths, Jawbreaker, and Weezer. The ska bands he was into the most—MU330, Slow Gherkin, The Impossibles—were incorporating similar influences. When music writers praise Joyce Manor and cite the band's influences, they're telling an incomplete story by leaving ska out of the equation. "Learning how ska works makes you a better song-writer," Johnson says. "Like how a ska bassline dives in. The role of the guitar in a ska band is way different than a rock band...counter-melody, dynamics. How to make a song move and be infectious. If you've never tried to write a ska song, you're doing yourself a disservice." Johnson remains an unabashed lover of ska. He's an encyclopedia of ska knowledge and is always ready to talk about the genre. Take note Joyce Manor fans!

He does understand to a certain degree why the media likes to ska-shame people. The genre can go into embarrassing territory at times.

"I thought some of the third wave ska stuff was a little too wacky for my taste," Johnson says. "Honestly, I dabbled in some wackiness. My ska past is brutal, but not that bad. It wasn't Skabba The Hut."

What exactly are all these people and publications doing when they are outing, or mocking people's ska past? They're trying to demolish these otherwise manicured images and expose something sincere, and vulnerable, like once being a silly kid who skanked their ass off at a Let's Go Bowling Show. Johnson is exactly what all of us with a ska-past need to model ourselves after. Change the narrative. If you grew up loving ska, embrace it. And if you look closely, you'll see that it probably impacted your life for the better.

Bands like The Bravery, who once trembled at the thought of anyone knowing their ska past, are completely gone from the musical landscape. Popular music has moved on to something different. Ska may never swing back, but it's clear the music will never go away, no matter how much pop culture mocks it to death. New bands continue to form, old ones keep touring, and new generations of kids keep coming out and declaring ska their all-time favorite musical genre. Some of these adults embarrassed by their checkered past will hopefully realize there's strength in numbers. Former and current ska fans are everywhere. There's no need to hide your ska roots when so many millions of people spent their formative years getting sweaty at a ska show.

ONE STEP BEYOND

My friends and I were at the nightclub One Step Beyond in Santa Clara, California, where the foul odor of booze and vomit wafted through the muggy, pressure-cooked air. We'd danced through four bands already, including a young, awkward, and poorly dressed Cherry Poppin' Daddies. Now it was time for the headliner. We stood by the stage, sweaty and shaking, willing the heavy theatre curtains to open.

The wait felt unbearably long. Finally, the lights went dim; everyone hushed. The buzz of the opening bass line rang out and the curtains whooshed apart to reveal Skankin' Pickle, a group of six misfits staring defiantly out into the crowd. The bass line continued to build slowly, each instrument joining in until the walls reverberated with eerie upbeats. Chills ran up my neck. The song reached peak volume and winded back down, each instrument dropping out one by one. The crowd roared.

Skankin' Pickle went right into their next song. The tall Korean-American sax player sang about missing the bus to work. He wore a karate uniform and jump kicked between each line. The song ended with the sing-along: *"I love Three's Company, but that's no excuse for missing the bus."*

"Singalong with Skankin' Pickle."

The remaining horn section pulled my focus away. They occupied the stage like two drunk frat guys. The slide trombonist lurched back and forth, pausing between blats to wave his arms like a windmill; he grabbed some devil sticks and did a short one-minute performance, while the valve trombonist leapt up and down with his arms glued to his side. He grabbed the mic and yelled, "pick it up pick it up pick it up," and glided into an ear-splitting '70s metal scream.

At the end of the song, the bass player approached the front of the stage. He pushed his bushy blonde hair from his face and turned to the side, posing like Jessica Rabbit. An obviously fake ass of cartoonish proportions bulged under his Hawaiian shirt and khaki shorts. Scattered applause from the audience. He pranced back and forth with a shit-eating grin.

Once he had our full regard, he said in a lousy talk-show voice, "Not only am I the president of the hair club for men...but I'm also a client." He pushed off all his hair—a wig!—and slapped his bass right into punky ska song twice as fast as the previous tune. It inspired a raging mosh pit. A friend and I leapt in, possessed by brutal punk rock demons. Our limbs flailed like broken marionettes as we ran in circles. The few lyrics I understood cracked me up. There was one line where he took an aggressive stance against blow dryers.

At last, the song ended and I caught my breath. Sweat dripped off me in rivulets. I'd never had this kind of fun at a live show before. I looked up just as the now-bald bass player mounted a unicycle and haphazardly pedaled across the stage. He dangled a moment precariously over the crowd but stumbled off and landed on his feet like a trained circus performer. Everyone cheered. An older, hairy, shirtless guy patted me on the back. "They rule!" he shouted. I threw my hand up and slapped his hand. We were brothers for life.

The sax player took the mic back and ordered all the Asians in the audience to join him on stage. He looked out and pointed at a guy near the back and said, "Get up here." A few other Asian people followed suit.

A bald—not-Asian—guy shouted: "Albinos too?"

The sax player laughed and motioned him up. "Come on up before I change my mind." He ran up and paced around with the others, arms raised like he'd won the lottery. The sax player looked back at the drummer, a stone-faced classic rocker with long stringy hair, and nodded. "This song is called 'Asian Man,'" the sax player said. The drummer counted off and broke into speed metal. The on-stage crew went ballistic.

Fifteen seconds in, and suddenly the song pulled back into a mid-tempo hip-hop beat. The spiky haired guitarist hung her tongue out the side of her mouth like a dopey dog and hopped up and down on the off-beats. The sax player slipped into a mock rap pose and began: *"I'm sick of people always telling me that dogs shouldn't be eaten as a delicacy. Yo, it tastes good, as a sandwich meat. Heck, I like it and it's low in calories!"*

The newly anointed stage dancers did their best wannabe rapper impressions. We all did. After the first verse, the sax player dove head-first into the audience, flipping around mid-air. The albino guy screamed and followed after him. They floated on the crowd's hands, returning to the stage in time for verse two.

I danced hard. Everyone around me danced just as hard. Punks with red mohawks, guys in loose-fitting suits, girls in polka dot dresses, long-haired hippies with tie-dye peace symbols, nerds with tucked in Atari sweaters, goths with painted black lipstick, metalheads draped in oversized Danzig shirts, and plain, old, fashion-free dorks like me. We were all dissimilar. Yet here we were, all moving together as one giant, heaving beast.

When I thought I'd pass out, the mood slowed into a down-tempo reggae song. The guitarist stepped forward to sing: *"We live in a racist world/where the colors of the land/won't keep us hand in hand."* People embraced each other, swayed back and forth, and sang along.

As I watched Skankin' Pickle from a sea of mismatched people, I felt a deep comfort. They were bizarre and flaunting it. And if they could, so could we.

Later that night I wrote the band a long bizarre fan letter. I made it extra weird to get their attention. It worked. The saxophonist, Mike Park, sent me an orange peel and told me to call him. I became friends with the band, toured with them as a roadie, and had my band open for them.

Gerry caught in mid-air keyboard solo

Aaron,
Read your letter!
Here's a piece of
TAPE For You!

Sincerely,

Bruce
Lee

I'd found my music. And it changed everything.

Skankin' Pickle logo circa 1990

FAT RANDY

I'm at Berkeley's legendary punk venue 924 Gilman Street in 2015 watching the Voodoo Glow Skulls rip through ska-core classics like it's 1996. Nothing has changed at Gilman. Teenage punks in patch-covered jackets circle-pit near the stage in nihilistic abandon while us old timers linger in the back calmly bobbing our heads. Twenty years ago, I would have sprinted to that pit. Now, I watch for openings, hoping I have one song in me.

The Glow Skulls open with "Shoot the Moon." The loveable green lowrider monster from the cover of their brilliant sophomore album, *Firme*, go-go dances drunkenly as the band thrashes around him. His presence drives the crowd bonkers like they're glimpsing a real-life celebrity. In reality, it's probably one of the roadies that will load gear after the show.

A few songs in, the horn section starts up the hyper-peppy "Fat Randy" intro, which leads right into copious distorted upbeats. Lead singer Frank Casillas bellows about Fat Randy shitting on his couch. Gilman's crowd howls. Some here are old enough to remember the release of the song 20 years ago. Others had yet to be born. Still, the feeling is the same: The band was finally playing their hit single.

But it wasn't their hit single.

"Fat Randy" should've been the band's breakout moment. It's catchy, while still staying true to Voodoo's chaotic ska-core elements of non-stop distortion, staccato brass and confrontational hardcore vocals. "Fat Randy" had decent airplay on LA's KROQ, hitting #87 in 1996, but never reached top ten status like Sublime or No Doubt.

The band wasn't really about singles, anyway. They honed their skills playing grimy backyard punk rock parties in Riverside, California. Dirty ska punk steez was their vibe in 1989 before they had a horn section, and it stayed that way, even in 1995, though they'd become better musicians. If the radio wanted to give them a few spins, it was fine, as long as it helped their draw.

Dirty ska punk steez

The Glow Skulls released *Firme* on Epitaph in 1995, a move which immediately increased their reach. Signing to Epitaph was controversial in the '90s. Some considered Epitaph an authentic punk label with more resources than your average indie. To other punkers, it was no different than signing to Warner Brothers. Epitaph bands Rancid and The Offspring were in heavy MTV rotation. Along with Green Day, they'd taken punk rock out of the basements and into the expensive car stereo systems of jocks, who, a few years earlier, were probably beating up those punk weirdos. No respectable punk band should have anything to do with all that capitalist bullshit. Even Gilman, ever self-righteous when it came to their "no major label bands" policy, banned Voodoo Glow Skulls upon signing to Epitaph 1995.

A lot of groups went through this with Gilman. Green Day was famously banned in 1994 when they released their Reprise album *Dookie*. A year later, lead singer Billi Joe Armstrong vented about it in their song "86" after sneaking into the club one night and finding "Billy Joe must die" scrawled on the bathroom wall. Rumor had it, he was on Gilman's official "86" (banned) list, which included his name right below George Bush. Ouch. The Green Day ban was lifted in 2015 when they played a secret benefit for AK Press, 1984 Printing and individuals displaced by the fire that devastated these businesses.

That same year, the Voodoos were also allowed back in the club. That night in 2015 was their first show at the venue since 95, despite being Epitaph-free since 2002. Bush, it should be noted is still banned.

Epitaph funded a couple music videos for the promotion of *Firme*. "Charlie Brown" was one of them--sort of a rap parody video. It wasn't anything special but it did have one hilarious moment where a hip-hop dancer fed trombonist Brodie Johnson a Big Mac as though it was part and parcel to the hip-hop ethos. There was also "Fat Randy," a mediocre wrestling themed video where the band is pitted against "Randy Gordo." Mostly, it's just a lot of Voodoo performance shots inside the wrestling ring. Both videos got some MTV love, but not much. Neither video particularly excited the band.

I had a chance to ask Voodoo's guitarist Eddie Casillas about the videos. "It was thrown together by a director that was on drugs. We never got to make the video that we truly thought represented the band," he tells me.

I'd heard a rumor back in the '90s that Voodoo casted Chris Farley in the "Fat Randy" video shoot, but that something went awry. Casillas told me that there was a discussion about bringing Farley into the shoot, but it never made it past the hypothetical. But there was an entire alternative partially-made video for "Fat Randy," casting the real Fat Randy (yes, Fat Randy was a real guy) as himself. I didn't know about any of this.

Who was the real Fat Randy? Casillas tells me Randy was an oddball Polish guy Eddie and his brothers—Eddie, Frank, and Jorge make up the core of the band—knew from their high school years at Riverside High. He was a social outcast who drank too much and got picked on by bullies. The song's lyrics were mostly true. The real Fat Randy was drunk and belligerent at a party, and the Voodoos' trumpet player, Joe McNally, told him to leave. Randy snuck back later and shit on the couch.

The song was later written to honor Randy and his weirdness in a funny way. "It was a light-hearted thing. We were trying to show him that we're not going to make fun of you. We're trying to immortalize you," Casillas says. They discussed the idea of him being in the video. Real Randy liked the idea and agreed to play himself.

The band rented an MTV Cribs-style house in Riverside and rounded up a bunch of old high school friends and acquaintances to be extras. They wanted to recreate the Riverside party vibe which Fat Randy would've inevitably crashed. Everyone thought it was going to be a hilariously endearing video.

On the day of the shoot, all the extras met up at the Voodoo's indie record store, Cheap Guy Records, just a few miles from the recording house. A couple of busses carted the roughly three-hundred people over to the shoot. Epitaph paid for copious food and beer for the cast.

All the extras had a bit too much to drink and things quickly got out of hand. When Randy showed up to the house, everyone broke from the script and acted like it was high school all over again. The extras started lightheartedly teasing Randy, thinking they were being hilarious. It grew more aggressive as more people joined in. Someone grabbed him and threw him to the ground. Mob mentality took over rational thought. Everyone dogpiled on him.

"They ripped off his clothes," Casillas tells me. "It was horrible, actually. It made me think of the movie *Carrie*."

The band was elsewhere in the house when the extras *Carrie*'d Fat Randy. As soon as they got word, they immediately shut it down and scrapped the whole thing, losing about $10,000 of production costs.

Come to 924 Gilman. 98% Dust-free

If everything had gone right, I wonder how Fat Randy would've felt to see himself on TV. It reminds me of a video I shot in college for local emo punk band My Former Self when I was studying film at San Jose State. My partners and I thought it would be funny to cast them as bullies, and surprisingly, they were into the idea.

They band called up a bunch of their fans to be extras for the shoot. One kid, a real-life nerd, was cast to play the band's primary target. In an early scene, a couple band members grabbed the nerd and gave him swirlies in the school bathroom. The nerd eventually got revenge by messing up their performance while they were playing a party. His bravery impressed a couple of girls at the party, and in the closing scene, they admired our beloved nerd and showered him with kisses. The actual guy was so awkward when we shot those scenes, but these two girls he co-acted with lightened up his anxiety by being super sweet to him.

A few years later, I bumped into someone from My Former Self at Barnes and Noble, and he told me the nerd kid had grown into a full-on mac daddy. I was shocked. I want to think that pretending to be a lady's man in the music video gave him higher self-esteem. But I'm not sure how I feel about turning a nerd into a player.

Voodoos may not have landed a hit single in the '90s but their legacy took an unexpected turn down the road, one I wasn't even aware of until that night at Gilman. Casillas told me about the vibrant ska scene in LA's Latino neighborhoods. These bands saw Voodoo as pioneers in Spanish-language alt-rock in the US since they sang in English and Spanish.

Despite no huge hits in '95, the band played to big crowds. Rather than following up *Firme* with another album in '96, they focused on a Spanish version of the record. It made sense. They always had one Spanish song on every album ("La Migra," "El Coo Cooi") but *Firme* completely embraced Spanish in a way that didn't exist in the American punk world. Musically it was different that anything happening in the *Rock en Español* scene of the mid-90s.

Epitaph hired a pro-level marketing team from the *Rock en Español* scene. The record got in the hands of people in US cities with large Latino populations (Chicago, L.A., New York, San Francisco) with no energy spent breaking them into Latin America. "It was a novelty since the band spoke Spanish and was primarily Mexican-American," Casillas explains. Two years later, LA Latin supergroup Ozomatli emerged with their debut record and received a lot of praise. A decade after that, a wave of cutting-edge, critically-revered LA alt-rock bands like Chicano Batman, La Santa Cecilia, and Las Cafeterias embraced Spanish. But Voodoo did it first. In '96, the band released a Spanish version of "Fat Randy" video ("Randy Gordo") utilizing the same wrestling footage. It wasn't a hit, but it got around. The entire Spanish *Firme* album had slow ripple effects.

Voodoo weren't even aware of the L.A. Latino scene they'd impacted until the mid-2000s when those bands reached out to them to play packed shows and massive DIY festivals. "Fans tell us to this day that they sometimes only had the Spanish version," Casillas says.

Voodoos didn't think much about recording a Spanish album in 1996. It was part of who they were as a punk band; they wanted to play gigs wherever people were excited to see them play. Now they can add to that list: DIY festivals in L.A., where they can choose between "Fat Randy" and "Randy Gordo" and the crowds will no doubt sing along word for word, as though it was their big hit.

DESIGNATED SKA FRIEND

If you know Brent Lawrence Friedman, you've probably tagged him in a ska meme. Maybe it had something to do with mozzarella sticks, Streetlight Manifesto or a skanking Andy Samberg. You pull out your phone, type his name, and hit send the moment you see anything ska related pop up on the web. You hope to be the first. But you're not. Believe me. Not even close.

Brent's flooded with ska tags. So much so, he's given in and changed his Instagram handle to @pleasetagmeinyourskaposts. "I'm everybody's designated ska friend," Brent tells me. "I'm the one ska kid everyone knows." We're sitting backstage at a Reel Big Fish show in Reno, Nevada. Brent slouches in his chair, low-key calm as he half-complains about the onslaught of ska memes directed at him. He's wearing a black Kemuri t-shirt and casual, no-frills, knee-length shorts.

Jeremy Andrew Hunter is with us. They're animated, perched on their chair and physically relating to every word Brent says. Jeremy runs the Skatune Network YouTube channel, covering non-ska songs, transforming them into ska perfection. It's far more popular than anyone outside of the ska community would have predicted. They wear a white Skankin' Pickle shirt, the one with the drawing of a dancing pickle. I'm pretty sure I wore the same shirt back when I was their age.

Jeremy's friendly, with hyper energy and talks twice as loud as

Brent. They're a hero in the ska community, on a mission to transform every song into ska, proving the theory that every song works in the ska format. Or as my publisher's designated ska friend (and award-winning horror-bizarro author) Jeff Burk likes to say—*ska improves every song ever.*

Both Jeremy and Brent play in the ska-punk band We Are The Union, currently on tour with Reel Big Fish. Brent rocks the drums, where he's in his element, calm and confident. Jeremy fills the role as the trombonist and lone horn section.

Every time Jeremy is tagged in a new ska meme a trombone gets its wings

Both Brent and Jeremy get tagged in ska memes non-stop. I ask Brent how often. When a new meme comes out, he estimates, conservatively, twenty people will tag him. ("Almost on a daily basis"). He even gets tagged in Jeremy's Skatune Network ska covers videos. People are so thirsty to surprise him with new ska content, they forget that Brent and Jeremy are already friends. "I'm like, 'I play in a band with Jeremy. How do you not know these things?'" Brent says.

Jeremy one-ups him by saying that they sometimes get tagged in their own videos. "Their instinct is just to tag me," Jeremy says.

who would win??

opening ska band	a couple of pluggy bois

We try to determine which of them are tagged most. It's too close to tell, so we call it a draw. What's clear is they're both designated ska friends to many people. Both of their identities are so enmeshed in ska, my friend Adam Davis ska-targets both of them on social media *constantly*. Adam's go-to move is responding with "SKA" to anything either of them posts. Anything. "He comments on all my stuff, even if it's not ska related," Jeremy says. "I'll post a selfie, and he'll say 'SKA.'"

Adam gets a pass for this obnoxious behavior because he's got the ska-punk bona fides. He played guitar in Link 80 back in the day and regales Brent and Jeremy with ska war stories all the time. Adam knows he's not the only person ska-teasing them. He's trolling. Most people, on the other hand, assume Brent or Jeremy will be grateful to be inundated with ska-related content and want to be teased ruthlessly about it in the process. The teasing only sharpened their resolve to stand up for ska.

"The ska thing is always a butt end of the joke. After a while it started annoying me to where I started defending ska on social media," Brent says. "I started talking about ska a lot. I became an exaggerated version of what these people thought I was. Then ska kids in bands across the country would tell me, 'Man I love that you defend ska so hard.' Apparently, this is making some people happy. I'm just going to keep fucking doing it."

Ska Kids Find A Way To Ruin Everything

When Jeremy was a teenager, they posted videos playing the trombone on YouTube. They loved ska and went to DIY ska shows in southern Florida, where they grew up. Around Christmas in 2016, an idea popped into their head: Record a ska version of "Feliz Navidad." It was mostly a goof. They posed the question to their Facebook friends, to see if it was a good idea and got an overwhelming *yes* in response. The video went viral. That led to more ska renditions of non-ska songs, which led to even more. Soon the Skatune Network YouTube channel was born, and Jeremy was cranking out ska cover versions of any non-ska song that popped in their mind. Jeremy plays all the instruments themselves (with occasional guest vocals). That includes guitar, bass, trumpet, sax, trombone, keys, vocals and drum machine. An insane feat. The videos are generally motionless shots in their room, cutting back and forth between Jeremy killing it on each instrument.

Some of Skatune's most popular videos are Blink 182's "Dammit," Green Day's "Basket Case," (which Billie Joe Armstrong shared on Twitter), My Chemical Romance's "I'm Not Ok (I Promise)," and a ska-medley of Nintendo Wii songs.

The name Skatune Network predates the channel. In the early 2010s, Jeremy, for no good reason, photoshopped the old checkered Cartoon Network logo to say "Skatoon Network." The image garnered a lot of online praise from friends, so they started using it for their handle on all social media accounts. When they had enough covers to start an official YouTube channel, Skatoon was the obvious name choice, though they changed the spelling to 'tune.'

Jeremy's channel has also become a safe entry point for people with misconceptions about ska. Jeremy gets comments from people saying that they don't like ska, but they like their covers. "I hate to break it to you—you like ska," Jeremy says. "If you like my covers, you just haven't heard the right bands. People are quick to generalize ska as one sound. I think of all of the types of music; ska is one of the more diverse."

Of course, plenty of people that trash Skatune Network. It is ska after all, and the internet. I prod Jeremy for some vicious negative comments. Brent interjects with a personal favorite on the "I'm Not Okay (I Promise)" video: *Ska kids find a way to ruin everything.* Jeremy adds with some delight: "People always tell me that ska sounds like Nickelodeon from the 90s. I'm like, 'yeah, I love Nickelodeon in the 90s.' Therefore, I love ska."

The Blink 182 cover is particularly special for Jeremy as it goes back to their teen years at the South Florida DIY ska scene space, The Talent Farm. Every punk and ska band back then covered, "Dammit." Jeremy remembers one Talent Farm show where all four bands on the bill pulled out their own "Dammit" cover. Fed up, the venue banned the song from future shows. Jeremy started wearing a shirt with Dammit and a slash through it, in solidarity with the policy. Years later, when the Skatune Network developed a national audience, they just had to revive it, dedicating the song to the South Florida scene that fostered their ska interest. *R.I.P The Talent Farm.*

Jeremy sees their channel as a beacon for defending ska. Not only do they shine a light on the music by covering indie, punk, and New Wave songs, but they have so much fun in the videos, that it's hard to deny ska's appeal. If you read some of the comments, people are thanking Jeremy repeatedly. "We need more ska heroes like you in this day and age," one poster proclaims on the Wii-ska-medley.

"One of my hopes for Skatune Network is to get people to think differently about ska. People take music too seriously sometimes. Ska is a great genre to not be so serious, and to have fun," they tell me. "Some people don't even know what ska is; they know it's cool to hate it. Why do you think it's cool to hate ska? Tell me your point, and I'll tell you why your genre is equally worth hating for the same reason."

A Joke To Most People

Even though he's always been super into ska, Brent didn't become the "ska guy" until recently. In 2013, he had a circle of friends who were big ska fans. A couple of years later, this same group of friends moved on to more "mature" music. Their ska past became so mortifying to them, these friends pretended they never liked ska in the first place, making fun of anyone who did. When they saw Brent around, they'd tease him ruthlessly for not growing out of ska.

"It was demeaning for no reason. They listened to ska and immediately were like 'I never listened to that shit,'" Brent says. "They'd introduce me to some friend. 'This is Brent; he's a ska guy.' You can listen to as many genres in the world. If ska is one of them, it defines your entire musical taste. I like Norwegian black metal, but nobody is making that part of my personality."

Many treat ska like a horrible phase you went through, and ardently erase from your permanent record. "It's a joke to most people. That's what I listened to in middle school," Brent explains. "Everyone was exposed to Less Than Jake and Reel Big Fish. What kept me engaged in the genre is bands that were doing different elements. Folly, Leftover Crack. Arrogant Sons of Bitches. We Are The Union." We all laugh. He shrugs his shoulders.

With all this talk of defending ska, Brent clarifies that it's the newer bands that most need defending. "The Specials aren't an embarrassing band. Hipsters listen to the fucking Selecter," Brent says. "I'm defending the bands that are embarrassing to listen to like third-wave and ska-punk."

A million ska bands have popped up since the '80s—all bringing different elements to the table—but most people think every post 2 Tone band sounds like Reel Big Fish. People aren't aware of the variety in the ska scene. Brent hopes that if anyone listens to him defend ska online, they'll understand this point.

I Still Play In My High School Ska Band

We Are The Union formed in 2005, years before Jeremy and Brent joined. It started as a ska band, but there were a couple of years in the 2010s where We Are The Union inched away from ska, a "respectable musician" move. But then, Jeremy and Brent joined in 2015 and 2016 respectively. Maybe it was a coincidence, but more than likely not. Having two of the internet's strongest ska defenders in their band pushed We Are The Union to do the right thing and brazenly embrace ska again. Any urge We Are The Union had to go "rock with horns" was squelched. The band returned to ska, and then some, now proudly taking a stand for ska. "[We Are The Union] was like, 'Fuck it. We're going to play on all the stereotypes of third-wave ska. We're going to fucking double down on it because whatever, fuck you guys, we like ska.'"

Later, after the interview, I watch from the crowd as We Are The

Union take the stage. The band members are dancing hard, but Jeremy is dancing the hardest. Jeremy's infectious skanking is inspiring. A blown-up meme behind the band reads: Who would win: Opening Ska Band We Are The Union or A Couple of Pluggy Bois (includes picture of disgruntled music snob plugging their ears.) Even better is the We Are The Union shirts on sale that read *I still play in my high school ska band*. The fans love it: We Are The Union acknowledging how embarrassing ska is supposed to be, but embracing the silly aspects loudly and proudly anyway. Ska fans react to this pride of ownership in earnest because they know how much the world ridicules them. It's why We Are The Union are one of the biggest post-90s bands out there on the touring circuit right now. They're deep in the trenches doing the hard, thankless work the ska community needs. Brent and Jeremy are more than just designated ska friends; they're ska warriors, making it okay to love ska out in the open, and not feel like you have to downplay how happy the music makes you. It's a lot of energy defending ska on a daily basis. It might explain why We Are The Union named their last album *Self-Care*.

SYNTH-POP FESTIVAL

It wasn't uncommon with '90s DIY touring to head out on the road with nothing but an address and vague directions to that night's gig. If you were lucky, you might get a phone number, which most likely went to someone's voicemail. Or their mom.

Our vague directions led us to a suburban park outside of Houston. We were midway through Flat Planet's second tour. Touring in 1994 as a ska band meant playing for audiences in small-town America who'd never heard a band blasting through hyper upbeats or seen a punk band with horns. It also meant playing at non-venues, like basements, community centers, and storage units.

We once played at an isolated desert spot somewhere outside of Vegas, powered only by loud generators and aggressive, Miller-drinking teens. At least that show had escorts—a few punks from Vegas in a beaten-up van met us in a casino parking lot and led us on a thirty-minute drive into the desolate desert. But in Houston we were sans escorts, wandering around a public park on Sunday afternoon, looking for a festival, trying not to alarm the well-dressed picnicking families.

"Should we backtrack?" I asked my wary bandmates, eying the sizzling hot dogs being grilled by the nearby picnicking family.

"Let's keep looking," said Alex, the lead singer, his eye on the same hot dogs.

Geoff and Seth, somewhere in Truth Or Consequences, New Mexico

We'd had a successful tour so far. We'd gone to Florida and were headed back, covering the entire Southern US, much farther than our first tour, a simple trek from Northern California to San Antonio. That first time, my parents had been petrified and tried to talk me out of going. I went anyway. Now it's a funny story they like to tell their friends. That time their 18-year-old son went on tour in two minivans. *Hey mom, guess where I am?*

We had stationed ourselves in San Antonio for a while, staying at our bass player Rudy's friend's house. From there we drove to various Texas towns each night. The matriarch of the household made fresh flour tortillas every day, the best I've ever tasted. She called Rudy *mijo* and made tasty dinners like *mole* and *menudo* from scratch. It was heaven.

The family came to see us play one night. They puzzled at our music and our nutty, full-throttle stage energy, but smiled proudly at Rudy standing like a bass god in his Azteca outfit. Rudy claimed to be 50% Aztec and the outfit to be 100% culturally accurate. I had no way to prove or disprove his assertions. The outfit must have cost him a pretty penny. It included a green, black and redhead dress, and warrior plated chest. I liked that he didn't match anyone else in the band. None of us did.

We worshiped Skankin' Pickle and used their stage chaos as a treasure map. Alex was our lead singer, a heavy-set guy of Mexican and Puerto Rican descent. He created alternate personas to act as front men for Flat Planet, like the hick pimp, Papa Don, named after his old boss at *Papa Don's Pizzeria*. The real Papa Don was a southern white man with a thick, indecipherable drawl. Alex re-imagined Papa Don as a pimp in his off hours. He donned an afro, a purple Parliament shirt, and perfected a spot-on impression of Papa Don's Texas accent. Once on stage, he'd sing how he'd think Papa Don would: left hand up like a Shakspearian actor pondering the meaning of life and stomping around on stage like an angry child. It didn't make sense. But it was entertaining.

Our two horn players, Seth and Geoff, were the dictionary version of punks: spastic energy, spikey mohawks, studded boots, ripped anarchy shirts, skinny as hell, and as white as freshly fallen snow. Before shows, they took turns doing each other's hair and studiously practiced synchronized sexy moves for the stage, in hopes of wooing ladies, and to my disappointment were occasionally successful. Years later, Seth became a real estate agent and Geoff a cop. When Geoff went into cadet training, he shaved off his Mohawk, stored it in a Ziplock bag and pinned it to his wall. A single tear rolled down his face that day, or so I imagine. Years later he joined his precinct's cop band, Kathy and the Bad Boys. They made trading cards and everything.

Mike kept the upbeats with his guitar. He was tall with soft Italian features that made him seem wholesome and unassuming. But he had a lot of nervous energy and an urge to provoke awkward social situations. On stage, Mike would randomly go bonkers and make the audience cringe. He'd wear something absurd, like only his tighty-whities, so people would be too uncomfortable to stare directly. Mike was most satisfied after those shows, having had expressed an unnamable emotion within him.

Alex befriends the shitfaced lead singer of The Real McKenzies

I was behind the drums, so no one gave a shit about me. That meant I could wear sweatpants, go shirtless, shave the crown of my head, call myself Uncle Elmer, and skank in my seat as much as I wanted.

After wandering around the park for fifteen minutes, we found a nondescript building far away from the parking lot. It looked promising, but when we got there, it was locked. Things weren't looking good. I didn't mind taking the afternoon off per se, but we needed some cash to fill up the gas tank and re-stock our bellies with Taco Bell.

"Do you hear something?" asked Rudy.

"It sounds like '80s dance music," said Alex, shaking his booty. He bumped and grinded, shouting "Yeah!" as we walked around the building trying to solve the mystery of the venue. A gazebo stood in the distance with a gathering of forty-five people. Faint strains of moody keyboard riffs wafted from their direction. It had to be the "festival." We headed over.

Within the gazebo, two keyboardists, one vocalist, and a single clear intention to mimic *Violator*-era Depeche Mode held reign. The keyboardists stood listless behind their instruments, like children forced into manual labor. Any enthusiasm they'd managed to generate had gone into matching black skin-tight outfits and applying meticulous *Crow*-worthy makeup. I surveyed the crowd, disappointed to see the same perfectly manicured *Crow* face-paintings and painfully bored expressions as the band.

Rudy: Every band has a van story

"Is this where we're playing?" Mike asked.

"I don't know." I searched the crowd and found someone not in makeup. A tall, lanky guy with a self-made laminated VIP card that read, "Chet," stood arms crossed against a cement pillar. I headed over to him.

"Hi, uh, I think my band is playing today," I said.

"What's your band's name?" he said. His accent landed somewhere between Texan and British.

"Flat Planet."

"You made it!" he said. "Great! You guys are on fifth. You can load your gear right over there." He pointed to a section of concrete underneath the gazebo.

After slogging our gear through the park, we watched the other bands. All were cut from the same 1990-era Depeche Mode cloth.

The only variance was the number of keyboards per band and the specific style of clothing. Some were traditional goth, others were dark punk goths, one was Steampunk. Next would be us. Flat Planet: a ska band.

As big as ska had gotten by 1994, ska bands were outnumbered in the millions by punk, funk, and alt-rock bands. It wasn't unusual to be the only ska band at a show. But a bill with nothing but synth-pop-loving goths was new.

Mr. Happy goes full on Mr. Crow

Alex fortuitously had chosen his goth wrestler character, Mr. Happy, for the gig. He spent more time than normal applying black and white facial makeup. He finessed Mr. Happy to be a bit more Mr. Crow. Alex heard the challenger's call and accepted. Mr. Happy Crow would earn this crowd's respect. All hail your new suburban goth overlord!

"They'll hate us, so let's make this a memory that'll live forever in their heads," I said. Everyone nodded. We always strived for an exciting show, but when up against a potentially hostile audience, we added a certain venom to our energy.

We played with one intent: to blow goth minds.

The audience of not-quite-fifty made a wide circle around us, keeping their space. We occupied their circle and claimed it as our own. Seth and Geoff synchronized moves and locked eyes with the cutest goth-girls. Alex mimicked Robert Smith and danced so hard his makeup smeared like Tammy Faye Bakker. I pounded the shit out of the drums, jumping mid-beat to smash down on my cymbals. Mike and Rudy jogged back and forth the length of the gazebo, daring the crowd to join in their mad dash. I didn't quite get what they were going for, but it was a spectacle.

"All-American ska band"

No one left the circle. No one danced. No one smiled. They didn't clap their hands. They stared at us like pod people. Their non-reaction turned our energy aggressive. Alex and the punk twins danced right up to their faces. During our song "Holding Up The Wall," I took over on lead vocals and Alex, walked around the crowd with his hate upside-down, asking for tips to help us on our long trek through the US. The pod people didn't budge. And then, just like that, we finished our last song, failing to get a rise out of anyone in the crowd. As quickly as I could, I packed up my drums, ready to bolt, avoiding everyone's eyes.

Original, unused Flat Planet mascot "Junior," designed by Alex

To my surprise, the goths flocked to the merch table, where our roadie Mark sold shirts and tapes. We fielded a lot of *what the hell kind of music were you playing* questions and gave them a Complete History of Ska TED Talk. We sold more merch than any other show on tour.

No one had yet told weird, suburban goth kids how to react to ska. Once they heard it, and had a chance to process it, they loved it. It was a brief moment of unfiltered appreciation. A few years later, MTV would take over as ska's official ambassador, and kids would no longer be shocked speechless or fall in love when a ska band crashed their show. They'd know the truth: marching band kids can't be real rock stars.

BOOK YOUR OWN FUCKING LIFE

The first time I imagined Flat Planet going on tour, it seemed like a pipe dream. But then, in 1993, Mike Park told me about a magazine called *Book Your Own Fucking Life*, designed specifically for nobody bands with only a single box of self-released demo tapes and mono-color band t-shirts. A band like mine. All you needed was an almanac from the local drug store and hours of precious time clogging up your parent's landline pestering punks for shows. These were DIY gigs: dingy basements, anarchist coffee shops, rented out VFW Halls, and unsanitary skate parks. *BYOFL* listed promoters, bands, indie records stores, even random punk shit like vegan cafes, where one could swipe some food if they showed up at closing time on Tuesdays when "Corin was working." Park encouraged me to book a *BYOFL* tour even though our music wasn't punk. We mixed ska with diverse genres and abstained from suits and doc martens in favor of a crazy spectacle of a show ala Skankin' Pickle and Fishbone. To me, that didn't equal punk rock. It didn't matter. From '94-95, we toured three times, all DIY punk shows—all great tours.

What I learned was *BYOFL* was a portal into the vibrant punk scene of the '90s that embraced ska with open arms. We did better gigging with sloppy punk bands in crust punks' backyards than on stacked bills with stylish rude boys at twenty-one-and-over bars. A decade earlier, American ska bands were viewed as live dance music,

46

an oasis from the aggression of hardcore. Early-to-mid-80s bands Culture Shock (U.K.), Kortatu (Spain), and The Offs (U.S.) blurred these lines. But as the '80s progressed, California legends Operation Ivy showed that punk rockers could play ska too. By the '90s, punk rock had absorbed enough of the ska scene to obliterate any line separating them. There was still a traditional scene, but they were a minority. Most ska bands were honorary punks.

So how exactly did ska and punk become so entangled?

Touring is fun! Flat Planet newsletter photo collage

The Next Obvious Step After Punk

The story of punk begins in the mid-70s, where bizarre, and eclectic stripped-down rock 'n' roll bands, inspired by The Stooges, MC5, The New York Dolls, Velvet Underground and countless '60s teenage garage rock bands, thrived in urban wastelands: New York had The Ramones, Television, and Patti Smith. L.A. had The Germs, The Dickies, and The Weirdos. London had The Sex Pistols, The Clash, Wire, and The Damned. San Francisco had The Avengers, The Nuns, and Flipper. Most of the punk scenes were inclusive, particularly for women and queer folks.

While punk was raging in England, memories of ska existed in used record stores—over a decade since the music filled dancehalls in West Indian neighborhoods. There was nothing cool about the music. It was old upbeat dance music that white kids were vaguely aware of (apart from working-class kids that lived near Caribbean neighborhoods) and an unhip style that West Indian kids viewed as their dad's music. The late '70s kids all liked the newer roots reggae, for its deep bass, and politically defiant lyrics. Reggae helped the second generation of West Indian immigrants claim their cultural heritage in a predominately white country.

The white British punks got a heavy dose of reggae at punk club The Roxy where DJ Don Letts spun the music exclusively between bands. "They dug the basslines, beats and attitude of the tunes I played," Letts wrote in a piece for the *Guardian* in 2001. The Clash and The Members were huge reggae fans. It informed their music.

At the same time, the Rock Against Racism movement was bringing the anti-authoritarian punk bands together with Britain's homegrown reggae scene, bands like Steel Pulse and Aswad. Together they fought off racists who were trying to kick Caribbean immigrants out of the country. Bob Marley even released the corny "Punky Reggae Party" in 1978, celebrating the unlikely alliance he witnessed first-hand after Letts showed him around and explained that "dem crazy baldheads are my mates."

Jerry Dammers on the 2 Tone Tour

The Specials formed in Coventry in the midst of this political and musical atmosphere. They originally got together in 1977 as the Automatics. Keyboardist Jerry Dammers' vision for the band was to mix roots reggae with punk rock, bridge these scenes together, and make it political. But trying to combine the two didn't work; the energy was too dissimilar. He realized the upbeat pace of ska could combine with punk and could still be made politically potent. From this, The Specials sound was born. He punked up a lot of old Jamaican ska tunes to honor the pioneers, and to make sure they got paid. But to recontextualize the music, he tweaked some of the originals' lyrics to make them politically relevant to the racism, the corruption, and the crumbling economy of late '70s England. "Our take on ska was mixed with the present-day punk and socialist politics of the '70s," says Specials guitarist Roddy Radiation.

Madness got going around the same time in London with their own nutty spin, influenced by Ian Dury's style of British 'everyman' storytelling. The Selecter followed the Specials in Coventry along with The Beat in Birmingham and The Bodysnatchers later in London. When punk died in England, 2 Tone ska took off like wild-fire. "2 Tone was very much this anti-racism thing. High energy music, but with its roots firmly in Jamaica. We were conscious of the politics that were around The Anti-Nazi League, Rock Against Racism. All of those things were coming up as an antidote to the flaccid, white, prog-rock nonsense that had flowered during the early '70s," says Pauline Black, singer for the Selecter.

2 Tone was technically the name of The Specials' indie label that released music from all these bands, but they presented themselves as a movement. That they were mixed-race bands was a statement in and of itself. They also sang overtly anti-racist and politically-progressive lyrics. The 2 Tone bands surpassed any of what the punk bands were able to achieve on British radio and television. "2 Tone was the next obvious step after punk. It melded the iconoclastic attitude of punk with the righteousness of the roots culture in reggae at the time, then produced this third thing," says Bodysnatchers singer Rhoda Dakar. "There was a style to it. It was something that people could adopt immediately. It spread further abroad."

Punk Rock Dogma

In the states, punk rock gave way to hardcore; bands like Minor Threat, Black Flag and Bad Brains funneled anger into faster and more aggressive songs. A few years later, a second wave of hardcore followed, even more pissed-off, much of it fueled by suburban angst. When 2 Tone ska bands came to the US around the same time, the small cult fanbase of kids that found it had little context for it. The US had nearly as many Caribbean immigrants as England, but many inte-grated into the existing black culture, like hip-hop architect Kool Herc, who took Jamaican sound system DJ culture and used it to spin Amer-ican soul music. In the UK, the West Indians kept much of their culture intact. 2 Tone Ska emerged as a clear melding of existing British cultures. But to the kids in the US, it was this whole new thing;

they didn't particularly grasp the individual components—old Jamaican music mixed with British punk. A small handful of these kids, enamored with 2 Tone ska, started their own bands modeled after 2 Tone. They were few and far between, unlike hardcore, which dominated the underground landscape.

Hardcore thrived so well that every major US city had its own distinct, vibrant scene. San Francisco's was initially led by oddballs Dead Kennedys, who sped up garage rock and spouted satirical lyrics to mock yuppie Reagan conservatism and the American war machine. The bands around them grew less sophisticated. As this scene flourished, some fragments split off and grew darker, more violent, and attracted a scary right-wing element, even Nazis in some cases.

Punk rock in the '70s was about being open-minded. Hardcore became dogmatic about what was and what was *not* punk rock. It also got macho. Others felt left out, abandoned by what was once an inclusive community of outcasts. Many no longer wanted to be involved with a scene full of potential violence, particularly women and people of color. Eventually people stopped caring about punk. The shows got smaller; the fear-mongering media exposés became non-existent. It was as if it wasn't there anymore.

The pissed off hardcore bands were in stark contrast to the danceable, suit-wearing American ska bands. These bands rarely shared the same stage. The Bay Area's main ska band, The Uptones, from Berkeley, were drawing big crowds. As much as they intended to model themselves after 2 Tone, their high school spastic energy and appetite for politically left-leaning lyrics gave them a punk rock edge in their early years not seen in most early American ska bands like LA's Untouchables, New York's Toasters and Boston's Bim Skala Bim. It wore off as they got older and mastered the mid-tempo ska grooves, but those early shows made an impression on Albany high schoolers Tim Armstrong and Matt Freeman, who would join the '80s ska scene with their group,Basic Radio and later form Operation Ivy and then Rancid. The Uptones even impressed future Operation Ivy singer Jesse Michaels, not much of a ska guy. "I saw them play at the Keystone Berkeley in '82 or '83 and they won me over because their show was essentially like a punk show including stage diving and confrontational, though light spirited, lyrics," Michaels says.

In the mid-80s, as The Uptones were packing clubs, melodic punk rock bands were almost non-existent. Aggressive bands still ruled the scene. "You were either playing hardcore, or there was a big speed metal scene. There wasn't many punk bands," says Operation Ivy drummer Dave Mello, who at the time was playing in Distorted Truth. For the few punk bands out there, spaces were hard to come by. Local DIY promoter Kamala Lyn Parks did everything she could starting in 1984 to book all-ages DIY punk shows in San Francisco, Berkeley and Emeryville. "I wanted to make sure that young people could see bands," she tells me. She booked amazing shows for punk groups like 7 Seconds, the Asexuals, and Nomeansno. The spaces were unreliable, and it was always a crapshoot whether the promoters would demand more money for the venue than what was negotiated.

Her and her associate, promoter Victor Hayden, were on the lookout for a place they could put on punk shows on a consistent basis. They spotted 924 Gilman Street in Berkeley and saw the potential for a dependable all-ages venue where their scene could thrive, but they didn't have the resources to lease it. They mentioned the place to Tim Yohannan, founder of San Francisco punk rock magazine *Maximum Rocknroll*, who happened to be searching for a space in San Francisco. It took some convincing that Berkeley would be just as cool. Yohannan signed a lease in April 1986, and Gilman was born. Gilman would impact not just the future of punk, but also ska.

Gutter-Punks, Goths, And Anarchists

Basic Radio was not a traditional ska band, or even trying to emulate 2 Tone is any way. The group played rock, punk, and hip-hop but used ska as its glue. "This diversity of influences was typical of bands in those days because Berkeley in the early 80s was a real melting pot of musical cultures and different types of kids," says Michaels. One of Basic Radio's final shows was in Mello's tiny garage in Albany; they got a feeling for how well their breed of jumbled-up ska would go over within the small community of East Bay punk rockers.

When Basic Radio broke up, Armstrong wanted to form a strictly punk rock group. He invited Freeman, Michaels, and Mello. Armstrong envisioned Operation Ivy to be somewhere between East Bay punk band Crimpshrine, early Social Distortion and The Clash. In the first few practices, those elements came together well. However, ska also seeped in, but with the same hyper energy as their punk songs. "Once we started playing, the ska influences quickly emerged because of Tim's familiarity and natural talent with that type of music and because the ska songs we wrote sounded good," says Michaels.

THE JOHN BROWN ANTI-KLAN COMMITTEE
AND
THE GILMAN STREET PROJECT PRESENT

ROCK AGAINST RACISM

WITH BEATNIGS
M.D.C.
OPERATION IVY
DEAD JACKSONS
BO
PARANOIA

FRI. JUNE 24

9PM $5 PLUS $2.00 LIFETIME MEMBERSHIP

924 GILMAN STREET IN BERKELEY

PLUS SPEAKERS, FILMS AND INFORMATION

ACTION AGAINST IGNORANCE

Once Operation Ivy was playing ska, Armstrong gave the rest of the group a crash course in the music. "I had never really played ska," says Mello. "I remember Tim saying, you got to listen to these records: The Specials, Madness, English Beat and the Selecter. He just said those four records." At their heart, the members of Operation Ivy were punk rockers, even when they were playing upbeats. Operation Ivy only rehearsed for a few months before they played their first show in Mello's garage, along with Crimpshrine, Bitch Fight, and Isocracy, which was jammed packed with friends and other bands. The crowd surrounded the band tight enough that they could literally touch the musicians as they played. The energy was so punk rock the wooden shelfing unit on the garage wall nearly fell on Mello mid-set, but a few audience members caught it in the nick of time.

The next day, the group played its second show at the recently opened Gilman where they opened for MDC. Gilman was a natural fit for Operation Ivy. Initially, Yohannan ran Gilman somewhere between a socialist collective and a community center with a whole network of people sharing duties. Outcasts from every subculture flocked to Gilman: Goths, gutter-punks, skaters, art students, anarchists—all rebels against the status quo. Creative kids formed friendships and took care of the venue, even volunteering to do menial tasks like sweeping the floors and taking out the trash. Bands weren't listed on flyers, in newspaper ads, or even on the venue itself. You would show up and find out what was going on that night.

Sometimes bands didn't even play, in which case, kids just hung out. There was hardly a line separating the band from the audience. Anyone could hop on stage and sing another band's songs. Musicians were interchangeable or ambidextrous, spontaneously joining and leaving other groups. Unlike emerging punk scenes in other cities, these bands were wildly diverse. Pre-Gilman, most of these kids didn't know each other and had developed their own styles. Gilman brought them all together. The environment supported originality and creative thinking. Even Gilman's famously posted wall rules (No racism, no sexism, etc), were thoroughly debated from the beginning by its volunteers as to how strictly it should be enforced.

The moment when everyone is Op Ivy

At Gilman, no one watching Op Ivy told them they were playing ska wrong. Had Operation Ivy tried to join the mid-80s ska scene, they would have been laughed off the stage. Early Uptones may have had punk energy, but they didn't play punk songs. You couldn't be a ska band that dressed like dirty punks, played sloppy upbeats and fell off the stage mid-song, accidentally unplugging your guitar cable. Like-wise, Operation Ivy would have never fit in the hardcore scene a few years early where dogma demolished outliers. At Gilman in the late '80s, with the small crew of kids that brought this scene to life, the very notion of punk rock was being redefined. What everyone did was punk; it wasn't defined by how the music sounded. Operation Ivy's adventurous approach to melding late-80s East Bay punk with ska came at just the right moment. Parks explains this liberating spirit of Gilman: "It was the attitude, the energy, the political bent, challenging the norms—you were part of it."

In this landscape, a diverse free-spirited group of East Bay punk bands all cropped up together that said *fuck you* to punk rock dogma. There was the metal adjacent Neurosis, a confrontational, funny feminist rap trio called The Yeastie Girlz, the light-hearted pop of Sweet Baby Jesus. There was the Beatnigs, an all-black, industrial-punk group who banged on metal objects. And within all of that, there was a single group playing ska songs: Operation Ivy, who all these bands loved dearly.

No stage required

Mysterious Hybrid

Punks in other cities got a taste of Gilman in 1987 when *Maximum Rocknroll* made its first attempt to document these bands with a two seven-inch record compilation called *Turn It Around*. Local engineer Kevin Army recorded most of the bands in two short sessions, one band after another. Later Army would record several seminal punk albums from bands like Jawbreaker, Mr. T Experience, and Green Day, but at the time he wasn't familiar with this current crop of bands. He was the only engineer in the area *Maximum Rocknroll* could find that wasn't scared of recording punks. Once he started the *Turn It Around* session, he recognized immediately the thread connecting all these musically diverse punk bands: They were all great pop songwriters.

Army was especially impressed with Operation Ivy. They were a sloppy, raw punk band throwing ska riffs into their songs. Their politically charged anti-cop anthem "Officer" was unlike anything he'd ever heard. "It's this mysterious hybrid. It's simultaneously ska, hardcore and pop-punk," says Army. "It's melodic and catchy."

The kind of ska Operation Ivy played was totally new territory. It went way beyond having punk elements. That was already happening. The Mighty Mighty Bosstones had released hardcore and metal influenced ska, but the Bosstones still adhered to ska traditions. They wore suits, they had a horn section, and played as tight and in-tune as possible. The N.Y. Citizens, though much less famous, formed in the mid-80s and were also very untraditional and punky in their approach. "We had this fuck the world approach to everything. A lot of our stuff didn't come out very ska. We would meld it all together," says N.Y. Citizens bassist Paul Gil. They too didn't stray from the core mission of being a dance band. Some Op Ivy songs were power chord punk blasters; others were upbeat-driven ska songs. But it wasn't a dance party. It was unleased, unapologetic punk rock fury. "We never really played ska shows; only punk shows," says Michaels. "Some ska people distinctly didn't like us because we had no horns or suits and I was too much of a spaz for them," says Michaels. Op Ivy was doing something no band before them dared: recontextualizing ska within the punk genre.

Other cities around the country had growing underground punk scenes, many with great bands and killer DIY venues, or at least local promoters that could navigate through the halls and basements to sustain a scene. Parks soon discovered this. She may have been instrumental in opening Gilman, but she didn't heavily participate once it got going. She wanted something of her own. With Gilman providing a stable place for East Bay punk bands, she transferred her energy to helping bands book elsewhere. San Francisco punk band Clown Alley, who she was the unofficial manager for, asked if she would book them some west coast dates. With a little research, she spotted DIY scenes up and down the coast. The tour went splendidly. The drummer then asked Parks how she booked shows so he could do the same for his other band, Sacrilege B.C. She gave him her contacts, figuring this would be her final time booking a tour.

Larry Livermore, co-founder of Lookout Records, heard what Parks had done for Clown Alley and asked if she would get Operation Ivy on the road. He had just released the group's debut EP *Hectic* at the beginning of 1988 and they were itching to tour. That was an easy yes. She loved that band and was friends with all the members. Operation Ivy became the first Lookout band to hit the road.

The tour was six weeks across the country in a beat-up 1969 Chrysler Newport. Leading up to the tour, they'd spent the prior year playing every weekend, usually at Gilman or other DIY spaces in the region. Their whole life revolved around Operation Ivy. "We had a routine where we would make stickers and we would do this thing called doh-ing where we would stick them on people's backs and stick them on cars and walls, wherever we would go," says Mello. "We talked about our band as much as we could. We were always at Gilman Street."

The shows Parks booked were mostly punk rock DIY shows that she located from copious research. The audiences ranged from five to a couple hundred people, though usually it was in the fifty-to-one-hundred range. In Chicago, Op Ivy played a big show with Screeching Weasel and headliner Zero Boys, who were reuniting. Operation Ivy had developed in the unusual bubble that was Gilman, but word was spreading in the deepest punk rock circles about them from their two tracks on the *Turn It Around* comp and their *Hectic* EP. Most of these people they played to on that tour had never seen a punk band play ska, but they took to it right away. "Even though ska and punk were different, they still knew ska. They listened to The Descendants, they listened to So Cal Punk, they listened to The

Specials," Mello says. "It wasn't like we were blowing people's minds. We were just playing something that they were like 'of course those things mix together.'"

For The Love, Not For The Money

In no time, Parks was booking several East Bay band's tours like Stikky, Dead and Gone, and of course bands she played in like Cringer, The Gr'ups and Naked Aggression. She was building a network, but also, she was recognizing its distinct culture. DIY touring didn't work like typical showbiz: hire a manager, show up, get drunk, play, and walk out with a wad of cash. DIY required a code of conduct. Whenever she booked a tour, she would give bands a little lecture on *how* to tour. "I didn't want people screwing up my network," she tells me. "People relied on me to provide bands that were good but also people that were not jerks." The code of conduct was a lot like the Golden Rule. Be considerate and view everyone you work with as part of your community. Be respectful of anyone that lets you stay in their homes. Leave their house cleaner than when you arrived. Do your dishes. If five-year-olds could Do Unto Others, so could crusty punks.

One time, she booked an epic three-month long tour for Crimpshrine. When they got to Pensacola, Florida, the bass player Pete Rypins got so fed up with the unglamorous, non-stop grind of DIY touring, he up and left. His fill-in, Paul Curran showed up a week later, which was great, but unfortunately, Rypins took the van—his van—with him.

Crimpshrine continued the tour, anyway, hitchhiking and taking the train whenever possible. They didn't know day-to-day whether they were going to make the dates. Parks and the band called the promoters and updated them daily on the band's status. "It was insane in terms of trying to manage it," she says. When Curran showed up with his unreliable Ford Pinto a week later, it made them only slightly more mobile. Rypins later joined Neurosis and when they asked Parks to book their next tour, before she would agree to it, he had to promise her he wouldn't do the same thing once Neurosis was out on the road.

Parks typically only booked tours for the East Bay punk bands she was friends with, though she would sometimes meet out of town bands at Gilman and like them so much she'd offer to send them on the road.

One night, she caught LA band The Offspring. A few days later, she called their singer Dexter Holland and offered to book their next tour.

Parks didn't make money off bands. She only asked them to pay for her phone expenses. Neurosis gave her an extra $80 for the second tour she booked for them, the only time she got paid for her efforts. Ian McKaye, who considered hiring Parks as Fugazi's booker, told her she really should get paid for booking bands. "He said, 'You're doing work, you should earn money for it.' I responded, 'I don't want to mix up my love of music with being profit-motivated,'" Parks says. "I came from that *Maximum Rocknroll* mantra of 'do it for the love, not for the money.' He said, 'That's just ridiculous.'"

Mistakes Are Ok

That first Operation Ivy tour had a big impact on the band's sound. It pushed them in a more ska direction, a natural evolution that grew from playing every night to new crowds. If there was a down moment in the sets, they'd start to play a ska or reggae jam to fill the silence. Mello and Freeman were locking in on their grooves better every time. Armstrong would inevitably hop in with a skanking guitar and get it going. If Michaels was feeling it, he might start improvising lyrics or pull out words from a song like Journey's "Lights." The audience would go crazy. The consistently positive response they got from audiences gave them the confidence to slow down some of their ska and let it actually have more of a dance feel. They wrote "Unity" on tour and started working out ideas for what would be "Sound System" and "Take Warning."

When the band returned home, they already had material for a full length, but it took a while to record. Gilman sound guy Radley Hirsch had a vision for the recording and the band were willing to follow him on it. He started by recording demos at Gilman. He then recorded the band's instrumental takes at a nearby empty warehouse and did a bunch of overdubs at his apartment basement in San Francisco. It took a while to get what he was hoping to get. He nitpicked parts of it, like the snare drum sound. He overdubbed Mello playing just the snare parts in his bathroom because it wasn't popping in the warehouse recordings. Regardless, the whole recording wasn't sounding right to the band. "It was too hollow of a sound. We didn't hear the actual instruments. It was too much noise, too much bleed.

He wanted us to feel like this is going to be a great thing, but it was taking so long, we just got bored of the whole process."

They went back to the man that captured them so well on the *Turn It Around* tracks and the *Hectic* EP: Kevin Army. The objective was to get it done and not dawdle around. They had spent so much time trying to record what would be their first album, *Energy,* in the warehouse that they'd already updated their song "Freeze Up" to say that it was 1989, instead of 1988.

Army recorded the basic tracks at Sound and Vision in a single eight-hour session in early 1989. Fortunately, they'd been practicing the songs for nearly a year, so it wasn't tough. Army got solid, immediate takes. He focused on capturing the band's live sound, and making sure you could hear the quality of that pop-songwriting he spotted when he first fell in love with the group during the *Turn It Around* recordings.

Every song was recorded in one-to-two takes, no more. "I had seen them play live. I knew, don't fuck that up. Don't make them freaked out and uncomfortable. You throw up the mics as quick as possible and you get them to play," says Army. "Mistakes are okay. Chuck Berry records are filled with them. Music business people are over-focused on perfection. Later I would be laughed out of an A&R office for my demo tape when it came to the Op Ivy song. People would fast forward or laugh."

He positioned the members in a semi-circle, facing each other inside the tiny space at Sound and Vision. The drums sat in front of the door, which was left open so the sound would bounce around and create natural reverb. Overdubs were minimal, though guitarist Tim Armstrong did some "scrape" guitar overdubs, some leads and some random rhythm parts to give the songs dynamic. And that saxophone in "Bad Town" was overdubbed by friend of the band, Paul Bany, who was the guitarist for Mello's old band Distorted Truth. Michaels was so focused and thoughtful when he sang, he'd re-write lyrics in the studio.

Army mostly kept his comments to a minimum. The band was almost perfect on their own. But he interceded during vocal overdubs when the band pushed to add gang "oi oi oi" vocals on every single song. "Left to his own devices, Tim will do that," Army says. "I went, 'You guys are starting to sound like the Village People.' I deliberately used 'The Village People' to bother them." It worked. They eased up on the gang vocals. Army told them to think about the magic that happened when it was just Michaels and Armstrong's vocals going back and forth.

Mixing went quickly. Army adjusted the levels of reverb, bass, and treble differently on every track. "If it's a ten-song album, you can blaze through it with all the songs sounding the same. But I think if it's that many songs, you want to mix it up." Army captured the band exactly as they were: Raw, fast, loose and with Armstrong's almost grating, dissonant tone. Michaels' lyrics were political but also intellectual, thoughtful and personally relatable. He railed against the oppressive, corrupt system, but made you think about your own role in perpetuating its power, and how you felt about that. "He was always writing lyrics. He was always trying to stress different syllables and come up with different words or different lines," Mello says. "Jesse would think about what he wanted to say, what the song meant and just rework the way he wanted to sing it. And it would come out more meaningful." Several songs started with a chorus hook that Armstrong or the group would make up, usually something that spontaneously came to them that they thought sounded cool. Michaels would pour over what he could say in the verses to give it meaning. "We came up with 'I got no nothing in mind.' Jesse would sit there and think about the meaning of that and what he could say about an empty generation, about not knowing and trying to make my way in this world but not saying anything meaningful." Few punk or ska vocalists have come out since with lyrics as good and as universally relatable as what Michaels wrote for Op Ivy as a teenager.

Heartbreaking On Every Level

Ever since they'd gotten back from tour, Op Ivy was getting a buzz in the larger punk community. They'd started as part of Gilman's scene, now they were a draw unto themselves. The group had a European tour scheduled for the summer of 1989 to coincide with the release of *Energy*. They would tour alongside UK ska-punk band Culture Shock. But before Op Ivy left for tour, they broke up due to interpersonal conflicts and an inability to hold together this thing that seemed to be growing bigger than they ever imagined. "One of the saddest days of my life," Parks says. "It was heartbreaking on every level. They were a very magical band to see."

Even with the momentum they had, Op Ivy might have been lost in obscurity forever had Lookout not released *Energy*. In 1989, the ska world wasn't sold on Op Ivy. Ska label Moon Records, to whom they'd sent *Energy* demos to in the late '80s, passed on the group. Tim Armstrong mentioned this to Moon owner Rob Hingley years later in 1998. Hingley told him he passed on it because he didn't have the funds, but the reality was he wouldn't have put it out anyway. Whatever it was this band sent them, it was not ska. It certainly didn't fit the Moon brand of 2 Tone influenced ska. Lookout released *Energy* two months after Op Ivy broke up. Even though they never toured to support *Energy*, it was *the* record for an entire generation of punk and hardcore kids. The same would be true for ska kids, but it took a while.

"We were starting to get a good reputation and good crowds," Mello says. "It's a shame we broke up, and [to think about] what we could have done if we would have still been together. But it doesn't do any good to think of it that way. It's better to think of what we did accomplish, how much fun we had, and how much we inspired people," Mello says.

As more ska bands heard *Energy*, it forever changed the rules of ska-punk. It set the foundation for a new way of thinking in the ska world. Fishbone had influenced nearly every '80s ska band to broaden what styles they mixed with ska, but Op Ivy inspired bands to rethink the culture of ska itself.

Eric Din's band The Uptones may have inspired the members of Op Ivy, but he quickly became a fan, and sees them as a distinct line in the sand for American ska. "Whatever the Uptones did, what Fishbone did, Crazy 8, all those other bands. It was a moment in time. Through that little funnel of Op Ivy, it just spat a thousand other bands," Din says.

Goofy Ass Motherfuckers

Free karate lessons

The Uptones only played one show in the '90s—their biggest—at the Greek Theater in Berkeley in 1990, in front of roughly 8,000 people as part of the International Ska Festival & Earth Day Celebration. They wouldn't play again until 2002. Operation Ivy had already broken up, so they couldn't play this festival, but Dance Hall Crashers, who Armstrong and Freeman formed and promptly quit, played the show. Armstrong was there but stayed backstage; he hosted a goofy behind the scenes public access segment for UC Berkeley.

Local booker Rick Bonde caught the show and loved The Uptones' set. Bonde, a hardcore Deadhead at the time, was unfamiliar with ska and primarily booked hippie jam bands. But he was utterly amazed by the energy he saw on stage and saw a great local band he wanted to work with immediately. It was a no-go since it was the group's last show. Din invited Bonde to check out his new four-piece rock 'n' roll band, Hobo, who were playing Slim's in San Francisco. Bonde came through. He liked Hobo but felt more curious about the headlining band, Skankin' Pickle. What an odd band name.

They played ska, but it was also a chaotic vaudeville show with props and costumes. If you asked Skankin' Pickle their main influences, they would have said Fishbone and Operation Ivy along with Oingo Boingo and Devo. "We were goofy ass motherfuckers," says valve trombonist Lars Nylander. "We didn't even know what it was. We were like, 'It's going to be weird and crazy.'"

Bonde handed the sound guy his business card to pass on to Skankin' Pickle. The band was on board right away and asked to be put on the road immediately—they didn't care where. Since Bonde came from the jam band scene, he booked them at bars and ski resorts where the money was good, but you had to play to older, drunken crowds.

Skankin' Pickle approached each show, no matter the venue and crowd size as an amphitheater level spectacle. They preferred to stay away from traditional ska shows—those crowds hated them. Every other kind of band was fair game. They played a bar near UCLA called Nomads. They had a guarantee with the club for $150. Only one person strolled in, but he was wearing a Fishbone shirt, so the band saw him as a potential fan. The club owner told Pickle it would be cheaper to pay the band and have them not play. The band asked if they could forfeit their $150 and play to the one guy and give him the show of his life. The club owner figured why not. "We are going so crazy," says Skankin' Pickle saxophonist Mike Park. "That one guy was dancing by himself, having a good time. He bought a shirt, a CD. We hung out, talked to him. The owner just gave us the $150 and said, 'That was great.'"

Skankin' Pickle was excited to go on tour. They'd been dreaming about touring since first picking up instruments as kids, but the bar scene quickly wore thin. "We did every ski resort. It was horrible," says Park. "Actually, it was super fun the first time; you're 21 years old getting free alcohol and getting free ski resort tickets. But man, that got old fast." Fortunately, a lot changed in the '90s for ska bands

Book Your Own Fucking Life

It was in 1991 when Dave Mello first realized that people were really into Operation Ivy. His old band broke up two years ago. He was on tour with Schlong and he suddenly received an $800 royalty check for sales on *Energy*. Not only that, he was suddenly meeting all these kids at shows that wanted to talk to him about the album. "I was amazed at how long it kept selling. It would sell and sell and then it seemed like it was *the* album," Mello says.

Kamala Lynn Parks found herself booking even more DIY tours. In fact, she was heavily in demand, so much that she couldn't keep up with requests. Every band wanted to hit the road using this diverse, supportive punk rock network, but no one knew how to do it. Parks was happy to book friends' bands' tours without pay, but she was getting daily calls from bands outside of the bay whom she'd never heard of. There were so many requests from strangers that she stopped having time to book tours for the bands she knew personally. She complained about it to Tim Yohannan one day and said, "I just want to tell them to book your own fucking tour."

Kamala Lynn Parks: Book Your Own Fuckin' Promoter

Yohannan responded, "Oh my God, that's a great article."

She wrote this piece for *Maximum Rocknroll* in June of 1989. True to Yohannan's word, he called it "Book Your Own Fucking Tour." Parks didn't include any specific contact names or numbers in the article but did break down how she was able to build her own DIY touring network in seven steps ("Step 4: Start calling for Chrissakes!") and encouraged everybody to do the same.

Much of her network was created by reading *Maximum Rocknroll*'s "scene reports," and then contacting the reporters in each city. With their help, she meticulously tracked down all reliable DIY promoters within each city and kept copious notes to update on any changes. She had to foster those relationships, and not treat them like mere clubs trying to fill dates. A lot of trust was involved with DIY touring.

Her article got a really positive response from the *Maximum Rocknroll* readers. Yohannan got to thinking. What if he took it a step further and created an actual resource for bands? He presented the idea in *Maximum Rocknroll* of including a "Book Your Own Fucking Tour" section in the magazine, with bookers sending in their info via postcard, and bands encouraged to send in feedback on these promoters. The response was so overwhelming, it turned into its own magazine in 1992, which included contacts, promoters, radio stations, distributors, bookstores, zines, and other miscellaneous items. And in honor of Parks, he'd call it *Book Your Own Fucking Life*. BYOFL became so popular that pretty much every indie punk and ska band in the '90s used it, eschewing the conventional channels needed to develop proper industry contacts.

Detroit ska-punk band Suicide Machines's first tour in the summer of 1994 was done entirely through *Book Your Own Fucking Life*. "You hoped the numbers worked. A lot of them did; a lot of them didn't. You called everybody and crossed your fingers," says singer Jason Navarro. "I remember we played an old mechanic's garage in Sacramento that had rolled-up doors and parked cars inside. Bowling allies. Living rooms. You're just in someone's room. It was fun. *Book Your Own Fucking life*; that's how you did it."

It's Still Punk Rock If You're Making A Couple Of Bucks

A few factors led to Skankin' Pickle wanting off the bar circuit.

For one thing, they were becoming more aware of this punk network that *BYOFL* was connecting. Plus, they were figuring out who they were and what they stood for. Park was getting heavily into the politics of punk rock, with Fugazi's Ian MacKaye as a role model, and *Book Your Own Fucking Life* as its manual. Do it yourself, challenge authority, fight racism. Punk rock encouraged him to think about everything he was doing and the motivations behind his actions.

Park wanted to embrace punk values with all-ages shows and low-ticket prices and have it be about the music, not selling booze for club owners. The bar crowds could care less about anti-racism and progressive messages. "It felt like being at the zoo. We are there for entertainment purposes, 'dance for me,'" Park says. "All-ages shows, they're there to see you. The bar scene sucked. I remember singing to the wall —Why am I doing this?"

Park convinced the band to change course, even though several members were pretty attached to the abundance of money and beer flowing their way. But they saw Park's perspective. When he told Bonde only all-ages shows from now on, it posed a dilemma. The mid-sized clubs and bars rarely did all-ages shows. Unsure of how to book them, Park handed Bonde a copy of *Book Your Own Fucking Life*. If clubs wouldn't book them, punks would.

"I'm like the only agent in the world that's got a copy of *Book Your Own Fucking Life*," Bonde tells me. "Some of the places—like, I could not book at Gilman Street because they don't deal with booking agents. I would call Mike and say, 'They won't take my phone calls. Can you call them?'"

Bonde developed a two-prong attack to build an all-ages network for Skankin' Pickle. First, he called the bars he already had a relationship with and tried to convince their talent buyers to allow a single all-ages night highlighting Skankin' Pickle. A few clubs were open to the concept, but most needed persuading. He asked them to look past the lost alcohol revenue they'd probably incur at this one show and invest in the future where they'd make up for it with future ticket sales.

"It was a challenge to shift into predominantly all-ages shows," Bonde says. "Gradually we opened up opportunities for more and more all-ages venues."

The second strategy involved working with the DIY promoters to help them develop a more dependable scene in their towns. When Bonde pulled out his copy of *Book Your Own Fucking Life*, he often spoke with kids who only got into booking because they wanted more all-ages shows in their area. He heard the same thing from them: "I don't want to make money on this show."

"I want you to make money," Bonde recalls telling them. "I want you to be successful in this business so that I can call you and we can do more shows. It's still punk rock if you're making a couple of bucks."

Skankin' Pickle became more noticeably punk rock in 1993 when they kicked out original bassist Mike Mattingly, who was behind a lot of the theatrics, props, and funk songs. New bassist Ian Miller came from ska-core band Hoodlum Empire. Pickle still had wacky elements but reined it in, focusing on diversifying their musical influences, writing politically poignant material and keeping the energy up.

As Skankin' Pickle drew larger audiences, Bonde and Park, who was always heavily involved with the booking, successfully bridged the wide gap between the hardcore basement circuit and the twenty-one-and-over bar scene. They helped create a streamlined path for bands to build all-ages tours. Bands could forge a DIY musical career without having to choose one path over the other. It also got a lot more bands on the road.

By the mid-90s, ska bands were choosing to position themselves within this all-ages punk-fueled scene. It was an attractive route because punks didn't care how weird your ska band was, if you drove scooters or had the right outfit like much of the traditional ska scene did at the time. The DIY scene encouraged ska bands to align with punk rock ethos and politics and think about the values they repre-sented with their music. Ska bands started reaching out to Bonde, figuring he'd be the one to know how to book a ska tour.

Eventually, Bonde was booking Reel Big Fish, the Aquabats, The Toasters, Let's Go Bowling, Less Than Jake, The Skatalites, The Blue Meanies, Sublime, Cherry Poppin Daddies, Mad Caddies, Voodoo Glow Skulls, Goldfinger, and more. He had some non-ska acts like Blink (later Blink 182), but his reputation was as a ska booker. The Blue Meanies dubbed his agency (The Tahoe Agency) the Ska-hoe Agency. Soon, everyone was calling it that.

"We built this reputation in the ska world because other agents weren't interested in these bands. It was before ska started becoming a thing," Bonde says. "As it progressed, I'd never had to say I needed it to be all-ages. They knew if I was calling and it was about one of these ska or punk bands, it had to be all-ages. It just developed."

Misfits Of Ska

By the early '90s, word spread quickly about Skankin' Pickle. Indie label Restless Records offered them a record deal in '91. The band was excited to be on the same label as other great bands like Fear and They Might Be Giants. But the more Park looked at the contract, the less excited he felt about it.

"It was a bad deal," says Nylander. "Mike was like, 'Do the math. This is not going to work.' We were trying to make this into a living. This is what we wanted to do for a long time. Mike is a good salesman."

The band decided the best course of action was to do everything themselves. The punk icons Park admired like Ian MacKaye and Greg Ginn were releasing their own music. No one was telling them what they could or couldn't sing about or what styles of music they could play. And most importantly, no one was taking their money. There was no reason Skankin' Pickle couldn't follow in Fugazi's footsteps.

Skankin' Pickle created Dill Records and self-released their first three full-lengths: *Skafunkrastapunk* (1991), *Fever* (1992) and *Sing Along With Skankin' Pickle* (1994). After *Sing Along*, they started releasing other bands, mostly from the same punk-ska scene, beginning with Tantra Monsters self-titled album in 1994. Other early Dill records include Slapstick's *Lookit!* and Less Than Jake's *Pezcore*.

"It was a lot of work. The fact that we did it DIY was more punk. It attracted all the bands who eventually came on Dill Records," Nylander says. "It was a family affair. I still talk to those guys to this day. All the fuckers."

Less Than Jake's pop-punk infused *Pezcore* was a breakout hit for Dill, a solid indicator that punk-influenced ska was gaining a larger audience. Skankin' Pickle met Less Than Jake on one of their tours when the band played Gainsville, Florida. Lead singer/guitarist Chris DeMakes didn't know Skankin' Pickle's members personally; he was just a fan. He handed Park a demo. Park liked it and could tell the band had the pop-chops to ascend to the next level. He called DeMakes, telling him wanted to release the band's full-length. "He felt in his heart that we could move records for his label. They were one of our favorite bands, and we knew that our popularity could only grow by being associated with a band that was running a primarily ska label," says DeMakes.

As Skankin' Pickle continued to tour, Park noticed most of the new bands didn't fit the "traditional ska" mold—a mold Skankin' Pickle had to work hard to get away from. Just like Less Than Jake, who identified more as a punk band, Pickle was playing with bands like Suicide Machines, Slapstick, Sublime, and the Voodoo Glow Skulls.

They all had different, unique sounds. People often referred to this as punk-ska, but it was never just punk and ska. With Fishbone as guidance, ska bands in the '90s became eclectic, experimental fusion bands, with punk rock being its spiritual engine.

Shortly after releasing *Pezcore* in the summer of 1995, Dill made its most significant statement as a label by releasing the first *Misfits of Ska* compilation. Compilations had been a considerable part of the ska scene the past decade, often compiling bands from specific regions. *Misfits of Ska* was the first deliberate ska-punk compilation. The record embraced punked up and stylistically diverse ska, almost defiantly. It proclaimed the music to be its own subculture separate from the ska scene. It was a message to skinheads and rude boys they didn't have sole ownership of ska.

"I could see the tide turning. Those bands are about to blow up. Sublime and Voodoo. I was like, they're going to pass us," Park says. "I never did it [mixed styles] because I thought this is going to be popular. We were into Fishbone. Fishbone mixed styles, so we thought let's do the same thing."

Misfits of Ska fell into some legal problems. Within months of its release, TOHO, a Japanese company that owned Godzilla, threatened to sue Park for using the Godzilla image on its back cover without permission. Around the same time, Caroline Records sent Park a cease-and-desist letter for the use of the band Misfits' logo on the front cover. Fearing more trouble from the unlicensed use of the Bride of Frankenstein image also on the front, Park changed the cover to a cartoon drawing of the grim reaper. Not satisfied with that one, Park made a third Mighty Morphin Power Ranger style cartoon album cover for *Misfits of Ska*.

Despite these problems, the record sold incredibly well, roughly 50,000 copies, an amazing number for a ska compilation on an indie label.

None of the bands on *Misfits of Ska* had major label deals when Park assembled the compilation. That changed after its release. Was it a coincidence? Park doesn't think so. "I truly believe the major labels went down this comp and scouted every band," he says.

Less Than Jake, whose song "Soundcheck" was on *Misfits of Ska*, got signed almost immediately after the release of *Pezcore* and *Misfits of Ska*. They released their Capitol Records debut *Losing Streak* in late 1996. "In the 90s, there was this cry of selling out and all that bullshit. We always stuck to our guns and did our thing," says DeMakes. "If you listen to *Losing Streak*, the fact that a major label put that out in 1996, it's a pretty punk rock and raw record. It wasn't until the next record that we worked with our first real producer."

Other bands from *Misfits of Ska* had major label deals when Park assembled the compilation. That changed after its release. Bands that landed deals included Blue Meanies, The Suicide Machines, Less Than Jake, Reel Big Fish, Sublime, and Voodoo Glow Skulls. Slapstick was being courted by Epitaph, but the band broke up before it could materialize. "A lot of people think that it was *Tony Hawk* that did a lot for us," says Suicide Machine's Jason Navarro. "*Misfits of ska*, that shit put us on the map."

Reject It And Be Assholes

In 1995, The Suicide Machines were scoped by several stuffy A&R guys, eager to cash in on the bubbling ska craze. The band passed on all of them. The band members were crazy punk rockers, influenced by the mania of Detroit's lawless hardcore scene. They saw right through the A&R bullshit and knew these guys didn't understand where The Suicide Machines were coming from. Then Hollywood's PR agent Julian Raymond flew out to Detroit suburb Redford to watch the band practice in guitarist Dan Lukacinsky's parents' tiny basement. He didn't say much, just that it was nice to meet them, and then left. A few months went by and he called the band while they were on tour and asked if he could meet up with them again, this time at an actual show. Raymond and his wife showed up at their Baltimore gig. This was days after someone broke into the band's touring van and stole their money, drummer Derek Grant's clothes, and one of Lukacinsky's guitars.

At the show, The Suicide Machines played to a dozen people, most of whom played in the band touring with them, Buck O' Nine. To top it off, they got ripped off by the promoter. The members of

Suicide Machines got revenge by taking their own fresh feces, stashing it under rugs and smashing down on it. Raymond looked on while the band that he wanted to sign lost their minds.

"We were like, dude, this is the sixth week of tour. All our money is stolen. Our drummer has no clothes. We're driving with no window. We're fucking miserable," Navarro says.

Raymond was oddly still interested. He hooked them up with a hotel and took their drummer clothing shopping. "He thought it was funny that the people who broke in went through our cooler and then just threw the food [out] on the bench just to be assholes. He bought us food too." Navarro says. Raymond offered to fly them out to LA to record some demos, with the promise that if they didn't want to move forward with Hollywood, they could keep the recordings and release the songs themselves. That sealed the deal for the band, who were reluctant to sign to a major label. Signing to a major at the time was considered the antithesis of punk. Navarro was comforted that Raymond wouldn't try to dampen their punk rock attitude or hard-edged sound, and that they could reach a larger audience in the process.

The band released its debut Hollywood album, *Destruction By Definition* in 1996. It's one of the best ska-punk albums of its mid-90s era, and a raging punk rock fueled album in the vein of Op Ivy. More punk than ska. Its success showed just how punk rock ska bands could be, even in the mainstream.

The band may have gotten to release the album they wanted to, but Hollywood still made them do bullshit band business events. This only propelled the members to rebel. In 1997, they got booked to play a KROQ promotion event in an LA Tower Records' parking lot. Annoyed to do "industry work," they played all their songs as grind-core. Grant wrote KCOQ on his chest (mocking KROQ), and the band were telling everyone to run inside and steal whatever they wanted from the store. KROQ wasn't amused. They told the band they'd never play Suicide Machines again. The folks in Hollywood Records' radio department were pissed too. The writing was on the wall for Suicide Machines, but with the constant cycling of staff that's all too common in the music industry, once the band released their next single "Sometimes I Don't Mind," the whole incident was ancient history and radio play commenced.

"When you're a bunch of fucking punk kids and all the sudden your shit's on the radio, and MTV, our natural reaction was to reject it and to be assholes. That's what we did," Navarro says.

Too Big To Keep Punk Rock

As ska gained mainstream acceptance, even though most of these bands had punk elements, Park looked on and worried that true punk ethos was slipping away. Money and large crowds will do that. The DIY touring network wasn't as important to ska anymore. Politics had been an important component of ska and punk, but bands seemed to be stepping away from having a message. And the bands that were getting big were more silly than political. As a result, Park started the Ska Against Racism tour in 1998 as a way to bring it back to its roots and to teach kids that anti-racism is a core tenet of ska. "I felt ska had become this corny circus act versus the political overtones of 2 Tone. I wanted to give it a kick in the right direction. I know how impactful music is on young people. I wanted to have a voice and influence in a positive manner," Park says.

The tour ended up being a big package with Mustard Plug, Five Iron Frenzy, Blue Meanies, Kemuri, Less Than Jake, The Toasters, MU330, and Mike Park solo. He raised $23,000 for Anti-Racist Action (ARA), Artists for a Hate Free America (AHFA) and the Museum of Tolerance. Park became uneasy with the tour, not really sure if the political activism was translating in everything. It was too big to contain. "I felt like it wasn't doing anything, other than being a slogan. I was turned off by the lack of activism at my own event. It became more about the fact that ska was big and that's why we were getting the exposure. That's not a bad thing, but I wanted 100% inclusion in terms of everyone being on board for what we're doing rather than it being a steppingstone to bigger and better things." The slogan "against racism" was a statement that needed to be heard. Even if there were issues with the tour, it was an improvement from other popular genres that weren't actively sloganeering anti-racism in the '90s. However, it was clear that some people in attendance didn't even understand the slogan. Blue Meanies singer Billy Spunke told the *Chicago Reader* in 1998 that the Phoenix crowd turned nasty after he mentioned the thirtieth-anniversary of Martin Luther King Jr's assassination. "A huge portion of the crowd was screaming, flipping me off, and telling me to get off the stage. It was one of the most tense moments I've ever had onstage. Finally, I said, 'I guess you're in the wrong place. I don't know what you're doing here.' I was terrified. I was afraid to go into the crowd that night," he told the *Reader*.

After Ska Against Racism, Park scaled down his operation with the Plea For Peace tour in 2000 and subsequent years, which encouraged the artists to talk more in-depth about ways they can get involved to fight racism and bigotry, and to contribute to their community in a meaningful way. And the shows were smaller. "Plea For Peace was a little bit more heartfelt. I feel like we stressed the importance of the cause more on that tour," says Chaz Linde, keyboardist of Blue Meanies. Park also made sure that the booths had more pamphlets available with real information for kids for when the show was over. He realized that sometimes to stay truly punk, you had to work on a small scale.

The Plea For Peace tours were an extension of his non-profit Plea For Peace Foundation, which he started in 1999 to "promote positive youth development through engagement in the arts and social change." Through the tours and other fund-raising events, he's raised money for a variety of organizations including Kristin Brooks Hope Center and 1-800-SUICIDE. He also ran food drives and in 2004, worked with Music for America to register people to vote. He made it be whatever he felt was politically urgent in the moment. "Once I branched out on my own with Plea For Peace, it felt more organic. I had done a few tours with Hopeless Records as the Plea For Peace/Take Action tour and it still felt too big to me. And made me question why the bands wanted to be involved. Was it because they really gave a shit, or it was something that looked good on their resume? Who am I to judge someone's character? It was just something that didn't feel right," Park says.

The Only Acceptable Dance Music For Punks

Anarchist-punker Scott "Stza" Sturgeon stands rail-thin, full of tattoos and has always played ska, no matter his project. From his early days in No Commercial Value to the '90s ska-core underdogs Choking Victims—who broke up in 1999, to the surprise of their record label Hellcat, while they were recording their only LP *No Gods, No Managers*—to the brutally political Leftover Crack and Star Fucking Hipsters. "Crack Rock Steady" has become his half-joking way to refer to his blend of ska, punk rock, black metal and growling vocals. "Rock 'n' roll seems like a silly thing to say," Sturgeon explains. "It's a joke as much as anything people make up."

Sturgeon is the exact opposite of popular culture's idea of a ska musician. But in a way, he's its natural extension in how its evolved alongside punk. He's lived much of his life off the radar. Since his teen years, he's squatted, hopped freight trains and slept in public parks. During the Choking Victim years, he and the other members squatted in abandoned New York City buildings. They never toured. They couldn't afford it. They didn't own cars; too punk and poor to even go on a *Book Your Own Fucking Life* tour.

Sturgeon sings anti-capitalist, anti-racist, anti-authoritarian lyrics, though his anti-police songs have gotten the most attention: "One Dead Cop," "Nazi White Trash," and "Operation M.O.V.E," a powerful statement about black liberation group MOVE that were bombed by the Philadelphia police, killing eleven members. "One of the reasons I started singing about [the police] was because Ice-T got into trouble with his record label, the policeman's association or whatever," Sturgeon says. "He had to apologize for 'Cop Killer.' You shouldn't have to apologize for that. First of all, it's art. Second, police are murderers. They need to be held accountable on some level."

He's had ongoing issues with the police. In 2008, he was arrested by the NYPD after throwing donuts at cops at Tompkins Square Park in protest over them gleefully enforcing the noise ordinance for Leftover Crack, shutting down their shows and effectively silencing their freedom of speech and not doing the same for pretty much every other musician that played the same venues.

A lot of other punks haven't wanted to deal with Sturgeon's bands. He recalls this punk venue Coney Island High that wouldn't let Choking Victim play. It was only two blocks from where they were squatting. "It was because we were squatters and crusties. That's why we got the most resistance. To this day we still get resistance because of that," Sturgeon says.

Leftover Crack formed in 2001, after ska left the mainstream. Leftover Crack would utilize *BYOFL* on their first tour in the early 2000s. "We played everything, bowling alleys. We didn't play too many legit clubs," Sturgeon says. Even if ska was no longer in vogue, its relationship to punk was so ingrained, it was never going to leave. "It's the only acceptable dance music for punks," he says of the two genres several-decade long relationship. The first ska band he saw was

Citizen Fish at Gilman in the late '80s. He would occasionally visit his dad in California. Some friends invited him to Gilman. That night he learned how much fun a punk show could be if there were some ska in it. "We skanked for the whole set, like an hour, non-stop, even when they weren't playing songs," Sturgeon says. "I couldn't do that at a punk show. I didn't have fun in the pit. I just got beat up."

The fact that ska is an ever-present part of Sturgeon's repertoire makes sense. As politically fierce as his lyrics can be, he loathes bands that are so serious, all they do is lecture their audience, and he's also got a weird sense of humor. During a legal dispute with Epitaph between the release of *Mediocre Generica* and *Fuck World Trade*, where he was unable to use the name Leftover Crack, he played under the name Crack Rock Steady 7, an oddly goofy jab at The Slackers' saxophone player David Hillyard—who he didn't even know—and his side project David Hillyard & The Rocksteady 7. Sturgeon saw Hillyard at a club once and told him all about his new band name. "I was like, 'Hey are you Dave Hillyard? Dude we're the Crack Rock Steady 7,'" Sturgeon says. "He reacted the same way as everything. Grumpy."

The way Sturgeon sees it, punk rock and ska have always been closely aligned since the 2 Tone days, and in some ways, punk-ska has remained closer to the spirit of 2 Tone than bands that emulated the sound. "The 2 Tone bands embraced anarchist politics more than the Moon Ska bands did—I mean, there were good bands that I'm sure cared about politics on Moon." When you think about how traditional ska developed in the US, he has a point. 2 Tone bands would never have encouraged its audience to stare angrily at a band that didn't dress or sound exactly right. What the 2 Tone bands were doing in 1979 was an evolving musical experiment, one that many of them grew out of in a few short years.

Every Generation Takes It Their Own Way

Ska evolved in the US differently than in the UK because most fans didn't fully grasp the history and context that created 2 Tone. Still, the impact of 2 Tone was critical; it created a whole new benchmark for ska music. Nearly every ska band that formed since 1979 started with 2 Tone as its primary reference point. Even traditional style bands like Hepcat, who were influenced by the Jamaican pioneers, dug into the music after first discovering 2 Tone. It makes the idea of a "pure" form of ska comically non-existent. Unless of course, you're Jamaican. "That beat, it can be fused easily with anything. It had that influence with rock music that made it interesting because the ska beat was for dancing and the rock beat was to keep the white people interested," says The Selecter's toaster Gaps.

Punk was instrumental in expanding ska into the highly diverse genre of music it is today—so diverse, it's been able to continually reinvent itself and find new life generation after generation. Musicians that understood this realized that you were honoring the 2 Tone musicians by reinventing ska in your own framework. "Ska-punk bands took what we did and put their own take on it, the same that we did with Toots and the Maytals," says the Specials' guitarist Roddy Radiation. "The Suicide Machines, they did a fast, sort of hardcore ska. They took it their own way. Every generation takes it their own way."

Perhaps it's not surprising that once ska melded with punk, it would stay that way. 2 Tone ska after all is the original punk-ska. Were it not for 2 Tone, ska would have forever remained reggae's predecessor, a footnote in Bob Marley's pre-70s roots reggae legacy. "It probably wouldn't have happened if you didn't have punk before it," says Gaz Mayall who's been spinning ska, R&B and Blues at his weekly Gaz's Rockin' Blues in London since July 1980. "The Specials, they said, 'Let's make this the most exciting thing.' The delivery that they picked up from punk bands, it did influence the world."

DEFENDING REEL BIG FISH

"Reel Big Fish is a good band. Their lyrics are dark, sad and upsetting, but also not too serious and kinda funny. The thirty bands from whatever city that didn't get those undertones, they would be like: 'Here's a song about ice cream.' People look at the genre and go 'This stinks.' It's a shame because so much of it is so good."

-Jeff Rosenstock

One of the first ska bands to sign a major label deal was Northern California band Dance Hall Crashers. The band signed to (510) Records, a newly formed Berkeley-based "joint venture" with major MCA, run by Green Day managers Elliot Kahn and Jeff Salzman. (510) Records' focus was to create a higher profile for rock and alternative. Dance Hall Crashers was the label's first signing. Their record, *Lockjaw*, came out in August 1995. Shortly after the record was released, (510) Records dissolved but MCA retained Dance Hall Crashers. MCA proper released their follow up album, *Honey I'm Homely* in 1997.

As soon as the band released *Lockjaw*, there was backlash, particularly in the Orange County ska scene, an opinioned bunch when it came to ska. In the mid-90s, Orange County had one of the biggest scenes in the country, and the O.C. kids loved DHC's prior album *The Old Record,* an early '90 poppy, horn-driven album with many nods to the more traditional ska sound. That a ska band they loved dearly dropped its horn section and signed to a big label worked them up into a tizzy.

The Old Record was a collection from their early years (1989-1992). By 1995, they'd broken up and reformed and were ready to write the kind of music they were feeling. They dropped the horns because it suited the twin-guitar, harmony-driven, pop-punk style of ska they wanted to create, and it made touring a whole lot easier. No label told them to change their sound. But there was no convincing the O.C. kids. They accused Dance Hall Crashers of selling out.

This chatter of selling out inspired a then-unknown Orange County band—who liked *Lockjaw*—to write a song poking fun at the scene's self-righteousness. The band was Reel Big Fish. A year and a half later, the song, "Sell Out" would be their major label debut single, and the ultimate ironic '90s tongue-in-cheek statement.

"People found their own meaning in the song. Some thought it was an anthem against selling out. It was really in defense of ska-punk," says Reel Big Fish singer/guitarist Aaron Barrett. "I was happy to see The Dance Hall Crashers getting some success and radio play," The opening riff of "Sell Out" even directly rips off Dance Hall Crasher's song "Go" from the *Lockjaw* record as a little wink wink, though it mostly goes unnoticed. One other *technical* detail about "Sell Out." Barrett wasn't flipping burgers like the song claims. He was working at Subway when he quit his job to be a big rock star. "I never flipped one burger. Totally bullshit. It's all lies," Barrett says. "It was too hard to say, 'making sandwiches at Subway.'"

When Barrett wrote the song, Reel Big Fish didn't have a deal yet. They never imagined themselves on MTV singing "Sell Out." Mojo signed them in 1996, and the next year, it was Mojo's idea to make it the lead single, thinking it'd be hilarious to have a young major label band debut with a song about selling out, something that so many bands at the time were terrified of being accused of. "It was nice that we had a record label that had a sense of humor," Barrett says. "It's ridiculous to me, watching what happened to the Dance Hall Crashers. I dreamt about getting my band to play in front of as many people as we can. That's all anybody's trying to do."

Why do Reel Big Fish rock so hard?

While Reel Big Fish were working on their follow-up album *Why Do We Rock So Hard?* in late '97, Universal Record's radio department, who had a joint venture deal with Mojo, requested a "no horns" mix of the album, you know something not quite so ska. "I laughed out loud during the conference call when they asked us for the 'no horn' mix," says Patrick McDowell Jr., Head of A&R at Mojo Records. "One of the things that I enjoyed about working with Reel Big Fish is that they did their own thing. Universal was never into horns. Their radio department always thought we could do better at radio, MTV, and sales if we just got rid of the horns. It was a ridiculous request. It wouldn't be a Reel Big Fish album." The band declined and released the horn-driven album as intended. Universal might have been right in a sense. *Why Do They Rock So Hard* had no hit singles, but it didn't matter; the group's fanbase could care less about what was popular and what wasn't.

"Selling out would be changing your music because the record label told you to, so you can sell more records. We're a horn band. We're going to keep doing it," Barrett says. "Some other bands dropped their horns and made albums that sounded really different. We didn't do that. We were little brats. *Fuck You. We do whatever we want.* Why would we make music that we don't like?"

That time Jimmy Eat World opened for "really big fish"

Ever since they resisted the temptation to abandon ska, Reel Big Fish have been a ska-punk touring machine with roughly 200-250 shows a year, releasing strictly ska-punk albums while still managing to experiment with the formula. They've never stopped drawing a loyal audience. For fans who found ska in the post-90s years, Reel Big Fish was often their point of entry. Yet, many people identify Reel Big Fish as the cause for how the '90s ruined ska by making it vapid, pointless, goofball music.

The nature of Reel Big Fish's goofiness is misunderstood. Yes, the band has a popular song called "Beer" and audiences at their shows joyously sing along about drinking said beer, but it's not a frat boy theme song. It's a statement about how people abuse alcohol instead of dealing with their emotions and relationships. Most fans get that and connect to Reel Big Fish's dark lyrics on a deep, emotional level.

"I'll say the most fucked up stuff and play the happiest music ever. I thought it was funny," Barrett tells me. "I'm really shy and awkward, so if I made it silly, then it was okay. A lot of kids have problems. People can relate to those lyrics. I feel terrible, but I'm glad to know that somebody feels like I do. But also, this is fun music, so dance it away."

Barrett argues the happy music/dark lyrics juxtaposition conveys a specific emotion you can't communicate in a strictly dreary or overtly angry sounding song. "Another F.U. Song" sounds upbeat, but it's pissed off and nihilistic. It ends up being cathartic. "It feels good to sing along to the 'Fuck You' song. It's for people that aren't angry all the time, just sometimes. It's not like Slipknot, where you want to be angry all the time," Barrett says.

The band's music holds meaning for awkward people who have a hard time expressing themselves. Barrett recalls being one of those kids when he was first going to ska shows. He hopes to give that back. "Cool people made me uncomfortable. I want to go where uncool people are welcome. That's what a lot of the ska-punk thing was about in the '90s," Barrett says. "I love horns and the fun of it. People hate horns. It makes them feel all weird."

Everything Sucks

"Sell Out" wasn't even Reel Big Fish's first single. In 1995, they had a surprise hit in Hawaii. An older version of "Beer" from their independently released 1995 album *Everything Sucks* took off on the islands. When the band arrived in Hawaii early in their career, they were greeted by fans at the airport. They didn't know the band's name, but they knew the beer song.

Reel Big Fish manager Vince Pileggi used this little factoid to lure Oingo Boingo bassist John Avila to produce Reel Big Fish's major label debut *Turn The Radio Off*, the album that would yield "Sell Out" and make the band MTV stars. At the time, Pileggi worked as the assistant to Linda Engle, the manager for Oingo Boingo. One of Pileggi's tasks was to drive Avila to interviews while on tour. One time, Pileggi pulled out a CD of *Everything Sucks*. Avila wasn't impressed.

When Oingo Boingo broke up, Pileggi kept angling. Avila agreed to come to RBF's practice and check them out. Up to then, he had a hard time understanding the band's appeal. Once he saw their live energy, he turned down an offer to tour with Steve Vai, and decided to work with RBF. He felt they were excellent pop songwriters, whose energy was refreshing. "There were so many good songs, and there was this teen angst about it. The youthful energy was infectious," Avila tells me. "They were the real deal. The people in the band matched the music."

McDowell signed Reel Big Fish to Mojo in early 96 a little while after Goldfinger. He liked the connection Reel Big Fish had with their audience. Universal wasn't happy with the signing because horns were a death sentence. He told them not to worry; the band would build up momentum by touring and sell records on the road. When *Turn The Radio Off* was released in August 1996, McDowell sent the band on tour to build said momentum. In the meantime, Carson Daly and Zeke Piestrup, excited about the record, were spinning the band's song "Everything Sucks" on the "locals only" program on LA's KROQ. The audience at the station dug it and were rapidly requesting more Reel Big Fish.

By the time Mojo was ready to release "Sell Out" in early 1997, the station had been begging for an official single to put into heavy rotation. Even Universal was suddenly (and briefly) on the Reel Big Fish train as potential stars. Avila, who'd help craft this album in 1996 was unaware a ska-craze was in full motion until his oldest daughter, a high schooler, told him this album he produced was everyone's favorite record at school. "A lot of kids still will come up to me and know me as the guy that produced Reel Big Fish, which is crazy. Their moms and dads know Oingo Boingo, but the kids love ska. The kids still love it," Avila says.

*No Doubt's Gwen Stefani hanging with Skankin Pickle bassist
Mike Mattingly*

A Brief History of Ska Selling Out

It took time before the industry was fully pushing ska in the culture. The two early bands to get signed were No Doubt in 1991 on the newly created Interscope subsidiary and Mighty Mighty Bosstones in 1993 on Mercury, thanks largely to their friend Alec Peters being on staff. No Doubt's debut record was mostly funk and didn't do well. An early, unreleased demo of some of the material was even produced by Red Hot Chili Pepper's Flea. No Doubt struggled for three years to write and record—in 11 studios—their massive 1995 hit record *Tragic Kingdom*. They nearly got dropped in the process. Mighty Mighty Bosstones put out a handful of records before finally landing a hit single, "The Impression That I Get," which was released on the same day as "Sell Out."

The two ska tracks in 1995 that got the ball rolling on the radio were Sublime's "Date Rape," a song from the band's 1992 indie record *40 Oz. To Freedom*, and Rancid's "Time Bomb." "Date Rape" went nowhere when it was originally released, but randomly got played on KROQ three years later, and suddenly got a ton of requests from the station's audience thanks to its "shocking" lyrics. As for Rancid, they were signed to indie Epitaph and already had established themselves as a successful punk band, so no one batted an eyelash when they wanted to release a 2 Tone sounding ska song as their next single. Voodoo Glow Skulls, also an Epitaph band, got some radio airplay that year. Dance Hall Crashers' *Lockjaw* had a few minor hits, like "Go" and "Enough," which got played on MTV's *120 Minutes* and was featured on the *Angus* soundtrack. In late 1995, No Doubt's *Tragic Kingdom* took off, but it was several steps removed from their ska sound from the late '80s.

Less Than Jake released their Capitol Records album *Losing Streak* in 1996. It didn't yield any singles, but they became one of the top touring ska bands of the time. The Suicide Machines had some success with "No Face." But it was Goldfinger who blew up that year and accelerated ska's popularity.

Goldfinger were Mojo's first band. Lead singer/guitarist John Feldmann was originally in funk-metal band Electric Love Hogs, which McDowell had seen in the early '90s in Seattle. "[Years later] I went to a hip clothing store in LA called NaNa and John [Feldmann] was the shoe salesman. I ask him what he was doing now, and he gave me a cassette of his new project, Goldfinger, with all different members. That demo was very Joe Jackson/Squeeze influenced. By the time we got around to recording the Goldfinger record, the ska thing was coming into fashion on an indie level. Goldfinger had been playing shows with Buck O Nine, Skeletones and Reel Big Fish, so that's how that influence came in on the record," says McDowell. He started working with the band before Mojo was even a label; he did whatever they needed. Jay Rifkin, who started Mojo, knew McDowell and told him he wanted to record a band. Goldfinger ended up being that band, but Rifkin needed a relationship with a more established label to make it happen at the level he wanted. McDowell shopped Goldfinger's debut EP around and no label wanted it. The band decided to record and release their own full-length. McDowell gave it to independent record promoter Del Williams who got it on KROQ and it immediately got put into heavy rotation, which led to interest from Universal Records. This paved the way for Jay Rifkin to officially form Mojo by establishing the joint deal with Universal.

Mojo sent Goldfinger packages to everyone, including Rick Bonde, who was already booking a lot of ska bands by then. He was so impressed with the band's ability to write pop songs, he signed them to Tahoe Agency. He remembers, before their single "Here In Your Bedroom" broke, the band played SXSW, and there was such a buzz around them that their showcase was filled with one-hundred-and-fifty industry people waiting to check this Goldfinger band out. "Industry people never stand around and wait for a band to come on. They show up minutes before you go on stage," says Bonde. "It was my impression that they [Goldfinger] were going to be the ones that hit. They saw the ska scene happening and they decided to be a ska band. My other clients had been busting their asses in this ska world for years, building the scene. They just swooped in and wrote some hit songs—they had great songs. An undeniable song is an undeniable song." "Here In Your Bedroom" peaked at #5 on the Billboard Modern Rock Tracks in the US.

Goldfinger advocated for Reel Big Fish. Back in early 1996, Feldmann was so impressed with Reel Big Fish at a show they played together—and Barrett standing up to an obnoxious sound guy—he borrowed their horn section for Goldfinger's debut Mojo album. He told McDowell to check out Reel Big Fish. McDowell loved them and demanded Mojo sign them. The plan was to cross-market them with Goldfinger. First, Mojo released a split cassette, followed by a split seven-inch album called *Teen Beef and Tiger Meat*. Eventually Mojo wanted to do a full length with Reel Big Fish.

Afterwards, Mojo signed Portland, Oregon swing—and previously ska—band Cherry Poppin' Daddies, and New York ska band The Pilfers. They also offered a deal to Riverside band The Skeletones, a ska band that didn't have punk elements. The group's singer Jonas Cabrera had one of the best, most soulful voices of any ska band at that time. But The Skeletones were also offered a deal with Maverick, a legit major with more money on the table, so they turned Mojo down. The band recorded a five-song demo, but Maverick wasn't impressed. They wanted more of that "Time Bomb" sound that Rancid were doing. "We could have easily been a part of that whole camp and signed with Mojo Records. It just didn't work out, unfortunately," says keyboardist Paul Hampton. "Mojo Records would have been our best bet. They knew how to market. They knew how to do it." The Skeletones were such a good band, they'd been offered several deals in their career. In 1992, Epitaph, still a fledgling punk label, offered them a contract, which they turned down. In 1994, Rondor Publishing who was connected to A&M Records were interested in giving them a publishing deal. They had the band record a few originals and a few old songs from A&M's back catalog like "Mr. Pitiful" and "Knock on Wood." A noncancerous growth in Cabrera's vocal cords led to some lackluster demos, and Rondor chose to not pursue the band.

For ska in the mainstream, the year everything got cooking was 1997. More bands released singles. Save Ferris came out with their cover of "Come On, Eileen." The year before, lead singer Monique Powell sang on Reel Big Fish's "She Has A Girlfriend Now" a last-minute replacement for Gwen Stefani. "She Has A Girlfriend Now," was a modest hit. "Come On Eileen" was much bigger. That year, Rancid's Tim Armstrong started Epitaph offshoot, Hellcat Records, to focus on ska, Oi! and psychobilly. In its first year, he released records by The Slackers, The Independents, Hepcat, Pietasters, Gadjits and more. Armstrong offered Skeletones a deal in 1998, but they turned it down. "We didn't want to consider ourselves punk rock, even though we were all punk rockers," Hampton says. "We wanted to be on a label that was broader." It was a shame. The Skeletones were an amazing band.

Other groups were getting swept up in the media's hyped-up ska craze whether they liked it or not, like San Jose's Smash Mouth. Their 1997 Interscope album, *Fush Yu Mang*, had some ska-punk songs on it. A ska cover of War's "Why Can't We Be Friends" got some MTV play, but their lounge-garage-retro-jam "Walking on The Sun" was the album's breakout hit and the song that got them signed in the first place, not their ska material. Back in San Jose, a young, then-unknown DJ, Carson Daly, was friends with the band and played the track all the time on his show. When he moved down to KROQ, he continued to spin the track. "We got lumped in with that whole ska thing," says

Smash Mouth guitarist Greg Camp. "We weren't trying to be a ska band. Some of the guys in the band were into reggae. Some people were into straight up metal. Some were into Elvis Presley. That band ended up being sort of a bric-a-brac of whatever. I wasn't going for some jumping on a bandwagon ska-punk thing."

Once radio stations took serious interest in ska, it took off fast. Bonde remembers driving around LA in 1997, hearing Sublime, No Doubt and Reel Big Fish, one song after another. "This is big now. The ska scene has made it," Bonde recalls thinking. As time progressed, ska went further and found its way into TV commercials. "As soon as a company is telling kids this is what they should be into, it's not as interesting. There was a lot of financial success for everybody. Alternative music is only alternative until it becomes commercial. Then something else has to become alternative."

Ska Revival Isn't Cool You Stupid Fuck

Ska was on its way out by 1998. Reel Big Fish kept plugging away without missing a beat. Reel Big Fish gets treated as a '90s one-hit wonder, but there's a lot more to the band than their brief time in the spotlight. They had a bigger impact than most '90s alt-rock hitmakers. Hell, they had a bigger impact than most radio ska bands. The reason: They never blinked twice at their dedication to ska. Even when it was the least trendy thing to do, Reel Big Fish continued to release ska music.

The ska defenders we need

It's unreal when you go online and see all the kids *now* covering Reel Big Fish on YouTube. New ska bands form and still try to imitate RBF, however poorly, which only adds to the narrative that they turned the genre into a circus sideshow. But their fun, catchy songs "reel in" kids who otherwise wouldn't have had an interest in ska. Many of those same kids go on to discover 'respectable' bands like Hepcat, The Slackers, The Specials, The Skatalites, Toots and the Maytals, all bands that have Reel Big Fish to thank for increasing the genre's overall fanbase. I know, I know, your brain refuses to accept that RBF may have had a positive impact on ska.

The Reel Big Fish story also says something about ska fans' commitment to the music. Even when ska was the most mocked genre in the world, Reel Big Fish packed clubs. Can you think of any other band from the '90s that had a couple of hits and successfully toured ten months of the year every single year, still to this day? It takes a band with persistence to never stop playing ska, no matter where the world stands. Like it or not, Reel Big Fish have been the ska defenders we needed. And they're still out there, closing their sets with "Sell Out" to clubs full of screaming ska fans, many of them so young, they don't even understand the concept of "selling out" to the once all-powerful major labels.

THE FOURTH WAVE

In 2017, *Thrillist* published an infuriating article about the supposed Fourth Wave, you know, what ska fans affectionately call ska's post-90s return to the mainstream. The article was called, "Are SoCal ska legends Reel Big Fish and Save Ferris opening the door for a ska revival?"

I interviewed Reel Big Fish in 2016 for the Santa Cruz *Good Times* weekly newspaper. Leader Aaron Barrett told me the group's popularity hasn't changed since they released *Turn The Radio* Off in '96. "In the 90s, we got to a certain level," he told me. "We were never playing stadiums. We were doing 500-1500 capacity venues. We're still playing all the same clubs we were back then. The ska scene has been going strong, at least from what we've seen."

How can there be a Fourth Wave if most of the bands still playing ska never stopped and continue to play to the same size crowds? People call it the Fourth Wave because it's drilled into their heads that mid-90s ska was Third Wave. Once 2 Tone (or Second Wave) revived Jamaican ska and mixed it with punk in the late '70s, it instantly proliferated across the planet. What we called a Third Wave in 1997 was just a flash of attention in popular culture in an otherwise unbreaking ska continuum since 2 Tone. When MTV lost interest in 1999, the Third Wave came to a screeching halt. At least that's the thinking, which is clearly false.

When Third Wave fans at a Less Than Jake show find out there's no Fourth Wave

Another article published in the *OC Weekly* in 2018 annoyed me: "Suburban Legends and Goldfinger are still riding high during Ska's Fourth Wave." In it, the author claims he predicted the Fourth Wave two years earlier and it officially happened on July 26, 2018, when the

Interrupters appeared on Jimmy Kimmel and performed "She's Kerosene." At that moment, everybody bowed down before ska, pledged their undying allegiance, and the Fourth Wave commenced.

I like the Interrupters, despite singer Aimee Interrupter thinking it's a good idea to appear on Infowars (and guitarist Kevin Bivona's extremely defensive non-response to Stephen Shafer's *Duff Guide To Ska* post discussing the band's "libertarian" politics. Google it.). But aren't we overstating the importance of a late-night talk show appearance? Besides, if we're talking about a wave, shouldn't we see multiple new ska bands clearly impacting the culture?

Why do ska fans need to divide ska into waves, anyway? My guess is it's rooted in a need for validation. *I sure hope that Thrillist article is right and ska is cool again so I can stop being the ska-dork my friends all make fun of and...hey have you heard the Interrupters? You might like them even though you hate ska and you hate me!*

It boggles my mind how much time ska fans burn talking about the mythical Fourth Wave. Will there be a Fourth Wave? Maybe there's already been a Fourth Wave, and we all missed it? What if the Fourth Wave is happening right now?! These debates are as endless as whether Streetlight Manifesto is a ska band or not (they are). Several ska bands continue to have sizable fan bases regardless of what wave we are in. We should own that. This wave discussion undermines how consistently popular ska has been, and continues to be, regardless of mainstream validation.

Let's assume the *OC Weekly* is right, and we're deep within ska's Fourth Wave. If so, we need to redefine the Fourth Wave. It has nothing to do with music; rather the plethora of memes, jokes, and ska references suddenly sprinkled in all our favorite TV shows the past decade. *Brooklyn 99, Last Man on Earth, Workaholics, Master of None.* In a cut *A.P. Bio scene that went viral,* Patton Oswalt plays a sad principal who performed in a ska band that once "blew the Tweed Sneakers off the stage," and who lost a demo deal because their drummer was dating the Pietasters' manager's sister—the relationship ended badly. These references are getting so specific, even obscure ska bands like The Impossibles and The Hippos got a shout out on *Crazy Ex-Girlfriend.* Link 80's Adam Davis complained to me about this clip after we watched the ska documentary *Pick It Up* in San Francisco in 2019. Not only was his band not mentioned in *Pick It Up's* recap of the Third Wave, but so far there's been no Link 80 in-jokes on TV shows. I get it, he wants to join the Fourth Wave.

Still, you have to admit, it's odd that every Fourth Wave joke on TV rips ska to shreds. Us fans are tickled pink every time a celebrity winks at the camera and pretends to be mortified when their ska roots are revealed. But why? We are the butt of the joke.

Skanking Is Problematic

Punk and hardcore satire site *The Hard Times* joined the Fourth Wave in 2017, posting some ruthless ska parody articles. One of the early ones: "The Term Skanking Is Problematic, and That's Not Even One of the Top 5 Reasons Ska Is Dead" performed well, much better than the editors anticipated. As a result, many more followed. I spoke with the article's author, Eric Navarro, himself a diehard ska fan, to see if we could understand why the Fourth Wave turns out to be ska fans' addiction to being mocked in the media.

"Ska fans are so stoked for people to talk about ska," Navarro tells me. "You have people that love metal, but they don't love everything about metal. Ska fans, their fervor for ska is absurd. Any ska content that comes out, ska fans are just dying to share it."

Navarro tells me he looked at the metrics and while there aren't necessarily more ska fans than other genres, ska fans are more likely to click the full article and share it. He assures me all the ska fans on the planet will flock to the store and buy my book the day it publishes. They'll read it and display it on their bookshelf and declare me their king. I sure hope this Navarro guy knows what he's talking about!

It Sucks

During our interview, Navarro tells me, as a *Hard Times* editor, he gets pitched lots of ska article ideas. He passes on most of them because they tend to not come from actual fans and rely on surface tropes.

I needed to know these ska tropes! He laid them out for me:

1. All the songs sound the same.

2. Lots of band members. (This one he tries to stay away from as much as possible because it gets old fast. When Wu-Tang released

their last album, he received several pitches joking it must be a ska album, since there are so many members—get it?)

3. Heavy association with the '90s.

4. The fashion.

5. It sucks.

Thoughtful Mockery

The Fourth Wave thrives on thoughtful mockery. Navarro wrote one in 2018 that was pulled directly from the nonstop Streetlight Manifesto arguments that clog the ska forums. It's called "Opinion: Streetlight Manifesto isn't ska—They're good." He had to convince his boss the article would strike a chord because to them it seemed like nothing. "Inside the community, it's such a fevered argument. Outside, nobody gives a shit. The band has horns; they're probably ska," Navarro says. "When I pitched that article, they were like, are people going to share this? Is the joke that ska sucks? No, the joke is a very specific thing that the in-culture will understand."

The article did incredibly well. Part of the reason is the glut of ska groups and online forums now inhabiting the internet. These groups crave an endless supply of Fourth Wave content. Justin Ackermann, who runs the Facebook page, *What Do You Know About Ska Punk* told me: "People are seeing that there are lots and lots of other people that still like ska as much as they secretly do—so they can be open about it."

Ackermann originally started the Facebook page *For The Love of Ska* in 2013, which shared memes he and his group of friends created. For instance, one of the members added the text "Reel Big Fish's new album" to a photo of Kraft Singles Cheese. In 2014, he and some other folks started *What Do You Know About Ska Punk?* They cranked out memes every day and watched as their number of followers surged faster than expected. Ackermann's favorite meme he ever created is a picture of philosopher Socrates with Operation Ivy's lyrics for "Knowledge," which is a few words different that Socrates' famous quote. There's just something about ska and memes that go together brilliantly.

"The music is fun. Some of the memes can touch on serious stuff and still be fun. It's like the music," Ackerman says. "I'm in a mushroom gathering group. There're people that jump on everybody, like there's some sort of expert—I can't believe you don't know this. [In the ska group] they're not as toxic."

Aquabats recruiting new cadets

Online groups are bringing in new fans just getting acquainted with ska and old timers who haven't skanked in eons. "Some people think, 'I used to like ska,' and then join as a joke," Ackermann says and then adds that in no time, these same people are discovering new ska bands and going to shows again. And the ska scene is growing. Several bands that formed after the '90s are energizing the scene in new and exciting way in the internet age, bands like Bad Operation, We Are The Union, Kill Lincoln, Delirians, Steady 45s, Catbite, Los Skagaleros, Omnigone, The Talks, Night Gaunts, and Popes of Chilli-town. Jeremy Hunter, who runs the Skatune Network and their JER project, has become one of the most important voices for this new generation of ska fans, a beacon for new, young fans just getting into the music. As has Bad Times Records, who have been releasing a lot of the newer bands' music and promoting them online relentlessly.

But excitement in the online groups is a double-edge sword. Rather than bask in the brilliance of these wonderful new bands, many people in these online groups are constantly in the thralls of self-parody, memes and long-running in-jokes. Navarro's Streetlight Manifesto article was shared in the same forums multiple times, one after another, making a joke out of their own urge to over-share Fourth Wave content. I can't help but wonder why they share this type of content. There's a line in the article that says, "ska is objectively terrible, and every single song in the genre sounds like my parents having sex."

I appreciate that ska fans don't take themselves seriously, but it's this same impulse to share a parody article that hinges on how bad the music is, that makes them so desperate for the validation of the Fourth Wave. And then the Fourth Wave turns out to be the very media-driven self-mockery they continue to feverishly share in hopes of their music once again gaining mainstream popularity when they could be spending their energy appreciating the awesome new DIY ska scene that exists right now. Whoa, my head is spinning. Like I was saying, the Fourth Wave is real, and everyone who bought this book immediately needs to share it on their Twitter and Instagram for all to see.

ONCE UPON A TIME IN RIVERSIDE

Fresno ska band Let's Go Bowling loved kicking off a wild jam session in the middle of their sets. Usually, they took an old Jamaican instrumental and twisted it around until it trailed off into psychedelic Pink Floyd territory. When this happened, sound guy Tom Mattot, a jam band fanatic, would go heavy on the reverb, creating otherworldly horn solos, mind-expanding guitar lines, and tripped-out drum sounds. Everyone slowly spiraled away into outer space, then circled back to lock in on the main groove, horns finally playing a refrain only ska fanatics knew by heart. Let's Go Bowling's longest jam was a thirteen-minute rendition of Skatalites' "Confucius," a woozy distinction from their original tunes: bouncy 2 Tone grooves with hooky barbershop vocals.

The band played at The Barn at UC Riverside in Southern California in October 1997, and it was one of those nights; a particularly incredible set. The Barn, a deep-set building with wooden rafters, was packed. "You had people pushing folks up and people air dancing, hanging from the beams," says Let's Go Bowling bass player Mark Michel. The band hung around the venue until well after 2 a.m., chatting with fans and having a good time.

Once the fans dispersed, some of the band drove off with friends to hang out in Southern California for a few days. That left Michel and keyboardist Darren Fletcher in the backseat of the band van with

Mattot at the wheel and trumpet player Pat Bush riding shotgun. Thus, began the late-night, four-hour journey home to Fresno.

The band van merged onto Highway 60 a little after 2:30 in the morning. Mattot put a recording of the evening's show in the tape deck so they could listen. Michel remembers being lost in the hazy reverb-soaked saxophone solo when, just outside of Riverside, three bullets pelted the van and tore into the metal frame: *Fwap! Fwap! Fwap!* "All the sudden you hear what sounds like a hammer on the hood," Michel recalls. "As soon as I saw sparks fly, I knew exactly what it was." He ducked his head and shouted for everyone else to take cover.

Everyone quickly reacted. Fletcher hid under his seat. Bush didn't have space to duck, so he froze. Mattot did his best to keep cool and not swerve. He sped up a little to get out of the line of fire. That was all he could do.

Michel clenched his jaw expecting another round of bullets, but nothing came. He checked on the band who were all stunned but still alive and seemingly with no serious injuries. "There was no panic," Michel says. "But then again, shock set in. What the hell just happened?"

They drove another couple of miles, pulled over at the nearest exit and called the CHP. An officer was on the scene a half-hour later. While they waited for him to arrive, the band members poured out of the van and inspected the damage. A bullet stuck out of the front dash. The side window had shattered. A bullet-sized exit wound was found at the back of the van.

While Michel patched up the window with cardboard and tape, Fletcher noticed blood on his leg. He'd been hit by two bullet fragments. One fragment must've flicked past his leg. The other was still lodged in his hand, sticking out like a bad splinter. Fletcher grabbed it and pulled it out. He kept it as a souvenir because how often does a bullet fragment fly into your hand?

The bullet hole locations in the van sent shivers down everyone's backs. Michel thought about the bullet stuck in the front dash and realized that had the shooter aimed just a hair higher, it would have pierced right through the front windshield and killed Bush. Likewise, the band were lucky they only had four members in the van, an unusual decision for an out-of-town show, but they had a lot of friends in Southern California. A few more people in the van and maybe they wouldn't have been so lucky.

When the CHP showed up, the band wanted to know what exactly was going on, and who shot at them. The CHP officer suspected it was a gang initiation coming from a housing project on the other side of the freeway, but he wasn't sure. He mentioned there'd been other incidents of random shootings recently. Just a week earlier a 35-year-old nurse was shot and killed on the same exact stretch of highway, also in the middle of the night.

The officer told the band members they needed to go back to

Riverside to file a police report. That was the last thing the band wanted to do. "Are you fucking high? We just got shot on the freeway, and you want us to drive back to Riverside?" Michel recalls thinking. The band instead filed a minimal report with the CHP officer and headed north, to Fresno, mostly silent the rest of the drive. As they got close to home, a few hours later, Fletcher blurted out:,"Did that really happen?"

Word spread quickly in the ska touring circuit that Let's Go Bowling's van got shot up. It grew into an artifact of touring folklore. As they continued to tour stateside, bands who shared bills with Let's Go Bowling would inevitably ask about the "Riverside shooting." Michel was more than happy to show them the bullet holes, which he never repaired because they were badges of honor. "It was good for a few laughs because nobody got seriously hurt."

Let's Go Bowling "Rude 69" cover shot, behind '80s strip mall bowling lane, Rodeo Lanes in Clovis, CA, 1988

A few months after the shooting, Bowling drove up to the San Francisco Bay Area to play a few shows and were pulled over for speeding. The cop noticed the group's van had a bullet wound in the front dashboard and asked them about it. They relayed this entire story, and impressed the officer, who saw this scrappy ska band as badass warriors. He let them go with a warning.

The band, who's spent most of the '90s on the road, quit their full-time touring schedule in 2000, but still play time to time. They used the same van, bullet holes intact, until 2005. In 2018 they sold it for scraps with 521,000 miles on it.

RUDE BOYS DON'T WIN

It's January 13, 1985, halfway through the decade; America's favorite talent show, *Star Search*, returns from commercial break. Host Ed McMahon charms the camera with faux Middle-American energy. His unremarkable sidekick persona turned celebrity makes a certain kind of sense in the upside-down, cocaine-fueled '80s, when the trust-fund brats of Republican strategists and corporate lawyers are cast as protagonists in teen-sex comedies—pretty much every John Hughes movie.

The stage slowly rotates, revealing an eight-piece multicultural band, each member spaz-dancing in place—horns, keys, percussion, and of course guitars and drums. The members wear tacky and colorful tucked in button-ups, snappy New Wave haircuts, and smirks instead of smiles.

What's so funny? Maybe the fact that they're a ska band on TV in front of millions of Americans who've never heard of the genre, nor have any idea they're hearing it right now. The band understands the absurdity of this moment. Their first gigs were in late 1981, and they'd yet to see a music industry interested in ska.

The band in question is Portland, Oregon's Crazy 8s, who mixed elements of ska, funk, college rock, and pop. Known for epic Bruce Springsteen-length marathon shows and an insanely ambitious drive, the 8s had a DIY ethos which helped them piecemeal an independent career, one that should have yielded them a deal by then. The band's debut 1983 record, *Law and Order*, released on their own label RedRum Records, sold well over 20,000 units at a time when indie distribution was practically non-existent. Their song "Johnny Q," with no label support, but tenacious cold calling by lead singer Todd Duncan & manager Marc Baker— who both had worked at their campus radio station and had solid connections with CMJ & the Gavin Report—surprisingly went into rotation in several markets; it hit #1 on over a dozen college radio stations and became the "Screamer of the Week" on New York's WLIR.

CRAZY 8s

Crazy 8s press photo circa 1986

On *Star Search*, they play that very same feel-good toe-tapper "Johnny Q." Not pure ska; the pop-elements are informed by Oingo Boingo as much as The Specials. There's an explicitly political message in there: Politicians, the media, and corporations work together to confuse the general public about issues like the military-industrial complex, the nuclear arms race, and the destruction of America's small business. (*"I don't know what's going on/The TV news has got me confused/Some puppet king is paying his dues/for*

bald-faced avarice/was it the CIA or the same/or the other side,
someone is lying.")

The band looks shocked when McMahon declares them the
week's champion. They may have flown all the way down from Portland to compete, but they didn't expect success out of it. When *TV
Guide* interviewed the band prior to their performance, the members
scoffed and joked. "It was an experience, not a shot at stardom," trombonist Tim Tubb tells me, reflecting on their attitude of the whole
experience. *TV Guide* wrote that Duncan had a cute personality that
reminded them of Alfred E. Neuman.

Tubb's cynicism wasn't unfounded. Trying to carve out a career in
the mid-80s playing ska was an uphill battle, and technically, Crazy 8s
wasn't even a ska band. Such is the power of ska: if it's an ingredient,
it's the only one that matters. One of their first shows of note was
opening for The English Beat at Corvallis in Oregon. After that, they
were permanently branded with the ska label. Besides, Crazy 8s
looked like a ska band.

"We wore ties, a couple guys wore pork pie hats. It doesn't matter
what we're playing, people are going to say that's a ska band," Duncan
says.

Some in the music industry knew about ska but weren't interested.
The consensus was if the popular 2 Tone ska bands from Europe (The
Specials, The Selecter, The Beat) couldn't crack the US Top 40, what
chance did an American knock-off have?

Despite anti-ska attitudes, Crazy 8s were doing well. When they
gigged in Portland, they packed venues. Auditioning for *Star Search*
was more of a goof than a serious attempt to sway the industry's eye.
Other bands came armed with hairdressers, make-up artists, and
nervous energy—their one shot at fame. The 8s showed up in their
shirts and jeans, played a song and quickly left. They had a Halloween
gig that night at a local college. And beer to drink. But even *Star
Search* was weird. Before the band flew down to LA, the execs didn't
want to send their contract to the band and told them to just come
down in good faith. If they didn't want to, a number of bands would be
happy to take their place. The band responded by telling them that
they'd be happy to tell the *TV Guide* this whole saga. *Star Search*
promptly sent them the contract.

You'd think an unexpected win would soften these guys up, but
no. They knew full well they had no shot at a normal hit-making

career. For week two, the band proved it by playing their most overt ska song, the pessimistic "Rude Boys Don't Win." (This choice of song was also a comment on the contract tug-of-war incident.) Ska without the New Wave elements of "Johnny Q" was not to the judges liking. They were sent packing.

Still, it wasn't over for Crazy 8s. The next year, *Billboard Magazine* predicted 1986 to be the year that the 8s would sign to a major, and *Rolling Stone* named Crazy 8s as one of nine bands to watch. Atlantic offered the band a single deal. They were interested in "Touchy Situation," a non-ska ballad. Director John Hughes supposedly wanted the song for his upcoming film *Pretty In Pink*.

The 8s rejected the offer, not wanting to be a one-hit-wonder, particularly with an outlier song. Warner Brothers countered by offering to cut a five-song demo and *see* about making an album. The band's demo failed to impress Michael Ostin at Warner Brothers who responded by saying that he was looking for the next Peter Cetera. Crazy 8s was on their own again. Even with no major label love, the group's unrelenting, independent drive yielded five self-released albums in the '80s, supported by relentless national tours and a loyal cult following. Like many other ska bands, they are forever lost in the obscurity of history.

This is the story of American ska, a scene built from nothing, that started at the beginning of the '80s but wouldn't see mainstream success for another decade-and-a-half. It's filled with incredible bands who built vibrant, local scenes, crisscrossed the country on successful DIY tours, and even produced hits on the radio and MTV. But due to a music industry with no interest whatsoever in ska, this is a story that's dominated by a series of miserable failures.

The success of a handful of zany mid-90s ska-punk bands didn't pop up out of nowhere; it was built off the graves of a thousand failed rude boys.

The Most Danceable Music In The World

From 1979 till early 1981, 2 Tone ska was huge in England. The only people in the States who knew about the popular 2 Tone bands were music fanatics who regularly read hip British music newspapers like *New Music Express* and *Melody Maker*. In 1980, ska bands flew to the States and played small sweaty club shows. On the coasts, these bands did well; less so elsewhere. The Specials and Madness both played *Saturday Night Live*. It was a promising start to what could have been pop stardom in the US but ended just as soon as it started. By 1981, The Specials, the Selecter and The Bodysnatcher broke up. English Beat lasted just a few more years. Madness continued all the way to 1986. By the time they scored their US hit "Our House" in 1983, they'd drifted away from ska.

As the decade progressed, 2 Tone ska seeped into the States, but not directly from the bands; it was from the film, *Dance Craze*, a UK concert film that documented these groups in their 1980 heyday. By the time it was released in early 1982, ska was dead and buried in the UK. The average music fan there already knew the bands as top 40 pop stars and could care less about the film. But it played a much more important role in the US. These groups were obscure, mysterious underground bands. *Dance Craze* in the US ran in the college midnight movie circuit; most audience's first exposure to the bands.

In 1982, Berkeley teenager Eric Din saw the film with a group of his friends at the UC Theater. He knew almost nothing about ska. He and his friends—all between thirteen-and-fifteen-years old—fell in love with the music. They, like the hundreds of other kids in the theater, danced the duration of the film in the aisles like they were at an actual concert. Some kids screamed for management to turn up the volume. They leaped up onto the mini-stage in front of the screen to the annoyance of the managers. "That movie made us realize this was the most danceable music in the world," says Din. "It was beautiful. The Specials, the Selector, Madness, The English Beat—it was foreign to us. Most of us didn't know this stuff existed until we saw that movie. It wasn't until a little later I came to recognize that this was something that had roots in Jamaica."

After seeing *Dance Craze*, Din realized that if he and his friends wanted to see these bands live, the best they could hope for was repeated viewings of *Dance Craze*. Din's friend, Erik Rader got the idea to start his own band that mixed ska, reggae, mod-rock and punk, and asked Din if he wanted in. Like that, The Uptones was born. In addition to Rader on vocals and Din on guitar, the original lineup included other *Dance Craze* lovers: Charles Stella (guitar), Ben Eastwood (bass), Thomas White (drums), Gregory Blanche (keys), Michael Wadman (trombone), Paul Jackson (trumpet) and Kenny Brooks (tenor sax). The group played their first show in 1982 in Wadman's backyard. "There were no other bands [In the bay area] doing what we were doing. There were no other ska bands. It was silence," Din says. "It was really natural for us to just go, 'If no one else is going to do this, let's do it ourselves.' The birth of the Uptones was basically trying to create something like English 2 Tone ska, our interpretation. It had an additional aspect which came from our Berkeley left-wing politics, our love for punk rock, and our experience as young jazz players."

Dance Craze was conceived by director Joe Massot. In the mid-70s, he'd directed the Led Zeppelin concert film *The Song Remains the Same*. He wanted to do the same for Madness, a band his son tipped him off to. He soon discovered there was a whole scene of bands playing this ska revival music and he expanded his idea to capture them all. Massot told camera operator Joe Dunton about his project. Massot knew Dunton from visiting his camera shop JDC Wilmington Camera and from talking about movies. Dunton had owned Steadicam cameras—which were new at the time—since 1978 and taught roughly fifty cameramen in England to use them. Dunton assembled a crew of five Steadicam operators. He was excited about documenting these bands. He also had the idea to shoot the film on Super 35, which hadn't been done in film since the '50s. It had wider shots than the traditional 35 mm, and made everything look more epic, and in the case of *Dance Craze*, added to the effect that you were right there on stage with them. Since Dance Craze, several films revived Super 35 like *The Abyss, Se7en, Terminator 2,* and *Gladiator*.

Dunton put up the initial funds to get the project rolling. To secure the remaining financing, Dunton reached out to Chrysalis, the record label that distributed 2 Tone bands and signed the Specials and the Selecter for US release. Dunton knew he would never be able to afford the rights to the music. Much of the material was covers and would involve tracking down the Jamaican authors for permission, an arduous task. Leave that to Chrysalis. Dunton and Massot filmed each of the bands at their own separate concerts on different days. After two shoots, Chrysalis fired Massot, who was erratic and weird around the bands. Dunton took the project over himself.

The released version of *Dance Craze* is the vision of Dunton, not Massot. He led the film crew and captured the bands at their peak. He cut it all together to appear as though it was a single concert. The idea was for the viewer to feel like they were on stage with the band, a woozy effect at times. He kept the movements and the soft edits on pace with the music, with the audio shifting to highlight the instruments that were on screen at the time. The shots were dimly lit and felt chaotic, an effect of fully utilizing the Steadicams. Dunton's vision for the film was to give it the illusion of being an old timey news-reel style documentary. He even inserted a fake newsreel mid-performance to break up the energy. Most audiences thought it was inserted accidentally. For later versions, the fake news reel was removed.

Even though Dunton gave *Dance Craze* a documentarylook, that's not how he intended it to be experienced. A proper documentary would have had interviews and an attempt to tell the 2 Tone story. *Dance Craze* had neither. It was supposed to be experienced as a concert and he wanted it played at concert volume level, not movie volume. And he wanted the audience to dance, not sit and stare at the bands performing. At the premiere in England, several rows of seats in the front of the theater were taken out, and he told the audience to let loose, an idea he got after seeing his sixty-year old aunt dancing at a re-showing of the 1956 film *Rock Around The Clock* with Bill Haley. The theaters in England were not excited by all this dancing. "Big theater owners don't want 1,000 kids dancing on their seats. In a certain way, it was misconceived," says *Dance Craze* producer Gavrik Losey. "The idea was that you could play it in Kansas City and the kids would come out and they would have a good time. Interviews would have been great, but we didn't do it."

It tanked in the UK as mainstream culture had moved on to New Romantics bands (Duran Duran, Culture Club). *Dance Craze* was quickly pulled from the screens. Dunton got a random call from a guy in L.A. named John Quinn who claimed he loved *Dance Craze* and wanted a reel for a showing. Dunton sent him all twenty-eight of his reels. "I was upset with the distributor. There was no future for it. There's one man coming out of the wilderness. I said, 'Good luck' and I sent it all to him. He must have made a lot of money. We never saw any money from that movie," says Dunton. The film was distributed to art houses and college theaters in the US by small company Nu-Image, owned by Quinn. Nu-Image also distributed the Fantastic Animation Festival, a package of old newly restored Laurel and Hardy shorts and other foreign films. Quinn was the one that recognized its potential on the cult midnight movie circuit where it found an audience. As for Chrysalis, who actually owned the rights to the film, they had no interest in *Dance Craze,* which they likely saw as small potatoes and made no attempt to stop Quinn from showing the film, if they were even aware of the full extent he was distributing it.

Landmark Theaters, which ran 25 arthouse/revival theaters in 1982 was one theater chain Quinn approached. They ran *Dance Craze* in select big cities (Berkeley, LA, San Diego, Seattle) during normal movie hours for a few days to a week, but then it fell into the midnight movie role for periodic runs. The other music-based midnight movie at the time *Stop Making Sense,* a Talking Heads concert film, had inspiring dancing, so it got promoted as a "midnight dance concert." Landmark took a similar strategy with *Dance Craze;* however, the dancing for 2 Tone ska was a bit more unwieldly than Talking Heads. "They were a tougher audience," says Gary Meyer, co-founder of Landmark Theater "I don't know what it was about that audience. I would get stories from several theater managers complaining about the midnight audience. They would say 'Can we stop playing it?'" Meyer wasn't clear on details, but more than likely, kids all over joined in Din's enthusiasm for this music and took over theaters, dancing as hard as they could any and everywhere, including on the stage in front of the screen. You can hardly blame them.

The reason audiences so passionately loved *Dance Craze* was everything that seemed off about it. No other concert film had been shot like it before with the aimless Steadicam movements; you felt like an honorary band member on stage as they performed at their most energetic. You rarely got the audience point of view in *Dance Craze.* Most importantly, *Dance Craze* is the only document of its kind that captures the 2 Tone bands' furious live performances in 1980, the height of these bands. All their TV appearances were tame by comparison. *Dance Craze* was the closest thing to experiencing these bands in the environment they shined best: shitty clubs. With the exception of Madness, once these bands broke up, they would never reform in their original lineup. "I felt that it was important that the film be seen in the future. Not today," Dunton says. "I knew we captured a point in time that wasn't going to happen again."

In Northern California, The Uptones took *Dance Craze* as their primary inspiration and built a ska scene in the bay area. It blew up fast. In a few short years, The Uptones were packing clubs. Kids were excited to dance to ska music. The Uptones got so big that when Fishbone, Red Hot Chili Peppers or The Untouchables came up north, they would open for the Uptones. "There would be a line out the door and the fire marshal shutting the place down because it's getting out of hand," Din says. "I saw our fan base growing and growing. In my mind, it was like, why *wouldn't* we get signed?"

In 1983, The Uptones, recorded their first single, the bouncy, defiant ska track "Get Out Of My Way." When they finished recording it, they immediately left the studio, excited, and drove to Berkeley radio station KALX. They waltzed into the station and asked for one of the DJs, with Din waving the reel-to-reel recording and telling him they were a ska band. Surprisingly, the DJ didn't send them packing. He put the song on the air. The DJ, it turned out, loved The Specials. He couldn't believe a group of Berkeley High kids were playing 2 Tone. He spun the shit out of the song. It was in heavy rotation for a few months and then The Uptones waltzed over to San Francisco station, The Quake (KQAK), a commercial alternative station. They handed the DJ their reel-to-reel. He happily put it on air too.

Early Uptones press photo, 1982

"We were the only band on the playlist that didn't have a record—just a fucking demo," Din tells me. "It just seemed perfectly normal.

We were kids." After the radio success of "Get Out Of My Way" came and went, The Uptones recorded the environmental protest song "Radiation Boy"—another raging ska song full of youth, vigor, political rage, and perfect for dancing. It got heavy airplay in several San Francisco and East Bay stations. In all these early songs, the band ranted and railed about the war economy, El Salvador and Iran Contra, the poverty draft. All the terrible Reagan-era politics.

By this point, The Uptones still hadn't released an actual album. Those recordings remain unreleased. The members brought in the original reel-to-reel recordings to the stations, had the DJs make copies, and then they failed to make the songs available to be purchased by their fans. The only thing they cared about at the time was the live show. Getting a song on local radio increased their draw, so why not? The idea of documenting these songs with releases seemed pointless. They were writing new songs so fast, they didn't want to go back and try to professionally record songs already a year old. They just wanted to move forward.

"The idea that we were in the middle of doing our best work never crossed my mind," Din tells me. By the mid-80s, they decided to make a proper recording. That EP, *K.U.S.A*, released on 415 Records, documented a new era of the band. Gone were the hyper-energetic political ska songs. Now the band was playing reggae-pop and funk tunes, singing mostly about love, though this EP did yield the anti-war anthem "Out to Sea," which became a local hit. Overall, the record was a disappointment to their early fanbase who wanted their old ska songs to listen to at home. Later that year they recorded a full length with UB40's producer Ray Pablo Falconer that was never released due to Erik Rader, the original Uptones singer quitting the band and Falconer dying shortly after in a tragic car accident in the U.K. This album would have been a collection from their entire catalog, including early ska songs. It was a nice balance between raw performance and good production and could have done well. In 1986, they released a six-song EP called *Outback* without Rader. More reggae-pop songs, with the anti-Reagan rocksteady style song "Burning Sky" getting major local radio play.

The band broke up in 1987 and did two packed reunion shows at Gilman in 1989 and played a set at the International Ska Festival & Earth Day Celebration at the Greek Theatre in Berkeley in 1990. Berserkley Records released a recording of that 1989 Gilman show in

1995 titled, *The Uptones Live!! 924 Gilman*, but they weren't around to benefit from any attention.

The Uptones helped lay the groundwork for ska in the Bay Area. Rancid played homage to the group by covering "Get Out Of My Way" on their debut 1993 record, transforming it into a dingy street punk tune. Din co-wrote a few subsequent Rancid songs, and Uptones' keyboardist Paul Jackson played the Hammond organ on Rancid's monster hit "Time Bomb."

House Of Sweat

In the late-70s, Brit and hardcore music fanatic Howard Paar moved to L.A. He loved the live music scene but was thoroughly annoyed by the DJs' taste of music when he went out to the Whiskey or the Roxy. He would see a cool band like the Undertones, and then have to listen to the DJ spin Doobie Brothers between sets.

Paar had left England just before 2 Tone ska happened but became aware of The Specials when they released their debut single, "Gangsters" from reading *NME*. He looked at the band's suits and haircuts, and saw that they were a racially mixed band. Without even hearing them, he immediately understood the British subcultures that were coming together to make 2 Tone. "I ran out and bought the song. I was like 'This is it. They got everything, this is exactly it,'" Paar says. He vowed to open his own space, one that would highlight ska, soul and reggae, which almost no club in LA at the time were playing. He would feature live bands, and *good* vinyl records spun in-between. "I wanted what I didn't have," Paar tells me. "I wanted somewhere I could go where I wouldn't be irritated by hippie DJs. I was 20; I was reacting to what I felt."

That space, opened in 1980, became known as The O.N. Klub, a tiny 150-person capacity oasis for anyone sick of LA's violent hardcore scene and looking for a positive experience dancing. The O.N. Klub building was originally a Vietnamese Restaurant called Oriental Nights. "The place was just a hole in the wall," Paar says. When he took it over, he couldn't afford to change the business license, so he kept the name. However, a rock club called 'Oriental Nights' seemed tacky—he had a particular hatred for L.A.'s famous Madame Wong's —so Paar shortened it to The O.N. Klub. The space was a comfortable environment for everyone: black, white, Latino, Asian, rich, poor, male, female. It was the place to be. People crammed themselves inside well beyond capacity, upward to two-hundred-to-three-hundred *LA Weekly*'s Bill Bentley dubbed it the "House of Sweat."

Some of the early bands Paar booked included short-lived L.A. ska bands the Boxboys and the Skanksters, reggae bands The Rebel Rockers and The Babylon Warriors, and soul icons Geno Washington & Marsha Hunt. He also brought in out of town bands like Phoenix's underrated ska band X-Streams. He also brought in out of town bands like Phoenix's underrated ska band X-Streams. Paar alone spun music between bands. Before opening the O.N. Klub, he never DJ'd. He took right to it and curated a careful selection. When doors opened at 8 p.m., he spun dub tunes. As more people wandered in, he'd switch over to ska and upbeat soul. Nothing from the radio.

In those early months, a group of slick-dressed, *Quadrophenia*-loving, scooter-riding, mostly black mod-kids started showing up. They were the coolest and best dancers in the house. They tried to out-dress and out-dance each other. In early 1981, this group of kids would form The Untouchables. Before discovering the O.N. Klub, The Untouchables, still just friends, frequented one of the only clubs in town that had good dance music: The Starwood, where DJ Phast Phreddie, founder of early rock zine *Back Door Man*, DJ'd on Monday nights, spinning soul, old rock, New Wave, punk and a few 2 Tone ska songs. "They looked cool. They danced to all the hip records," Phreddie says. One night he quipped that they should start a band, since they looked like a band already.

Paar became friends with The Untouchables, particularly guitarist Clyde Grimes. He and Grimes chatted about music frequently. He even let Grimes DJ a few nights, the only person he granted this responsibility. One day, Grimes begged Paar to let his band play the O.N. Klub. He handed Paar a demo recording that was amateurish, but fun. Paar gave them a Thursday night. Their first show was more enthusiastic than skillful. "Their hearts were in the right place," Paar recalls. It was mostly ska songs with a few soul tracks in the mix. But Paar was impressed enough to give them a regular spot every Thursday. Before their next O.N. Klub show, they played their official second show at a packed house in the Venice Canals, a birthday party for a dog named Woberta, whose owner, Marylou Johnson, was a local pot dealer.

The Untouchables became the mascots for L.A.'s huge mod scene.

Every Thursday, a row of scooters lined up in front of the club. "The first songs we wrote were about being a mod, and ska music," says vocalist Kevin Long. "We were writing about what we were doing. It was genuine, however unartful it might have come across."

The Untouchables at The Roxy in Los Angeles, 1981

An early fan of the band was Ramon Estevez, brother of actors

Emilio and Charlie Sheen. Estevez loved the band and came to see them play frequently. He became their first manager in 1982 and lasted a year. Estevez booked them at Marin Sheen's house in Malibu several times. For a year they went up there to play everyone's birthday: Martin, Charlie, Emilio, little sister Robin. "Martin was so happy that his son was a manager. It was crazy. Stuff like that would just happen," says singer/percussionist Jerry Miller.

Chuck Askerneese and Jerry Miller (The Untouchables) outside of Tower Records on the Sunset Strip, 1982

In late 1982, X were scheduled to play The Whiskey. Their guitarist Billy Zoom called his manager and said, "I want The Untouchables to play," and hung up. His manager called back and asked who The Untouchables were. Zoom replied that 'they had scooters.' Eventually he tracked them down and contacted the band's new manager John Switzer. The Untouchables opened for X, and like clockwork, rows of scooters were parked out front that night. Owner Mario Maglieri was so impressed, he asked if they wanted to move their Thursday night residency to his other club The Roxy, where they could play two shows nightly. "Traffic on the Sunset strip backed up because of all the scooters in front," says vocalist Chuck Askerneese. They were the 2nd band, after The Doors, to play a residency at The Roxy. They built a big local following and released their first few singles on their own label Dance Beat records: *Twist 'N' Shake* (1982) & *Tropical Bird/The General* (1983).

In 1983, Dave Lumian, who'd been running the Alliance For Survival, booked The Untouchables to play a big anti-Reagan protest that drew ten-thousand people and happened outside a Century Plaza hotel Regan was staying at. With partner Phillip Cramer, he saw how they galvanized the mod scene and wanted to help the band gain a better national image. He started publishing *Twist Magazine* to showcase LA's mod scene in 1983. He put The Untouchables on the cover of the premiere issue. "The band were getting bad press because they weren't 'like the 2 Tone bands.' I put the band on the cover so the press would write about them. It worked. The press liked The Untouchables after that. They saw them as a positive alternative for youth," Lumian says.

In 1984, Lumian took over as the band's manager. The group made a big push to get serious. The Untouchables restructured, got rid of several members, including Long, and hired some new faces. Around the same time, they also landed some roles in movies, like the curious role of "scooter gang" in the 1984 cult classic and Emilio Estevez-led *Repo Man*, a gig they scored likely due to how much the Estevez family liked the band. They also appeared in *Surf II*, *The Party Animal*, and *No Man's Land* (a film starring Charlie Sheen!). Lumian started getting the band lots of opening slots for big acts, like Psychedelic Furs and UB40.

One of those bigger shows was three nights at the Universal Amphitheater opening for Prince, Sheila E., and Morris Day and the Time. One night, after they finished their set, Prince shyly peered over at Askerneese backstage and said, "Hey UTs," and made the group's hand gesture. "I guess that was his stamp of approval that he liked our sound. That was pretty inspiring," Askerneese says.

Lumian and Cramer also created Twist Records and released the Untouchables debut EP, 1984's *Live And Let Dance*, and its associated singles. The record sold sixty-thousand units. Reggae-style "What's Gone Wrong," was the first single, which went to #1, but what really helped boost album sales was the Northern soul style "Free Yourself," which went into heavy rotation on KROQ. To make it happen, Lumian borrowed $7,000 from friends. $2,000 went to making the record, and $5,000 went to the "Free Yourself" video, which MTV played aplenty. In the video, the band performs with their typical high-energy fun, dressed as cool as ever, and dancing in front of moving artsy patterns. The song was #1 on KROQ for the year. The video won *Billboard*'s 1984 award for best independent video. Even with all this, no US label had any interest in them. Lumian can remember the cynical reaction he got when he talked to labels. "We think it's the same five-hundred people showing up," Lumian recalls. "2 Tone is over in the UK and it never happened in the US. They all said this."

Baby Brother Of The Hardcore Scene

In late '70s New York, there was one band playing ska: a group of white kids who loved Jamaican music and had an uncanny ability to mimic the old school ska and reggae grooves. They were called Terrorists. They formed in 1977, predating 2 Tone, and played Max's Kansas City and CBGB's alongside bands like The Ramones, Richard Hell, Talking Heads, Blondie, Patti Smith, Dead Boys and Television. The energy fueling Terrorists had the same spastic mania of their peers. The band's singer John Collins hollered over the tunes like a less sophisticated David Byrne. The Skatalites' Roland Alphonso and legendary Jamaican reggae producer Lee "Scratch" Perry were both impressed with the group and worked with them a short stint. Perry first saw the group backing Alphonso at Isaiah's, one of the few Jamaican dancehalls in New York. During the second set, Terrorists played a few originals. Perry got so inspired by the group's odd, punky interpretation of reggae, he hopped on stage, grabbed Alphonso's mic, pushed him back and started an impromptu rap over Terrorists' grooves. He worked with them to record a handful of tracks that are sublime, bizarre, and hard hitting. They broke up in 1982 and faded into obscurity.

Lower east side group Urban Blight quickly picked up the slack. The group formed in 1978 as a dance band and were playing the same CBGB's stage, though never at the same time. In 1980, Trombonist Keene Carse made a trip to England to visit friends and discovered The English Beat. He fell in love and was immediately incorporating ska into Urban Blight's repertoire, though he never aspired for it to become a pure ska band. "We were the first band [in New York] to play ska to a lot of people, for better or for worse. Record companies wouldn't sign us because we played ska. We're like, 'We're not [a ska band]," Carse says. The record labels may have been squeamish about ska, but Urban Blight were packing CBGB's. "New York kids, they didn't wear pork pie hats or Fred Perry kind of style yet, but they were definitely down to come to clubs and mosh."

Carse and other members of Urban Blight hung out at a run-down lower East Side Russian bar called Blanche's. It was surrounded by boarded up storefronts and old near-empty diners. They didn't card anyone; they'd pour drinks for whoever handed them crisp dollar bills. Soon, Carse recalls seeing a couple stylishly-dressed rude boys named Sean "Cavo" Dinsmore and Lionel "Nene" Bernard hanging out, along with their crew of about 10 rudies, who also included future Boilers trombonist Jeff Baker and future Second Step guitarist Constant Bernard. "They had the suits and hats and were committed. We became friends instantly," Carse says.

Blanche's is where New York's ska scene came together, even if it was just to dress up and get drunk. "We would drink 40 oz beers at the corner with a boombox in front of the bar or in a parked car nearby playing ska on the street, dancing around, smoking weed. If no one was getting killed, cops didn't fuck with you," says Baker. The budding scene was a hodgepodge of people mixing and matching the British subcultures they read about in NME and giving it their own New York spin. "Everyone was a little bit skinhead and a little bit rude boy, A little bit mod. It all depended on which direction you took it in. If you were a skinhead, maybe your girlfriend was a rude girl."

One of the people that would go see Urban Blight was 20-something British expat Rob Hingley, who would greatly impact New York's ska scene the coming two decades. Hingley, moved to the states in the early '80s to manage New York's comic bookstore Forbidden Planet. He experienced 2 Tone ska firsthand in England and was surprised to find out how unknown the music was in New York. Pulling from Forbidden Planet staff—most of whom were unfamiliar with ska—Hingley formed a band called Not Bob Marley, which became the Toasters. The Toasters played its first show in January 1983. The early lineup was shaky. Hingley often asked Urban Blight's horn section to play at shows he couldn't find reliable players.

Around the same time, several kids from surrounding high schools were forming their own ska bands: The Boilers, Second Step, Beat Brigade and The A-Kings. City Beat also formed. They played a multitude of styles, ska being one of them.

Live concerts were sporadic and held at whatever venue or person's house was willing to host them. Most of the respectable clubs at the time didn't want ska since it was "kid music." By the mid-80s, NY's hardcore scene was raging. CBGBs had hardcore matinees on Sundays, which did well because, unlike evening shows, matinees were for kids (i.e., all-ages). Hingley thought CGBGs might be where the strewn about bands playing ska could coalesce and flourish. He got Saturday ska matinees going with stacked ska bills, and a US ska scene finally came together. It wasn't just a single band or two, like in other US cities. "It was the baby brother of the hardcore scene," Carse says of the early CBs ska shows. "The ska crowd was cooler because there were more females. A lot of the hardcore guys would also come to ska shows just because of the energy."

At the CBs matinees, more people came dressed in their best suits, though most of these kids were scouring the local thrift stores or their dad's closets, as real, "authentic" rude boy clothing was expensive and hard to find. The ska shows were energetic and got out of hand on occasion. Fights broke out, bottles were thrown around, people were tossed out of the club. CBs' owner Hilly Kristal decided to ban the Saturday ska matinees after a short stint. "It was out of control," says Skinnerbox guitarist Steve Abrams. "Off-the-wall crazy." Kristal eventually allowed ska shows back at the club, but they would now be in the evenings, and therefore over twenty-one.

By this point, The Toasters were on fire and even had their own solid horn section. They were able to headline evening weekend shows at CBs and fill the venue. Their newest and arguably best lineup now included Blanche's rude boy crew Dinsmore and Bernard, who referred to themselves as Unity 2, a black-and-white rapping duo that "toasted" over ska riffs. Toasting was a Jamaican style of rap that dated back to early ska and reggae and seen in the 2 Tone bands via Rankin Roger, Gaps and Neville Staples. Unity 2 were also influenced by New York's vibrant hip-hop scene. It was a mish mash. Bucket sang and played guitar. The band was a high-energy, beautiful mess. Abrams recalls the Toasters being "so much fun, kind of like Fishbone—that kind of energy: crazy."

. . .

In May 1986, Moon Records (Hingley's fledging ska label) presented a packed show at the Danceteria, a multi-level nightclub famous for its early LL Cool J and Madonna shows. Danceteria didn't typically book ska bands, but this one was special. The show was called *Two Tone Two*. Hingley booked the royalty of New York's mid-80s ska scene: The Daybreakers, The Boilers, The Toasters, The A-Kings and Beat Brigade.

It was the release show for Moon's *N.Y. Beat: Hit and Run* compilation album, a snapshot of the New York ska scene featuring thirteen bands, most of whom were very much in line with the 2 Tone sound. To make this comp, Bucket scoured the city, searching for ska bands far and wide. Many never recorded more than a few songs in their entire career. Some were so obscure, Moon could never re-issue the comp because Hingley couldn't track them down later to get permission. "A lot of the bands that ended up on that first *New York Beat* Record were not really involved but they were drafted in to fill out track numbers," Baker says.

N.Y. Beat was the first American ska comp. A lot of the early comps, like *N.Y. Beat*, compiled bands by region: Boston's *Mash It Up* (1987), *California ska-quake* (1992) and the Midwest's *American Skathic* (1995). *N.Y. Beat: Hit and Run* documented something special happening in New York: a music scene full of potential.

Ska Heavyweight Championship

In the mid-80s, American ska bands hit the road, traveling from bar to bar, inspiring drunk strangers to dance, and introducing ska to cities that didn't have their own homegrown groups. One of the hardest touring bands in the '80s was Boston outfit Bim Skala Bim. The band had already built up a huge scene in their hometown. The Mighty Mighty Bosstones may be Boston's most famous ska band, but Bim, who formed in 1983, were the first Boston band to play the music.

They were a scrappy, head-strong bunch, some punk rockers, some with long hair, tie-dye shirts and bandanas on their heads, others sporting checkers and makeshift rude boy attire. Known as one of the best early '80s American ska bands, Bim had a sound that melded the bounce of 2 Tone, the rebellious energy of '80s east coast rock, and a songwriting style keyed into '60s British Invasion. And there was always love for fast, punky influence in their ska, as well as traditional reggae when the mood called for it. They wrote gritty, simple pop songs with a single slide trombone horn section with keyboardist John Cameron occasionally adding sax.

After Bim self-released their brilliant self-titled debut full-length in early 1986, it landed the band on the cover of College Music Journal (*CMJ*), a complete shock to the band. It pretty much guaranteed that college radio stations across the country would play their album. Bim called those stations and asked them to recommend local clubs that drew a crowd. This prompted them to book their first six-week US tour. "It was a break-through for us," bassist Mark Ferranti says.

New York's ska moment

The tour started in September 1986 at the Haunt in Ithaca, New York, followed by Bard College in Annandale, New York. The next day, while heading towards Michigan, as they were crossing the Tappan Zee Bridge, the crankshaft in their van broke. Half of the band drove the van to the trombonist's cousin's house in a nearby town, where it stayed parked for three months. The other half headed to the Bowery in New York City to purchase a new tour vehicle that they spotted in a classified ad: a Miller beer truck. They purchased it for $1,200 from a ramshackle taxi company. "The oddest part is that a homeless guy was living in it, and they had to get him out for us to buy it," says lead singer Dan Vitale.

As fun as it was to roll into each gig disguised as the local beer delivery crew, the Miller truck did pose a couple of problems. For one, it only got nine miles to the gallon and had a ten-gallon tank, basically meaning it had a ninety-mile range. It wasn't made to cross the long stretches of midwestern plains. They ran out of gas a few times. Second, when they drove through congested cities like San Francisco, it was challenging to navigate some of those skinny streets. Parking was impossible. Probably worst of all, the van had no heating. "As much chaos as it was, it was fun," Ferranti says.

Once they got the Miller truck going, their next show was in Arizona Navajo Nation town Tuba City. They got the gig because a friend of the band was teaching at the Tuba City high school. It turned out to be one of their most energetic shows, with people connecting to the music in a way they'd never experienced. It washed away any thoughts of trading band life for day jobs. "You go to a place like Tuba City, which is the other end of the world. They're digging the music we're playing. We're digging being able to play music for them. We're not looking for more than that out of this experience," Ferranti says. It wasn't just an exciting show; everyone there gave them a life-changing experience to always remember. "In Tuba City we learned a lot about the peyote rituals. My friend Drew's father-in-law was the medicine man there. We even got a tour of the sweat lodge, an honor forbidden to most visitors," Vitale says. It was such a critical experience for the band that they named their next album *Tuba City*.

As the band grew, they became an adopted member of the New York ska scene. The flyer for their first New York show with The Toasters at the Cat Club in 1986 was made to look like a boxing match. It said "Ska heavyweight championship: Boston vs. New York" with Bim and Toasters on opposite sides, ready to face off. "Matt

Dillon was there. *Rumblefish* had just come out. Matt Dillon was hanging at the bar and he was having this conversation with our drummer, talking about how much he liked the band. That was our first brush with celebrity," Ferranti says. "We did a ton of shows with The Toasters up and down the East Coast and the whole New England region."

A year after Bim self-released their 1986 self-titled album, The Toasters were ready to release their debut record, *Skaboom*. Moon Records didn't have the capital to handle a full-length—they'd only released EPs, singles and one compilation at that point—so Hingley struck a deal with French/American label Celluloid Records to release their first album in 1987. The label had good distribution and dealt primarily in jazz, reggae, and experimental music (Yellowman, Fred Frith, Kora Jazz Band). At the release of *Skaboom*, The Toasters' members all quit their jobs and hit the road in promotion of the album.

Skaboom sold over 25,000 units. The label then created an imprint called Skaloid. They released the Toasters next album, *Thrill Me Up* (1988) and at the recommendation of Hingley, Bim Skala Bim's *Tuba City* (1988). These were the two biggest East Coast ska bands, each representing a major US city. Bim Skala Bim followed in Toasters footsteps and helped curate a Boston ska comp, *Mash It Up*, and released it on Razorbeat Records in 1987.

In 1989, The Toasters were hot and seemed poised to break out to a larger audience. An Island Records A&R guy came to see the group at a sold-out show at The Ritz in Manhattan. He went backstage and talked to co-lead singer Dinsmore and said that the label wanted to sign him and Bernard (ie Unity 2) and not The Toasters. The timing was good for Unity 2; they'd already been thinking about doing their own dancehall-reggae-hip-hop thing. They quit the band and ended up going with Warner Brothers, who also offered them a deal. They brought in Urban Blight's Keen Carse to produce it. The album released that year on Warner Brothers imprint Reprise—*What Is It, Yo?!*—bombed. The Toasters scrambled for a few years to re-gain momentum and to find members as good as the *Thrill Me Up* lineup.

That same year, Celluloid/Skaloid went under. Nether The Toasters nor Bim Skala Bim got paid royalties for their albums. This killed momentum right when things were hitting the next level and set both bands back financially. Hingley put effort into making Moon a dependable entity for the Toasters, though he still kept an eye out for other label opportunities. Bim created BIB Records to self-release and put out other bands' music. *How's It Goin'?* (1990) was their first release on BIB. They put out albums by Johnny Socko, Six Feet Deep, and Dion Knibb and The Agitators.

Bim persisted through the '90s, staying in the realm of cult status, even as ska became a viable mainstream genre. They had one minor local hit, their 1992 ska-cover of Pink Floyd's "Brain Damage" off the *Bones* record.

Most kids getting into ska in the '90s were not interested in Bim Skala Bim. They played ska free of pop-punk and dressed like regular dudes, not a winning combination for the '90s. The Mighty Mighty Bosstones on the other hand mixed metal, hardcore and ska, and did so in plaid suits. Kids ate it up. "We didn't look the part. Nobody wore skinny ties or loafers," Ferranti says. "Other than Dan, nobody was wearing a pork pie hat. You'd end up with all these ska kids wearing plaid, not knowing that they were only doing that because of the Bosstones."

What's Gone Wrong

In 1985, The Untouchables toured up and down the west coast with UB40. The first two dates were at L.A.'s Universal Amphitheater. UB40's horn section joined the Untouchables during their set, and vice versa. During those shows, UB40 approached the members of The Untouchables seeing if they were interested in selling their song, "What's Gone Wrong." The Untouchables appreciated the compliment but politely declined.

Another big thing happened at Universal Amphitheater. Dave "Robbo" Robison from Stiff Records approached Lumian and said he was interested in signing The Untouchables to his label. This was huge. This came right after Island US had passed on the band. Stiff was second only to 2 Tone as the coolest British indie label of all time with releases from Elvis Costello, Ian Dury, Madness, and the Pogues.

Within weeks, the band was on a plane to London where they'd hopefully record an album that would break them into a whole new level of pop stardom. England was a good place for them since the band also played Northern Soul, a high-energy style based on a heavy beat and a fast tempo. The Brits loved Northern Soul way more than Americans. "When we landed in London, we saw all these big posters of us. It almost scared us," recalls percussionist/vocalist Jerry Miller. "We're thousands of miles from California, and here we are on the side of a building in a land we'd never been to. This stuff is serious." Word spread about the group. At one of their shows at Dingwalls in London, several members of Madness showed up to check out this Untouchables band they'd heard about.

They didn't return home for eight months. Stiff had them doing promotional tours in England and parts of Europe. They recorded the full-length *Wild Child* in Holland, a monthlong session, produced by Stewart Levine, who'd recently produced Simply Red's wildly successful soul-pop album *Picture Book*. Stiff re-released "Free Yourself" as a UK single; it climbed to #26 on the charts, hit top 40 in most of Europe, and random US stations continued to play it. For the second single, "I Spy For The FBI," they brought in The Specials' Jerry Dammers on the board. It also hit top 40 in the UK.

Despite this, *Wild Child* had some issues. As cool as Stiff was, they seemed to not quite understand The Untouchables. *Wild Child* was a bit too slick and didn't capture the group's live energy. There was also less ska. Worst of all was the cringy rap song "Freak in the Street" which was given to MCA (who had a deal with Stiff). Their "urban" division was very excited about this song. A video was made for it. It made it to the top ten on the dance charts, but it never crossed over.

"I think our varied sound threw people. As far as the record label, they weren't quite sure how to handle that," says lead singer Chuck Askerneese. "The rap at that time was getting to be popular in the black subculture. I think they were trying to focus on that. That wasn't our deal at all."

Jheryl Busby, the A&R rep at MCA who signed them to the "urban" division, wanted them to record songs from the label's catalogue. They performed new original songs for almost two years that MCA would not record. The Untouchables recorded a pop tune during that time that they and their producer Don Was were stoked on called "Quit Your Job." It was an anti-Reagan song, but catchy and full of hit-making potential. When they played the song at the Greek Theatre in Hollywood, opening for Peter Tosh, it brought the house down. "We almost had the packaging ready. All the sudden MCA just pulled out. The producers were pissed. The A&R people at MCA were pissed," Miller says. "It took the wind out of our sails. We were young and like, that's the way the business is?"

Stiff Records folded shortly after in 1986 and was purchased by ZTT Records. The owners of that label weren't impressed with the new material the band was producing. Over the next few years, the band struggled to write new material. What they did write didn't impress ZTT, who were continually dissatisfied and "didn't hear the single." Meanwhile, they re-released old singles and endless over-the-top remixes of songs off of *Wild Child*.

Eventually, Lumian got the band out of their deal. They released their next album *Agent Double O Soul* on Twist Records. The title track did well, but still there wasn't much momentum for the group. By that point, in the late '80s after a few years of spinning their wheels, members were quitting and moving on with their lives. As much as the group had flickering moments of success, The Untouchables were never able to crack the US pop market in a significant way and were lost to history. Subsequent generations never got a chance to know the brilliance that was The Untouchables.

Mad Mods

Fishbone were another '80s ska band making waves in LA. They signed to Columbia in 1984 shortly after most of the members graduated from high school. Their debut self-titled EP from 1985 would define the '90s third wave ska sound a decade before anyone uttered the words "third wave"—particularly, the upbeat, satirical anti-cold war anthem "Party At Ground Zero."

In the late '70s, five of the six members of what would become the all-black group Fishbone were living in South Central. As part of a Supreme Court decision intended to combat LA's deep segregation, they, along with several other black children in South Central were bussed to the mostly white San Fernando Valley schools. There, they met the nerdy, spazzy, and always smiling Angelo Moore, who desperately wanted to join their crew. In the ninth grade, they got together in "The Aquarium"—bassist Norwood Fisher's bedroom—and would rehearse and write songs for several hours a day.

After winning a talent show, the group played its first show in 1983 at legendary punk club Madame Wong's. They originally went by the name Megatron, but the members grew tired of people assuming they were a metal band, so they changed their name to Fishbone, drummer Philip Fisher's nickname. The group played a lot of different styles, but ska dominated their early catalog because they loved 2 Tone so much. "Ska was easy for us to play. It was born out of that because the shit we wanted to play was crazy," says keyboardist Chris Dowd. "It wasn't as extreme as punk. There was actual singing. We were all singers because we grew up listening to R&B and going to church. The idea of being Darby Crash didn't sound fucking appealing."

The group also modeled themselves after the thriving mod scene that The Untouchables helped to flourish. Sort of. They had their own take on mod fashion. They wore oddball thrift store suits and incorporated mismatched punk rock elements, like mohawks and ripped-sleeve shirts. They were playing ska songs faster than anyone else at the time and were mixing every other element. They referred to themselves as the "mad mods." "The mods that were pissed off," Dowd explains.

Like that first show at Madame Wong's, Fishbone immediately distinguished themselves from other US ska bands by deliberately playing with bands that sounded nothing like them. They admired The Untouchables and had listened to them on KROQ as teenagers, but they also saw them as competition. "When you're 18, you're super competitive," Dowd says. "They were the biggest band in LA. They had a target on their backs. We wanted their fucking audience."

Fishbone's influences were completely scatterbrain: Prince, The Specials, Van Halen, English Beat, Michael Jackson, Parliament, B-52s, Devo. They were also listening to complex jazz-fusion too but weren't able to play it yet. Two huge influences for them were Bad Brains and local band BusBoys. Keyboardist/vocalist Brian O'Neil from BusBoys came to Fishbone's first show at Madame Wong's and loved them. He connected Fishbone to their manager Roger Perry, who decided to manage Fishbone for most of the '80s.

Within a year of that first Madame Wong show, Fishbone were *the* underground LA band everyone was talking about. Eventually David Kahne from Columbia Records decided to check them out. He was blown away and told them he wanted to sign them. The group didn't believe him—he was this quiet, soft-spoken, Fred Armisen type. "This guy said he was from Columbia Records. We were very skeptical," Dowd says. Kahne got the group into a studio and cut a bunch of demos from the group's huge repertoire of songs—they had over 60 at that point. In three hours they cut raw, energetic versions of early Fishbone classics, like show opener "Mister Zero," hyper-fast "Skankin' To The Beat" and popular closer "Fishbone is Red Hot" as well as much of the songs that later landed on the six-song EP. Kahne showed the demo to his boss, who told him to take the tape to the "black music" department. There, they listened to it and told him to take it back to rock.

"I didn't think about music being so segregated even though the departments were segregated at Columbia," Kahn said in the film *Everyday Sunshine*. "What was going on in black music at the time was so far away from what Fishbone were doing."

Hide your mics from Fishbone, 1986

As much as Kahne was excited about Fishbone, Columbia didn't know how to market an all-black band playing super-fast ska songs with politically satirical lyrics, though they trusted Kahne enough to let him try. "The world was divided into R&B for black people, rock music for white people. When we started playing music, it was like, why can't we bring all these people together?" says Dowd. "We tried to have a sound that encompassed something for everyone: White kids, black kids, whatever. It stemmed out of the 2 Tone movement. Here's some metal shit for that guy, some reggae shit for that guy. Some soul shit for that girl. Some dub shit for that girl."

When Fishbone released their self-titled EP in 1985, most other US ska bands were desperately trying to emulate the British 2 Tone. Fishbone were on to something new. Unfortunately, there was no mainstream interest for ska in 1985. Still, the EP hit hard enough that it launched Fishbone into cult stardom and enabled them to tour the world to excited fans and build their "Fishbone army." The record was monumental in how it spoke to the fragmented youth of color that didn't see a place for themselves in the highly segregated music scene. "A lot of friends of mine who were African American, they thought there was nothing musically that spoke to what they were into at the time," Dowd says. "There will always be that one black punk rock kid, that one black skater kid. I feel like we were actually playing for that person and everybody else came along because anytime you're playing some music and there's some outcast shit, other outcast motherfuckers are going to show up. They relate to it. You're speaking their thoughts and feelings into existence."

In February 1986, Fishbone were on stage at the Fender's Ballroom in Long Beach, CA, opening for Bad Manners. Fishbone were at the top of their game. The fifteen-hundred-capacity venue was jam-packed. As they went into "Party At Ground Zero," the horn section of Moore on sax, Walt Kibby on trumpet and Dowd—normally keyboardist—on trombone, all danced in place while playing the opening line—and no one messed up.

During the mid-song guitar solo, Dowd fell on his back, mimicking guitarist Kendall Jones, flopping around like a dying fish. Meanwhile, Moore leapt as far into the audience as he could, lying on his back on top of the crowd like an otter peeling open a clam. It took three audience members to pull him back on stage. Once up, he and the rest of the band continued jumping all over, while a steady stream of audience members sang along in the on-stage mic, danced in place, or dove back into the audience. It was a leader-less chaotic revolt against boring concerts.

As far as Dowd is concerned, this is the moment third wave ska was born. It wasn't just Fishbone; the audience saw Bad Manners, one of the most underrated and silliest bands from the 2 Tone era. A band that never actually affiliated with 2 Tone, yet, they brought circus energy to their set.

"There were a lot of bands that came after Fishbone, and mostly they were Orange County ska," Dowd says. "Everybody that wanted to have a ska band [was there at Fender's Ballroom that night] and walked away and formed the Skeletones and No Doubt and Sublime." Fishbone introduced something to ska that impacted nearly every band that came after them. It wasn't punk exactly, though the energy was wilder than anything the 2 Tone bands produced. Fishbone played funk, metal, and alt-rock, and they spit it out in the framework of ska. Fishbone inspired bands to mix ska with any genre they could envision and to play it with so much energy, the audience had to decide whether to join in or stay stunned on the sidelines, watching all the fun pass them by.

Missed Opportunity

Back in New York, now 1990, Hingley was trying to rebound from the demise of Skaloid Records. As much as The Toasters were struggling financially from the debacle, he still hoped the US could foster an active and growing ska scene. Joe Massot, the credited director of *Dance Craze*, flew to New York and told Hingley he wanted to film a sequel, this time highlighting New York's ska scene. It would be called *NYC Ska Craze*.

Massot wanted to film everything in one night. Hingley set up the show, which he booked for March 26, 1990, at the Cat Club. The bands on the bill included Bigger Thomas, Skinnerbox, The Toasters, N.Y. Citizens, Steadys, Skadank and The Scofflaws. The bands were prepped in several pre-show meetings: no swearing, no smoking, and no drinking on stage while the cameras were rolling.

Suddenly, Massot backed out, telling them he'd had his camera gear stolen. Hingley already rented expensive lighting, special mics, and a remote sound truck, so the show went on as planned. Hingley recorded audio of the show, which he released on Moon later that year, calling it *N.Y. Ska Live*. The recording was good, though it didn't sell well. So much of the appeal of the original *Dance Craze* had to do with witnessing the energy of the shows. "It was a missed opportunity for the American ska scene. It would have been cool to have that as a document. There were hopes that this would lead to bigger things," says Marc Wasserman, bassist for Bigger Thomas and prolific *Marco on the Bass* ska blogger.

No one knew for sure, but many figured Massot must've never had financing for the film. None knew then that Massot was removed from *Dance Craze* before filming had finished. He hadn't even see the film until the premiere. Cameraman Joe Dunton gave Massot the director credit because he was a friend and felt bad that Massot had been taken off the project.

Even if Hingley and the bands were unaware of Massot's true relationship (or lack thereof) with *Dance Craze*, many of them had a feeling he was going to flake. "He always seemed like a suspicious guy," says N.Y. Citizens' Chris Acosta, who helped put together the show. "He came to some of the bars that we used to hang around at. I think he had a financial problem. I don't even recall ever seeing any film equipment to be honest."

Something changed in New York after the movie fizzled out. A sense of scene unity dissipated. Some bands broke up, others transitioned into other styles of music, most horrifically, funk. New York ska needed a scene to thrive. "The Untouchables and Fishbone didn't need a ska scene to be famous. In New York, a lot of these bands relied on each other to get people to shows. We needed a couple other ska bands on the bill to ensure there would be enough people," says Acosta.

The bands that stuck around New York focused less on the scene and more on themselves. The Toasters had high hopes for their third album, 1990's *This Gun For Hire*. They got a nice write-up in *Spin* and had people from CBS/Sony sniffing around. The group figured a major label deal was imminent. The Toasters deliberately wrote and produced *This Gun For Hire* to be more commercial in order to appeal to the majors. No deal was offered, and with Celluloid no longer an option, Hingley released the album on Moon. It got a mixed reaction from fans. Too commercial to appeal to their hardcore fans; not commercial enough to appeal to a new market. The record was the first official Toasters LP on Moon. Hingley now shifted focus to build up Moon Records as a legit indie label, no longer focusing on capturing the New York sound. He first showcased the national ska scene on 1988's *Ska-Face* compilation, the first non-regionally specific ska comp in the US. In the '90s, he wanted to be *the* label for American ska.

Things got better in the early '90s. In 1995 both BIB Records and Moon Records signed separate distribution deals with Relativity Records (later known as RED). With real distribution, both labels were doing great. Moon made a deal with Caroline in the Spring of 1995 and continued to have excellent distribution. A few years later, BIB had problems with RED. They made deals with other indie distribution channels, but it never worked out. Distribution kept on being tough. Moon, though, built an impressive catalog of American ska. Let's Go Bowling, Dance Hall Crashers, Scofflaws, and Hepcat released their debut records on Moon, all defining albums of this era. Moon also released *Skarmageddom* (1994) the first third wave compilation. If you played ska in the US in the early '90s, forget about signing to a major. The goal was to get your demo to Moon Records.

Back To The Real Shit

By the late '80s, Fishbone not only didn't have a song on the radio, they were feeling like the message of their music was being ignored. For 1988's *Truth and Soul*, they wanted to show people what life in South Central was really like without having to disguise their anger with humor. "Nobody was telling that story about growing up in South Central. That's what *Truth and Soul* was. We grew up in the hood. Your life is grim and nihilistic. We can go to my corner liquor store and I can show you actual fucking grim, not make-believe white guilt, entitlement, suburban angst. Bobby's mom *is* a crackhead," Dowd says. "Real shit."

The group had also recently discovered N.W.A. and connected to their message. For their first big show following *Truth and Soul*'s release, they wanted to join forces with the gangsta rap crew. Fishbone asked their management to reach out to N.W.A.'s people to see if they'd play a show together. Management reported back that N.W.A wanted a huge sum of money, so it never happened.

With no singles, *Truth and Soul* managed to sell a half million copies. Columbia was hoping the next album, *Reality Of My Surroundings,* would go platinum. This album was a big shift for the band musically, and their resolve to be taken seriously had only increased. It's a brilliant, cutting edge album, but more challenging than the group's previous records, particularly for a 1991 alt-rock audience, with elements of math rock, prog rock, and the jazz fusion they always wanted to play. Lead single "Everyday Sunshine" is a gospel-punk song about staying positive amid depressing times. The album details the very real, unfiltered problems black Americans faced—and still face—in this country: systematic racism, generational poverty, and the crack epidemic, something that other '90s alternative rock bands wouldn't touch with a ten-foot pole. In a 1991 *Rolling Stones* interview, bassist Norwood Fisher described the group's public image as "all entertainment and no mental stimulation." In the same article, guitarist Kendall Jones points out that Fishbone's music was always political, even if the songs seemed silly. For instance, "V.T.T.L.O.T.F.D.G.F.," from the debut EP is commentary on how Nazis pushed the narrative of the holocaust being fake. Fishbone used the metaphor of an alternative America that claimed to never have sent atomic bombs to Japan; it was just Godzilla fart. "We tried to make it funny so people would listen," Jones continues. "It was wrong. You try it that way, and it just cheapens everything you're trying to say. We went back to the real shit."

The people at Columbia all felt like "Everyday Sunshine" was destined to be the group's breakout moment. When that didn't happen, there was an attitude change from label executives. "I still like *Reality of My Surroundings*. I understand why it didn't blow up now that I have a healthy distance from it," says Dowd. "'Fight The Youth' had that Rush and Return to Forever embedded in there. The record we were trying to make, Outkast made with *The Love Below*. You got to have that song. Maybe 'Everyday Sunshine' was the closest we could have gotten or 'Party at Ground Zero' or 'Ma 'n' Pa.' Most people on the pop charts want something about love. When you're sitting there talking about how you grew up in the fucking hood, and racism, it makes it hard. [At least] people understand our artistic integrity and how much we influenced bands musically."

The group's next effort was even more ambitious with the schizophrenic *Give a Monkey a Brain, and He'll Swear He's The Center of the Universe* in 1993. They go into slow psych-metal, like on "Swim," but also upbeat ska, like "Unyielding Conditioning," one of the group's most profound songs. Reviews were mixed, though often tepid. "Everyone was like, Fishbone wants to be grunge. If you listen to 'Servitude' It sounds like some jazz fusion shit," Dowd says.

As they finished the record, Jones joined a Northern California cult. On April 28, 1993, some of the band members and Jones' family tried unsuccessfully to 'kidnap' him and bring him back to L.A. Fisher nearly faced jail time for it. In the summer of '94, without Jones, the group went on its biggest tour of their career: Lollapalooza. Afterwards, Dowd, unhappy with Jones' departure, and losing his pop-co-songwriter, left the band.

Fishbone wasn't the same without Jones and Dowd. The group lost its record deal that year, leaving them scrambling while this new crop of Fishbone inspired bands like No Doubt, Sublime and Reel Big Fish were getting blasted all over MTV. Fishbone was the standard they all tried to reach, but nobody could match their eclectic musicality and unbridled energy. Fishbone struggled with becoming almost too diverse for their own good.

One of the last shows Dowd played was at the Nice Jazz Festival in France. At one point, he pulled the promoter aside and asked why he booked Fishbone to play a jazz festival. He told them that in France what they were doing was jazz to them. "Because you're taking the styles and you're playing this music that nobody has combined before," Dowd says. "That's what we view as jazz."

The Real Beginning Of The Third Wave

David Wiens remembers how amazed he felt standing on the Greek Theatre stage in Berkeley, looking out at the sea of thousands of dancing people as his band Let's Go Bowling ripped through their set. It was 1990. They were at the International Ska Festival & Earth Day Celebration. The show drew roughly eight-thousand people, an unbelievable success for ska. "I was shocked," Wiens says. "I had no idea that many people would show up for a ska show. It was the real beginning of the third wave."

The show had a killer lineup: Dance Hall Crashers, The Uptones, Donkey Show, Me Mom and Morgentaler, Gangster Fun, The Skeletones, and Bad Manners. Roland Alphonso was hanging out at the show and hopped on stage when Let's Go Bowling went into The Skatalites' "Confucius." Before playing, he motioned for the band to slow down and bring the pace back to something The Skatalites would do. "We always played The Skatalites tunes pretty fast in those days," Wiens says. The headliner was International Beat, which featured Dave Wakeling and Rankin Roger from The English Beat and they played a mix of new songs and old English Beat tunes. It was a letdown after Bad Manners, who, by all accounts, brought the house down.

Who in the world had the audacity to book an eleven-hour ska festival at an amphitheater? That person would be Lou Avert, a guy who booked ska shows at Gilman and other Berkeley venues. Apparently, he knew something: there was a big audience for ska.

People traveled from all over the country to skank the day away. Karina Denike of the Dance Hall Crashers wasn't all that shocked by the turnout. "It didn't seem completely out of line—smaller bands like us were pulling good numbers at medium-sized clubs. The Skeletones, The Uptones, and Donkey Show were headlining larger rooms than us, and Bad Manners was still pretty big. It was an amazing lineup."

The festival's striking attendance numbers had zero impact on ska's viability with major labels or the music industry. The only thing that came from the International Ska Festival & Earth Day Celebration was a lot of people experiencing the best show of their lives. Not that's there's anything wrong with that! Afterwards, ska returned to the clubs.

As the '90s progressed, ska bands dutifully continued to build an independent touring network and record distribution channel. With new bands forming daily, it felt like only a matter of time before someone took notice.

Back in New York, after a lull, the scene was rebuilt with a new crop of ska bands like Mephiskapheles and The Slackers. On New Year's Eve 1992, The Toasters and the Scofflaws appeared on New York cable show *USA Up All Night*, for a broadcast of the comically bizarre "New Year's Eve Ska Party" with hosts Gilbert Gottfried and Rhoda Scheer. The bands played short, minute-long segments of their songs in the Palladium while groups of well-dressed rudies and skinheads skanked in the foreground and Gottfried and Scheer blathered in-between.

The short segments served as ads for the biggest ska show to ever hit New York: Skalapalooza, at the New Ritz (Old Studio 54) in

February 1993. Hingley and New York promoters Tom Gammino and Rebecca Ludgin put together the show, which sold out with 2,500 people in attendance to see Bad Manners, The Skatalites, The Toasters, The Scofflaws, Ruder Than You and The Skunks.

Hingley reckoned *now* was the right time to take ska to that elusive next level. He reached out to Larry Gold, booker for local club S.O.B.s to see if he'd book a big ska tour package, something bigger than had ever passed through the states. Hingley and Gold brought together ska bands from Jamaica (Skatalites), England (The Selecter, Special Beat—a mix of the Specials & English Beat) and the US (The Toasters, and local openers) to play 1,000-2,500 size spaces. The four-week tour, called Skavoovee was a huge success, with many sold out shows. The tour also hit smaller US cities that these bands individually were skipping on their solo tours for fear of empty houses. "It helped show that there could be a larger market for ska. Without question, it was a special moment," Gold says.

Toasters bassist Matt Malles said it was clear to him and everyone else on the tour that Skavoovee was major. "It was definitely a point in time where it seemed like this could be pretty big." The industry did take notice, but they were uninterested in 2 Tone-influenced ska. They wanted ska-punk.

The first U.S. ska band to ink a major label deal was ska-core maestros The Mighty Mighty Bosstones, who signed a seven-album deal with Mercury in 1993. More signings happened in the mid-90s—all ska-punk bands.

Bands playing regular ska still struggled. In an October 1995 *New York Times* article, "The Sound Of New York: Ska. Ska? Yes, Ska," Neil Strauss interviewed several New York ska bands who discussed how much the ska scene had grown while also lamenting how few people understood it. Mephiskapheles' drummer Mikal Reich told the reporter—in 1995 mind you—that labels were telling them that they didn't know how to market the music. "I used to think people in the record industry were barracudas and would jump on anything. Here you've got Rancid with a ska single in MTV's 'Buzz Bin,' and I still have to spell ska to people over the phone," he said in the article.

In ska's long-foretold mainstream explosion in 1997, it was ska-punk that got heavy rotation. None of the bands from the '80s enjoyed the success, aside from the Mighty Mighty Bosstones. All the original ska bands had either broken up, changed their sound, or continued to toil in the night club scene. The Toasters were the only other band from that era that were offered a major label deal.

Mercury A&R rep David Silver was really interested in The Toasters and had been courting them for a year. He showed up to several shows, always talking about how excited he was to work with the band. Hingley, Steve Shafer and one other Moon Staffer agreed to sit down with Silver for a meeting to discuss a possible signing with The Toasters and the potential of working out a distribution deal with Moon. It was early 1997. Mercury CEO Danny Goldberg walked into the meeting unannounced. He looked at Moon's bank statements. He shook Hingley's hand and commented on what a great fourth quarter Moon had in 1996. Goldberg was there for a few minutes and then departed, leaving the actual meeting to his underlings.

Everyone at Moon was hopeful that Mercury would want to build a relationship with the label or at least with The Toasters. Since Mercury had signed Mighty Mighty Bosstones in 1993, they had some clout in the ska world. But Mercury wanted a full acquisition of Moon. In their offer, everyone but Hingley would be cut. Hingley would consult for two years and then also be cut. Ostensibly most of the bands on Moon's catalog would get dropped while Mercury cherry-picked the big sellers. There was no guarantee that The Toasters would stay on. The offer, according to my sources, was obscenely low, an amount they'd take in from mail order in a few months. It was a "take it or leave it" situation. Hingley said no thank you.

Moon continued to profit for a few years. Then in 1999, when ska fell out of fashion and magazines started publishing "ska is dead" articles, record stores panicked and completely unloaded their ska inventory. Small artists, big artists. All of it. In 2000, Moon filed for bankruptcy.

It's a shame The Toasters, all the '80s bands, and most of the talent at Moon never reached a larger audience than the underground scene they'd built. These bands worked their asses off to build a healthy, sustainable ska scene in the US over the course of a decade and a half, only to be quickly torn down by big labels coming in and scooping up a handful of wacky punk-ska bands that formed in the '90s that had no hand in building the vibrant ska network they benefited from. In the end, there's no denying the bitter truth. Rude boys don't win.

RUN SCREAMING

"Ska sounds like a bunch of cheesy game shows and Jewish themes that try to be a half-assed form of jazz mixed with the weird pseudo-reggae guitar riffs that sound like super Mario Bros...pretty terrible."

-some random asshole online

Believe it or not, there was a time when being in a ska band was considered embarrassing. I know, crazy huh! You should've heard the wild accusations people made:

Every song sounds the same!

Out of tune marching band horns over pop-punk riffs!

Nothing but silly songs about food!

Ok, that last one is sort of true, at least for Flat Planet. We had a song that was an ode to cheese but sung in Spanish. (*"Queso en el dia, Queso en el Noche! Queso! Queso! Dame Mas!"*)

We also had a song about Taco Bravo, our favorite late-night dive in San Jose, California. It was the go-to place for bands of every genre. And jocks. And just plain 'ol drunks. Many fights ensued alongside absurdly heaping Super Nachos and refried bean-stuffed Taco Delights. The Taco Bravo staff served everything with a superabundance of cheese and treated you like garbage, which was a major part of the appeal. Whenever Flat Planet showed up after a gig or band practice, the late-night manager would shake his head and say, "You guys again...don't you have lives?" "No," we'd proclaim, shoving crumpled dollar bills in the tip jar, asking for *even more* cheese, as the ashes from the staff's cigarettes fell into the beans. We were so obsessed with Taco Bravo--and always talking about it—my mom decided to go there to see what the all the hubbub was. She ordered a decaf coffee with her meal. When they handed it to her, she confirmed, "This is decaf, right?" The guy told her, "Yes...it's coffee." She couldn't sleep that night, wired from having caffeine for the first time in a decade.

Our songs were influenced by the general silliness that defined a lot of the '90s ska scene, which I know people hate. Let's defend "ska silliness" for a minute and describe what it was like to be in a '90s ska band.

In 1993, our local San Jose music scene consisted of bands playing grunge, dreary alt-rock, and worse, rap-metal. There were maybe three ska bands in the whole city. This scene took itself seriously. Too seriously. I can't tell you how many times some shitty rock band was on stage at the local 18+ venue, Cactus Club, acting like disaffected rock stars to a crowd of twenty people who cared more about their ice-cold beer than the cool poses of random local band.

For us, getting on stage and giving our set a considerable dose of silliness was a *fuck you* to the self-indulgent, pretentious rock star bullshit we saw at the Cactus Club and on MTV. When we played in front of twenty people, we weren't trying to be cool or get signed. We wanted to make everyone in the venue smile despite themselves. Yes, it was also an outlet for all our crazy, awkward energy, but we were trying to get people to join us and have a fun night, not admire our cool threads and perfectly disheveled hairdos.

Ashamed To Be A Ska Band

In the early '90s, most ska bands weren't riding the silly-train. The priority was to play danceable music with creative hooks and unique song structures that kept things interesting. People in this era liked the clothing, the dancing, and usually understood basic ska history, like how 2 Tone was born from British punks and Caribbean immigrants combining forces to make an exciting new musical style with a strong anti-racist message.

The Pacers formed in 1990 and built an impressive scene in Milwaukee, their hometown, and later Minneapolis, where they would relocate, as well as several nearby Midwest cities where they regularly gigged. They weren't Milwaukee's first ska band. Bands that predated them were International Jet Set, Invaders, Wild Kingdom, all of whom started in the late '80s. These were popular local bands, but the Pacers applied some business smarts by pushing shows to be all-ages. They went to the Unicorn, a local twenty-one-and-older club, and told the venue owner if they let the them play an all-ages show, they would draw three-hundred kids. The club owner agreed to it reluctantly. It was a success, but due to some disagreements, the relationship didn't last. The Pacers took the same deal over to Peter Jest at the Shank Hall, and that started a three-to-four year run of really packed, successful shows. It was a captive and consistent audience. The band was making a couple thousand dollars a show just because they recognized how eager kids were to go out and dance.

"We never wanted to be a group where everybody showed up in Fred Perrys. We also weren't skate punks either. We wanted to be popular with kids our age," Pacers bassist Andy Noble says. The Pacers didn't play punky sounding ska songs or dress in wacky costumes. They were closer to a 2 Tone sound, with mid-tempo upbeats and Specials' style grooves that were mixed with subtle rock and soul beats and some New Wave melodies influencing the group's intricate sound.

By the mid-90s, the Pacers were witnessing a shift happen as younger bands joined the scene. It wasn't a shift they liked.

"We were extremely ashamed to be a ska band," Noble says. "When we started, we were really proud of it. We thought we were the only motherfuckers on to that stuff. We had this pride of ownership. By the time we were done, we perceived the music to be jazz band nerds wearing mismatched suits, recruited by one guy who realized he could have a popular group."

They weren't too stoked by the growing number of ska bands in the Midwest, either. Or how those bands were making the genre look like nothing but a bunch of kids spazzing out at Chuck E. Cheese on a permanent sugar high.

"The first time we saw Skankin' Pickle, we all thought it was really funny. Two years later it was like every ska band was a joke novelty band. We were not proud to be part of that scene anymore. We thought it was nerdy," Noble says. By 1994, because of this and some other internal band factors, the band lost steam and broke up.

Ska had a moment in the mainstream a few years later, which softened the "nerd" vibe temporarily. It also validated the wackiness. Suddenly bands on TV were wearing colorful shirts, checkered shorts, and pork pie hats. The Mighty Mighty Bosstones showed off their plaid suits in *Clueless*; Reel Big Fish sported cabbie hats and colorful, tucked-in button-up shirts in *BASEketball*. Save Ferris represented the rainbow's full spectrum with their members' bold single-color t-shirts and laid-back skater shorts in their "Come On Eileen" video. When ska fell out of its short-lived favor, all those offbeat checkered V-neck sweaters and bowling suspenders were as mortifying as MC Hammer parachute pants.

The Lamest Guys Around

James Rickman of Santa Cruz, CA band Slow Gherkin tells me about his experience living through the peculiar era of ska during the late '90s.

"We felt like we were just the lamest guys around all of a sudden," he says.

Slow Gherkin formed in 1993 and were an underrated band that never reached a large audience outside of their hometown, where they would sell out the largest venues. On tour, they'd draw anywhere between 50-150 people. Not bad, but not enough to give them the satisfaction of quitting their day jobs. As they pushed forward, they were handicapped by ska's rise and fall in the mainstream.

The bad boys of Slow Gherkin

In 1998, they released their brilliant Squeeze-meets-Nick Lowe-infused, peppy, rock-ska sophomore album, *Shed Some Skin*. It still holds up as a unique record during a year when one-thousand ska records were released. They'd gone on multiple tours that year and were rehearsing daily to make something happen.

And then in late 1998, just after their record released, they were approached at a show in New York by John Avila, bassist for Oingo Boingo (85-95) and producer of Reel Big Fish's *Turn The Radio Off*. Gherkin were playing their final show on the Independent's Day tour with The Toasters, Edna's Goldfish and Skoidats. (The band The Independents were unfortunately *not* on that tour. They were the answer to the question: What would The Misfits sound like if they played ska?). Avila asked the band to send him some new songs. One of Avila's kids was a Gherkin fan who liked the band's catchy New Wave-y sound.

It seemed entirely possible Slow Gherkin could gain a wider audience if they had just the right push. They were great pop songwriters. But it took the band a good six months to demo two new songs ("Tap Dancing" and Salsipuedes"). By then, now 1999, they'd lost a few members which sucked momentum from the group, and Avila never got back to them. They grew frustrated with pushing hard and living life on the road, eating nothing but peanut butter and jelly sandwiches and unhealthy portions of Waffle House, all while still having to maintain shitty day jobs. Not to mention they were starting to feel their first few waves of ska-shame, which would only grow in the coming years.

Post Waffle House nap

Mike Park, who ran Asian Man Records, the label that released Gherkin's first album and already agreed to release its second, was already feeling ska trepidation by early 1998 as Slow Gherkin was recording *Shed Some Skin*. It was clear to Park the ska boom was not going to last much longer. But the band was already set to record in the lovely twenty-four-track studio SoundTek and had a thick twenty-four-page booklet planned for the album release. Rickman tells me that Park would show up in the studio as they were recording, pace back and forth and say, "No one is going to buy this record" and then leave.

Park's nervous foresight turned out to be correct. The album sold less than the band's debut record. The tides were changing in pop culture, and Slow Gherkin looked on, suffering a band identity crisis. By the end of the century, post-*Shed Some Skin*, they were writing songs deliberately lacking upbeats, as if to signal to the world they, too, were no longer part of that horrid ska scene. Other bands did the same. Orange County ska band The Hippos released their major label debut *Heads Are Gonna Roll* in 1999, now as a ska-free, synth-rock band, with an album cover fabricated to look like a hip '60s rock 'n' roll group, ala The Kinks. In subsequent years, The Hippos singer/guitarist Ariel Rechtshaid furthered his cold-hearted ska abandonment by carving out a hipster producer career, working with artists like Vampire Weekend, HAIM, Adele and Charli XCX

"We did what so many other ska bands did, which was suddenly get totally self-conscious. That was the real sell out moment, I think. All ska bands got mocked all of a sudden, and we were like, 'Abandon ship!'" Rickman says. "I like *Run Screaming* [the band's third album]. We wrote great songs, but it's not a ska album. It's a pretty chicken shit move. On one hand, we were getting to be a better band, but we were having a total identity meltdown right in the middle of that."

Ska may have dropped in popularity but trying to pretend you never were a ska band only brought on greater ridicule. 2002's *Run Screaming* was Slow Gherkin's lowest selling album. Only two-thousand copies were pressed, and not all of them sold.

Ska's never been as hated as it was in the early 2000s, but since then it's never lost its stigma. Even now if you tell people you like ska, you must do so with a big fat asterisk, acknowledging all the bad, bad ska bands out there before admitting to the ones you like. Ska seems more than any other genre to be defined by its worst bands and least creative tendencies.

The problem with ska in the '90s is only a few bands reached mainstream audiences, so the general music loving population never received proper exposure to the genre. Trying to explain to the average music listener why ska is one of the most diverse musical styles out there requires a couple of pie charts, a lengthy powerpoint presentation, and a history lesson that spans several decades. To most people, all ska sounds the same.

"I hope at our best we shined through that [third wave] and sounded different," Noble says, reflecting on his time in the ska scene with the Pacers. "Now the huge bulk of what people think of as '90s ska is background music for Food Network shows. We did not want to sound like that. That's for sure. But we probably did sometimes."

It's so entrenched in culture to make fun of ska as wacky nerd music, no one questions why nerdy music is such a bad thing. Are we also throwing They Might Be Giants, Weird Al and Devo under the bus, because last time I checked, they were some of the best artists to come out in the past forty years? Besides, if I had to choose between some douchebag rock star flexing his muscles on stage while playing an uninspired guitar solo to woo groupies to his hotel room later that night, or some silly kids who spent hours discussing the pentatonic scale and all the tacos they want to eat after the show, I say long live band nerds and pass me a taco.

SKA SUCKS

In 1993, Winnipeg ska band Whole Lotta Milka were so strapped for
cash, Geoff Crowe couldn't afford to buy a baritone saxophone to play
in the group. Fortunately, the band's tenor sax player bought one at a
garage sale for $50 and let him use it. It was completely out of tune.
The band referred to it as a "gibble sax." A little later, one of Geoff's
friends, a fellow music major at University of Manitoba, took pity on
him and his gibble sax, and lent him one of the University's baritone
saxes. Geoff was so glad to be able to use it for Whole Lotta Milka that
he never gave it back. This horn was an improvement, but not much
better than the gibble sax, which explains why the University never
put much energy into retrieving it. In 2000, when Whole Lotta Milka
broke up, Geoff donated the horn to a middle school in need, a "seven-
year loan," so no biggie.

Guitarist Greg Crowe (not Geoff's brother as some lazy Canadian
journalists have speculated) tells me this anecdote to illustrate exactly
how broke his band was. "There was no money to be had. We had
eight people in the band. Nothing was ever cheap." We're on the topic
of Propagandhi's infamous "Ska Sucks," and Greg is especially honed-
in on the most irksome of lines about how ska bands were only in it for
the bucks.

Propagandhi were infamous in the DIY scene as confrontational
left-leaning, anarchist punk rockers who railed against capitalism,

sexism, and racism. And, apparently, ska. To make it sting a little more, "Ska Sucks" *is* a ska song—the only one in their catalog. And it's a ruthless jab. Lead singer Chris Hannah sings all about how uncool the ska revival is and how he hopes it will die out with any luck.

For Greg, it took three years of festering annoyance after the song appeared on Propagandhi's debut record *How To Clean Everything* to formulate his official response. He called the song "A Message to you, Chris." *Would you have guessed/that we would be so goddamn in debt/playing for peanuts every show/forced to steal our saxophone.* Greg wasn't mad per say; he just needed to stand up for ska. Greg was a huge Propagandhi fan. Still is. In Winnipeg, they're hometown punk rock heroes.

Whole Lotta Milka's monthly Ska Don't Suck! *meeting*

Everyone a part of ska scene in the '90s knew about "Ska Sucks," but no one could decide what the best way to react to it was. Some ska kids were pissed off that the almighty punk rock overlords were viciously slamming their music; others embraced it as their own. "Ska bands would get up onstage in Winnipeg and play that song," Greg says. "Almost a point of reclamation."

Greg's rebuttal also got mixed reactions. He shares with me a letter he got in the mail shortly after releasing "A Message To You,

Chris." It was from a fan, suspiciously named Chris. "Chris" claimed to like Whole Lotta Milka's music, but wouldn't be dancing to "A Message to You, Chris" anytime soon: *Your song is just an insult to the intelligence of Propagandhi fans, not to mention a waste of one of your best dance riffs,*" the letter goes. "*...Just because Chris says 'Ska Sucks' doesn't mean we aren't going to support ska bands anymore. We aren't that dumb (most of the time).*"

The stolen saxophone

Strangely, of everything Propagandhi took a stand against in their career, ska became one of the most talked about. The band mostly stopped playing the song, even though fans continued to request it. On a live version of the song from the 1998 album, *Where Quantity is Job #1*, Chris mutters: "I hate this song. We hate this song," repeatedly during the opening bass line.

I reached out to Chris on several occasions to chat about "Ska Sucks" and got no reply. I even sent him a physical letter at the advice of a knowledgeable punk friend. Punks like physical mail, he suggested—still nothing.

Fortunately, Chris opened up to Damian Abraham about the song on his podcast, *Turned Out a Punk*. During the interview, Damian referred to "Ska Sucks" as the song that has "plagued you so much," eliciting a knowing laugh out of Chris. "That song wasn't meant to be heard by anybody but skins at the Albert," he explained. "Everything we wrote back then was meant to be played at the Albert. We had no idea that anybody besides the ten people that came to see us at the Albert, which included nine skinheads, would ever fucking hear it." It should be noted that he *did* record the song on the band's debut Fat Wreck Chords album, which was sure to be heard by more than 10 people.

He offered the song's official backstory. Nazi skinheads promulgated within the late '80s and early '90s Winnipeg punk scene, becoming a serious problem no one knew how to handle. "They would march into a show and start kicking ass—inside and out of the shows," Chris tells Damian.

The Winnipeg Nazis walked around aggressively espousing white power ideology in spaces nobody wanted them at while co-opting Jamaican fashion and wanting to dance to ska music and rocksteady. And for some reason, they felt inclined to destroy this tolerant punk rock subculture as they did so. Not the brightest bunch. When Toronto hardcore band Bunchofuckinggoofs came to town, they told Chris the best way to deal with Nazis was to kick their asses. The band presented their evidence: Toronto's scene wasn't overrun by Nazis because asses were kicked. Nazis were cowards once someone stood up to them.

Nazi-scene-invaders weren't something unique to Winnipeg. Punk scenes all over the US and Canada in the '80s and '90s found Nazis infiltrators in their midst. Director Corbett Redford showed me and my friend Keith Lowell Jensen a cut scene from his film *Turn It Around: The Story of East Bay Punk* about such an incident that became legendary among East Bay punks. On September 16, 1989, Green Day, Samiam, Econochrist and other East Bay punk bands drove out to Clunie Community Center in Sacramento and were greeted by an audience of eighty punk rock nerds. Among them, a handful of skinheads. Were they good skinheads or Nazis? Nobody was quite sure.

Things went fine at first. Green Day and Samiam didn't want to choose a headliner, so they played two songs apiece, and went back and forth. The skinheads proved to be the not-good type and were tripping people and pulling the oh-so-clever move of deliberately going the opposite direction in the pit with fists swinging. Everyone hoped the skinheads would get bored and leave, but it only escalated. During one of Green Day's two-song sets, a dozen more skinheads entered, these ones bigger and more aggressive. They shoved punks down on the floor and made a big show of themselves. Filth guitarist Len Rokk tried to stop them. A Nazi clocked him in the face. That was it. The venue brought the house lights up. A full-on brawl ensued, with the object being to remove the skinheads as quickly as possible. Samiam guitarist James Brogan and Green Day bassist Mike Dirnt hopped off the stage and joined in.

"They were probably just kids from Rancho Cordova that shaved their heads. They weren't the really scary kind of skinheads we would encounter in San Francisco, which were hardened criminal skinheads —murderers that were in skinhead gangs," Samiam guitarist Sergie Loobkoff tells me. "These guys were suburban dudes that probably lived in tract homes. They didn't expect everybody in the room would turn on them." Econocrhist singer Ben Sizemore grabbed a large oak chair inside the venue and broke it over the back of a large skinhead who was seig heiling. East Bay scenester James Washburn single-handedly beat up three skinheads—at once. Econochrist roadie Shammy broke a bottle on stage intending a makeshift knife, instead cutting up his own hand.

The punks removed the Nazis from the venue and chased them off into the sunset. Once everything seemed safe, most of the bands packed up and left. But Green Day and a few other folks lingered around the venue, slowly loading their gear. They were pulled out of their blissful lollygagging state by the rumble of what sounded like an army of Doc Marten-wearing soldiers sprinting down the street. The Nazis returned, now 30 of them and ready to fight. They had bats, knives, 2x4s, and chains. This larger crew of Nazis chased Green Day and anyone else still around. Fortunately, these punk rockers were fast; they ran for their lives. When they managed to ditch the skin-heads and circle back, they found their van windows broken and tires slashed.

Green Day released the *Slappy* seven-inch shortly after this epic rumble. The liner notes said: *Green Day Won't Play Sacto*. They kept their words until their *Dookie* tour when they were able to play larger venues. On the spine of the group's debut album *39/Smooth*, they wrote "James, put down that skinhead," in honor of the skinhead slayer, James Washburn.

Back in Winnipeg, Chris wasn't prepared to fight Nazis with fisticuffs, but he wanted them to know they weren't welcome. In 1991, "Ska Sucks" was born as a way to publicly ridicule the skinheads who were causing problems at their shows. It was a message the Nazis understood. "As pencil neck geeks, what we could do was mock them. It got under their skin," Chris tells Damian. Nazis stopped showing up to Winnipeg punk shows. In retrospect, it's hard to determine the actual effect the song had because around the same time, several Winnipeg Nazis murdered a gay man in what became a high-profile hate crime. The remaining Nazis weren't so publicly bold about their hateful ideology once four were implicated for the murder. They hid from public spaces.

"Ska Sucks" may have been written to annoy Nazis, but once it got out of Winnipeg, it mutated into an anthem of ska mockery. By the mid-90s, ska became commercially viable, and with the song floating around, everyone who hated ska—and there were plenty—found a theme song. Chris has gone on record multiple times stating he doesn't hate ska. So he claims.

When Greg wrote his rebuttal, he was well aware of the complex history behind "Ska Sucks" and Winnipeg's Nazi problem. His band wrote their own song ("Intense") about Winnipeg Nazis, which appeared on Whole Lotta Milka's *Al's Diner*. Still, it got on his nerves that even when something as fucked up as Nazis was being discussed, somehow ska still ends the butt end of the joke.

In case you're wondering, Chris knows about Greg's song and has a better sense of humor about it than he does for his own ska-hating propaganda piece. Greg saw Chris at a Public Enemy show in Winnipeg shortly after releasing "A Message To You, Chris." He introduced himself as Greg from Whole Lotta Milka.

"He went, 'Oh *you*,'" Greg says. They talked about their respective songs and had a good laugh. There's a clear-as-day reference to the song on the *Where Quantity is Job #1*'s liner notes. Next to the song "Ska Sucks," it says: *See 'How to Clean' for the brilliant lyrics to the opus that inspired ska bands to write songs about Chris, oh dear.*

"I left honored," Greg says of the liner note shoutout. "They're one of my favorite bands of all time."

RENAISSANCE OF THE MIDWEST

In 1997, Grand Rapids, Michigan ska band Mustard Plug recorded a ska-punk rendition of the melodramatic hit single "The Freshman," by alt-rockers The Verve Pipe. The recording was for a benefit CD for local radio station WGRD. The Verve Pipe were also from Grand Rapids. It seemed like something funny to do, so why not?

"In Grand Rapids, the Verve Pipe walked on water. So, we gave them [the station] a ska-punk version of this song that was sacred to them," says Mustard Plug lead singer David Kirchgessner. "We weren't sure how anyone was going to react. Would the station get pissed off? Would the band get pissed off?"

The radio station loved it. The original version is breathy, yearning, and teeters on grunge. Mustard Plug turned it into an upbeat sing-along ska song with a double-time punk rock chorus. Not only did the song translate well, it was better than the original. Mustard Plug sent their version to several radio stations on a CD that also had their original "You," with hopes that DJs enticed by the wacky ska cover would check out the Mustard Plug original.

"The Freshman" found radio airplay in multiple markets, including several Midwest commercial rock stations. But none of the DJs were interested in "You." Disappointing, but Mustard Plug sensed an opportunity. "The commercial stations were already receptive to ska covers. There was that Save Ferris version of 'Come on

Eileen.' Reel Big Fish had 'Take On Me,'" Kirchgessner says. Mustard Plug's label, Hopeless Records, were eager to capitalize on the band's sudden flirtation with radio success. But the band didn't want to get famous off a ska cover.

So, what did Mustard Plug do? Nothing. Literally. They didn't push the song. They didn't put it on their album. They didn't shoot a video for it. They didn't even make it available as a single. They let the moment pass. "We would have been up for becoming more successful if it was our own music. With Save Ferris, I don't think anyone can name any of their other songs. I'm not saying there is anything wrong with their music. They'll always be known as that ska band that did that 'Come On Eileen' song. We were confident that's what would have happened to us," Kirchgessner says. "I still don't know if that was a good decision or not."

Mustard Plug never did jump to the next level, though they spent most of the '90s on the road with two-hundred-plus dates a year and built an especially strong fanbase in the greater Midwest. When the band formed in 1991, no one in Grand Rapids knew what ska was. "There was ten people familiar with it. We got most of those ten people to join the band," Kirchgessner says. The sudden interest from radio stations for "The Freshman" created not only a unique opportunity for the band to reach a larger audience, but also a chance to show the MTV ska-consuming crowd what an important contribution the Midwest gave to American ska. Ska's success in the mid-90s was built on a vibrant national independent network. The Midwest's role was substantial, allowing bands to string together full tours, and not just fly from coast to coast.

The radio-ready Orange County bands were the ones that got most of the MTV attention. This handful of mostly California bands didn't reflect the geographically diverse nature of the ska scene. The Midwest had a particularly deep affection for ska and produced some of the best and most daring bands. They had little regard for what ska was supposed to look or feel like, and they broke a lot of the rules. "We're a lot less pretentious. That's just how life is in the Midwest," says Chaz Linde, keyboardist for Chicago-based Blue Meanies. "We're not trying to be flashy. We weren't following anybody's lead. We all listened to Op Ivy. I don't think we were trying to ape anybody. It's a Midwest thing."

I Don't Wanna Be Too Cool

In the early to mid '80s, a small handful of ska bands emerged from the Midwest. SLK out of Ann Arbor, Michigan. Bop (Harvey) from East Lansing. Bop (Harvey) would gain modest fame in the '90s as a funky, world-beat, alt-rock band, but their roots were in reggae and old school ska. The initial ad for the band was, "drummer seeks bass player to start reggae band." Their first record, *Nation From Nation* (1984) is pure ska and reggae. St. Louis had The Urge, who had the 311-style minor hit "Jump Right In" in 1998. In the '80s, they played Fishbone-inspired frenetic ska and funk.

The Midwest's first band—one the US' first ska bands—was Chicago's Heavy Manners, who dubbed themselves "America's Premiere ska band." They played their first show on Halloween in 1980, billed as *SKAlloween*, a successful debut gig, proving that even in 1980, ska puns were an effective marketing tool.

Before Heavy Manners formed, lead singer Kate Fagan was a late '70s New York punk rocker. She liked the grimy CBGBs scene but felt annoyed watching the image-centric Studio 54 vibe take over the city while the punks and freaks struggled. Chicago seemed much less glamorous, so she relocated. She got together with some local musicians and recorded the offbeat post-punk single "I Don't Wanna Be Too Cool" as commentary on the New York scene. The single, which had the anti-Regan B-side "Waiting For The Crisis" did well in town. Wanting to dive further into the Chicago music scene, she started jamming with her neighbor, reggae bassist Jimmy Robinson and his friend, reggae guitarist Mitch Kohlhagen. Robinson had recently gone to England and discovered 2 Tone ska. It was a nice bridge between their reggae and punk interests.

They found several more musicians to collaborate with in the summer of 1980 and formed Heavy Manners. They realized that a small group of passionate individuals in the city loved 2 Tone, but no band played it. "People that were into ska started to come and see us," says Fagan. "It created a scene around us." The group's second single, 1981's "Flamin' First" became an underground Chicago hit.

Heavy Manners: America's original ska sweethearts

It was not financially feasible to tour as a six-piece ska band in the early '80s, and there was hardly interest in the Midwest outside of Chicago, though they did occasionally scrape together enough funds to tour the region, but their focus was on the longshot: scoring a major label deal. Money earned from sold out shows was invested in cutting demos. Several labels, including Columbia and A&M Records gave a listen, but continuously passed. "They kept saying, 'We really like it, but we're not sure if we hear the single yet,'" says drummer Shel Lustig. "We pretty much heard the same thing, several times."

The band self-funded a video for "Flamin' First" in hopes of getting on MTV, something possible in those days, but exceedingly hard for a band not on one of the coasts. A couple of local TV shows played it, and that was it. The video increased their local status but didn't build anything beyond that.

In October 1982, they released their debut record, *Politics and Pleasure* at local Chicago club Park West. Lustig recalls going to sound check in the afternoon, worried they might have aimed too high by picking a one-thousand-person capacity club for their record release. After dinner, he saw a line formed around the block. "We were happily surprised," Lustig tells me.

Attendance that night reached twelve-hundred, a new record for the club. In the first week of release, Heavy Manners sold two-thousand copies of their LP. Things were looking bright. But still, the biggest obstacle the band faced was geography. In the '80s, if you were from Chicago, you might as well have been from Greenland.

An opportunity came to the group in 1983. They were asked to open for reggae legend Peter Tosh at the Aragon Ballroom. Tosh approached Robinson after the set and told him he liked how the band mixed reggae, punk, and politics, and would be interested in working with them.

The band was on board. Tosh was an idol. The band's attorney, Linda Mensch, who they hired to find them a record contract, negotiated a deal where Tosh would produce some tracks and give them the industry push and connections they needed to get on a label. Tosh brought engineer Dennis Thompson (Bob Marley's live engineer) to run the board. In five days, they recorded four songs. Tosh sang vocals on a couple of the tracks.

Nothing came of it. Even Tosh couldn't land the band a deal. The group felt they really had no opportunity to take themselves any farther. They'd already gotten as big as they were going to get in Chicago, and they couldn't get anyone else to pay attention to them. Heavy Manners played their final show in July 1984 at Park West as a farewell to their fans, some of whom would go on to form ska bands years later, like Skapone. It was a sold-out show, but the band was already seeing ska's popularity fading in Chicago. "It was getting harder to attract new fans to our shows because we were heading towards the mid-80s," Lustig says. "New Wave stuff was coming in. The novelty of ska was beginning to wear off."

When It's Time To Party, It's Time To Party

In 1986, a group of Detroit college friends got the bright idea to start a ska band because no one else in town was playing the music.

They called the band Gangster Fun. The underground scene was dominated by rock 'n' roll, garage-rock and funk. "There wasn't a lot of people thinking about ska in Detroit back then. It's like we got the whole community to ourselves," says drummer Brian Bowie. Lead singer John Bunkley, who formed Gangster Fun with Bowie, keyboardist Dan Cogswell, trombonist/guitarist Pete Zura, and percussionist Josh Silverstein, was an exception. He had long identified as a rude boy and regularly wore suits. He liked the Equators and The Selector. His mom also played him old Jamaican oldies like Millie Small's "My Boy Lollipop" and Desmond Dekker's "The Israelites." The group's sound would align closely with 2 Tone grooves, using minor key chords, but would often go in a more lighthearted direction ala Bad Manners with songs like "Mario's Hideout" and "Fat Lady Skank," while also discussing serious issues. On "Bank of Love," they talked about the serious issue of racial equality though the absurd metaphor of a sperm bank. On "I'd Buy A Gun," they discussed the droll of working-class life but through the fantasy of having a gun to wield power. The group's name, Gangster Fun, itself an amalgam of ska culture and their brand of insanity, was inspired by the Specials' "Gangsters" but with "Fun" tacked on to demonstrate that they wanted to make their shows a party.

Just by the virtue of being a Midwestern ska band in the '80s, they faced an uphill battle. Their first show was at Oakland University in Rochester, where the members attended college. They played six songs that would eventually land on their debut album *Come See Come Ska*. They closed with a straight punk rock cover of Iggy Pop's "Lust For Life," with Bowie taking lead vocals. "All our friends loved us, basically the punk rock community at college," Bunkley says. "[Everyone else], they despised us. They were into Huey Lewis and the News and whatever was popular like the *Footloose* soundtrack. They didn't have a clue what we were doing."

Gangster Fun wouldn't toil in obscurity for long. At their second show, they played in front of nine-hundred people at a battle of the bands at local club Saint Andrews Hall, and finished second place, losing to pseudo country band Last Calgary.

Time flies when you're Gangster Fun

As the group moved to the clubs, they played with bands from every imaginable genre, but rarely ska: goth, psychedelic, glam bands, funk. "There weren't genre-specific shows. I don't think we saw a complete ska bill until we started touring," Bunkely says. The underground scene may have not known much about ska, but they fell for the wild out-of-control shows immediately. Bunkely tried to exude more energy than anyone else in the club without ever loosening his tie (that was the challenge!) and would stage-dive off of a two-story balcony, given a chance. The rest of the band was competing to see who could sweat the most. Silverstein brought the spectacle of magic tricks in-between banging on drums. "He would be pulling scarfs out of his mouth. He would have flashes and lightning coming out of his hands," Bunkley says.

Within five months, Detroit was fully converted. Gangster Fun was headlining clubs, drawing eight-hundred-to-twelve-hundred people each night. "We weren't the biggest ska band in Detroit. We were the biggest *band* in Detroit," Bunkley says. Clubs were so eager to book them, they would put them in the calendar without even asking. "We would be looking in the newspaper to see where we were playing next," Bowie says. "We would sell a lot of beer at Saint Andrews Hall and the bouncers would get beat up. They all considered that proof that we were worth having there a lot."

Gangster Fun started out as a suit-band, mostly Bunkley's influence. But everyone went their own direction with how they felt like dressing: t-shirts, jeans, silly hats, uniforms. One show at Paycheck's in Hamtramck, Michigan, they all wore mechanics' jumpsuits. At that same show, Bunkley distributed one-hundred stale cigars to the crowd, and told them to light up mid-show, pissing off the club owners. As they branched out into other Midwest cities, they got big nearly as fast as they had in Detroit. Most of these cities didn't have a ska band to speak of; Gangster Fun became their surrogate hometown band. The first time they played Akron, Ohio, thirty people came out. The next time, the club was packed with four-hundred people. Word travelled quick.

The band's debut album *Come See Come Ska* was released in 1989. Their second album, *Time Flies When Your Gangster Fun* (1992), now with the addition of guitarist David Minnick, got a little bit sillier. "He has a funny sense of humor," Bunkley says. "I have a sociology background. I take things seriously when I think they should be taken seriously. But when it's time to party, it's time to party."

Part of their party vibe heavily emphasized covers; turning non-ska songs into ska. The first song to make the transformation was a reggae rendition of The Ramones' "Blitzkrieg Bop," but with an added verse: (*"The Rudy and the Rasta/Going out to praise Jah/And he's toking all the ganja. Blitzkrieg Bop."*) They recorded it in 1988 but didn't play it live much. They learned that taking guilty pleasure rock and New Wave songs that were all over Midwest radio and transforming them into danceable ska tunes was the way to go. This would become a '90s ska staple; it started with Gangster Fun. A few examples include Kansas' "Carry On Wayward Son," AC/DC's "She Shook Me All Night," Bob Seger's "Turn The Page," and Duran Duran's "Hungry Like A Wolf." "The rock of the '70s and early '80s took itself seriously," Minnick says. "You can throw any song in that [ska] formula. It was funny."

Ska covers were an easy way to get the crowd pumped. Crowds might not have known Gangster Fun's music, or had the vaguest familiarity with ska, but they knew the lyrics to "Carry On Wayward Son." It's no wonder Gangster Fun was so popular in Midwest. "It gave them something they could immediately grab ahold of. They would sing along to it. It was stupid. It was fun. I don't remember bands doing that before," says Bunkley. One of their favorite covers was the

Rocky theme song, which they played anytime there was a fight, which was almost every show. "Our shows had a lot of violence. A lot of people would admonish them. We egged them on," Bunkley says. One show Bunkley recalls, a large skinhead guy was trying to grope a tiny 4'8" woman. She pulled out a knife and chased him around the club, stabbing him. Like clockwork, the band jumped into the *Rocky* theme.

Taking these macho rock songs and spinning them into ska gold wasn't just a goof. It was a way to grapple with their outsider Midwest identity. Even if they hated some of these cliché rock songs and the meathead mindset of their peers, it was still part of their culture. This was an inescapable truth for all Midwest ska bands of the time. "Classic rock, that's the background music to being in the Midwest," says MU330's Dan Potthast, whose early batch of songs melded '70s style arena rock with ska. "The Midwest is about ten years behind the coasts. We were drawing from older stuff than bands that were coming out at the same time in the East Coast and the West Coast. I didn't hear Op Ivy till we were touring. That wasn't a part of the melting pot that made up our songwriting."

The love-hate relationship with their own Midwest culture induced Gangster Fun to push the chaotic vibe to an almost dangerous level. The goal was to be the opposite of everything else around them. In doing so they created a frenzied style of ska that was nutty and berserk for its own sake, a dance party that was sort of loony but never safe—a new way to view ska.

Slayer Of Ska

In 1991, a new ska band emerged from Detroit called Jack Kevorkian and the Suicide Machines, later shortened to The Suicide Machines. They described themselves as the "Slayer of ska" for their brutal punk rock edge and hardcore live shows. Because their shows were so off-the-wall intense, a lot of ska bands—even a lot of punk bands—didn't want to share a bill with them.

"Our crowds were wilder than normal ska crowds. I came up in the fucking gutter punk scene In Detroit. I was more used to going to hardcore shows than punk shows," says singer Jason Navarro. "Dan and I incorporated that into how we played ska. It was normal to pass the mic to the crowd at a hardcore show. That's what a lot of ska bands didn't do it the time. People would do a front flip off the stage. Kids that came to see us danced like they were at a hardcore show. They would skank too, but shit got crazy all the time. It was reckless. A lot of people were really put off by that, especially in that ska world."

With that kind of energy, why didn't Suicide Machines just play hardcore? A big reason is the influence Gangster Fun had on them. Like every other Midwest ska band that emerged in the late '80s and early '90s, Suicide Machines worshipped Gangster Fun. Navarro remembers being a kid and going to Gangster Fun shows. He particularly loved seeing the sheer joy on audience members' faces as the band hopped around on stage and sang *I'd buy a gun if I had a million dollars* in-between ska covers of "Achy Breaky Heart" and "Blue Monday."

"There was zero elitism when you went to a Gangster Fun show. It was college frat boys, punks, hardcore kids, skinheads, Rastas, fucking hip-hop kids, skaters, The BMXers. Black, white, gay," Navarro says. "I wanted to be around something uplifting. We tried to do that with The Suicide Machines but obviously probably isolated people by playing as hard as we could sometimes. Gangster Fun shows is how it should be."

We Were Always The Ones On The Outside

In addition to The Suicide Machines, several other ska bands emerged from the Midwest in the early '90s: MU330 (St. Louis), Mustard Plug (Grand Rapids), Pacers (Milwaukee), Weaker Youth Ensemble (Madison), Johnny Socko (Bloomington), and Skapone (Chicago). Scrappy punk-ska group Slapstick formed in Chicago in 1993 and seemed poised to break out to a larger audience but broke up in 1996. The members split off and formed several successful bands, most notably Alkaline Trio and The Lawrence Arms. All these Midwest ska bands carved out new and unique versions of ska music as they were most likely the only band in their town playing the genre, so they had little input in how ska was supposed to sound. No Midwest ska band was more out there than Chicago's Blue Meanies, the weirdest of all. They formed in 1989 in Carbondale, Illinois by Jay Vance, who eventually played bass in Skankin' Pickle, and then quit to start robot-noise project Captured By Robots. A true weirdo.

Blue Meanies returning home from Mars

Blue Meanies started out as a Fishbone-meets-Red Hot Chili Peppers party band, albeit with a darker edge. "There was a lot of slapping bass and horns," says keyboardist Chaz Linde, who joined the band a year-and-a-half-later when the band relocated to Chicago. The party vibes got a whole lot darker in Chicago. Linde wrote much of The Blue Meanies' material. "It wasn't such a sunny, fun college town vibe. That's where my head was at," Linde says.

The group was channeling their inner Mr. Bungle with odd time signatures, demented circus horn lines, discordant sections, and mixing all of it with ska. "I wanted it to be as fast and loud and dissonant as possible just to fuck with people," Linde says.

In Chicago, they weren't viewed as a ska band—more a weirdo punk rock band with horns. But once the Blue Meanies hit the road, a funny thing happened: the Midwest ska scene welcomed them. The Blue Meanies went with it. "People wanted to book us because we had horns and keyboards," says Linde. "We didn't look like a ska band. We didn't sound like a ska band. It worked out great because we got on cool tours. We were embraced by the ska scene. We were the ones always on the outside."

Whatever Kind Of Bread You Want

Midwest bands had no unifying sound. The New York scene was connected by a strong jazz and traditional ska sound. The Orange County scene was dominated by pop-punk. The Midwest scene was characterized by its lack of definition.

"We played hundreds of shows with MU330. We're nothing close to being alike in terms of style," says Linde. "But we're both from the Midwest and our fan bases were kind of the same. Same with Mustard Plug or Suicide Machines. These were all our dudes. But we didn't have much in common with them musically."

United as a loose collective rather than a rigidly defined scene, the bands naturally pushed each other to be more different than one another. Dan Potthast recalls an early show at the Outhouse in Lawrence, Kansas where MU330 opened for Blue Meanies and Skankin' Pickle. "I recognized that there's a lot of flexibility in this genre. Seeing The Blue Meanies, which blew my mind, and Skankin' Pickle—this all falls under the same ska-punk umbrella, but all three of us are doing something different," he says. "Ska is the flour. You can make whatever kind of bread you want out of this stuff. It felt like anything was possible. There's no rules."

In 1995, the national ska scene got a proper taste of the eclectic mania these Midwest ska bands were baking with Chicago based Jump Up! Records' *American Skathic* compilation. It featured twenty-one Midwest bands. The four bands on the album that broke out of the Midwest were MU330, Mustard Plug, Blue Meanies, and The Suicide Machines.

The Suicide Machines had the fortune of signing to Hollywood Records in 1995. Their Op Ivy-style single "No Face" charted in 1996. The other three bands built underground careers from grinding out never-ending tours. It didn't hurt that rent in the Midwest was considerably lower than the coastal towns, which enabled the band members to sidestep day jobs. The Blues Meanies, as weird as they were, somehow landed on some big mainstream ska tours. In 1996, they opened for Goldfinger and Reel Big Fish, two California bands fusing pop-punk and ska.

The Blue Meanies weird approach to ska confused most of their crowds. Singer Billy Spunke screamed atonally into a megaphone while the band performed the marching parade of doom to young, impressionable teenagers. "There would be people just standing, looking at us like what's going on? We would always grab those twenty-to-thirty fringe kids. The people that liked our band grabbed on. 'We're going to come see you every time you come through.' That's how we got our fan base."

Gangster Fun, who set the tone for Midwest's lawless approach to ska, would never reach a larger audience outside of the Midwest, where they were considered gods. They were unable to tour two-hundred-plus dates a year in their early '90s heyday. They only made it out to the coasts a few times and didn't have many connections. Bunkley and some of the other original members left in '95. A new version of the band continued on for a little while longer and released two more albums. "We had been pounding on our own for so long with no help. There were more opportunities for bands after us, like Suicide Machines. They could play Warped Tour. A booking agent would never exist for us being from the Midwest at that time. You didn't have a booking agent that would even want to help a Midwest band."

The story of ska in the U.S. may have not originated in the Midwest, but the Midwest evolved ska to be the diverse genre it became. These bands argued that anything could be ska if you tried hard enough. The bands on the coast attained a higher degree of national fame, but the ska shows in the Midwest were always huge and wild. They took an approach that was opposite from how a lot of other ska bands approached the music: not as hip, fashionably dressed, 2 Tone homage bands, or pop-punk infused. They made it their own and showed that ska was more than a genre. It was something you mixed with your own identity.

SO FAR AWAY

I dubbed a copy of *Sing Along with Skankin' Pickle* for my nine-year-old-brother Matt when it came out in 1994. He listened to it on his old beat-up portable cassette player on infinite repeat. His absolute favorite song was "20 Nothing" by the band's new bass player Ian Miller.

The song had a gritty, East Bay pop-punk edge never previously part of Pickle's lexicon. Ian grew up obsessed with hardcore, then got into ska by way of Op Ivy. All these elements, mixed with a pre-*Dookie* Green Day vibe, went into "20 Nothing." To Matt, it was musical perfection. He danced around to it with careless abandon and sang along, slightly incorrectly. It was those incorrect lyrics that had me dying.

Rather than, "I can't even think about the proletariat revolution 'til after noon or 1 o'clock" Matt sang, "...till after noon *at* 1 o'clock." I don't know why this minor error was so hilarious to me. Maybe it was because he somehow managed to pronounce "proletariat revolution" correctly but would earnestly belt out "after noon *at* 1 o'clock," like Ian needed to take the time in his song to point out that one o'clock was after noon.

I called up Kevin Dill, Skankin' Pickle's merch guy, to tell him about my little brother's obsession with "20 Nothing." As I'd gotten to know the band, Kevin and I hit it off, even though he was ten years older than me. We talked for hours about the stupidest, most ridiculous things, like bad TV shows, or obscure punk bands singing about breakfast pastries, and exalted the brilliance of life's constant supply of everyday absurdity. "That's genius," he said. "You have to get him to crank-call Ian and sing that song. It would be amazing." He gave me Ian's number.

I'd do him one better. Not only would I get Matt to call Ian, but I'd tape it. I had an ancient answering machine the size of a suitcase that recorded messages on full-sized cassettes. I used it in high school to record crank calls.

I had a character named Sammy who was obsessed with soda, or *Shody* as Sammy called it. Sammy had a nasally, raspy voice, and pseudo-lisped a "sh" out of every "s." I called up random businesses and enthusiastically asked them if they had *Shodys*.

They never knew it was a crank call and were always extra polite. I kept them on the phone as long as possible, running through every single soda brand I could think of to confirm if they had it. (*"Do you have Shrpite shody? What about Sheven up shody? Pepshi shody, too? Shimpshons shody?"*) They informed me that they carried all of these but Simpsons Sody and "wouldn't be surprised if that's on the market soon." I could hear them holding back laughter but still trying to be helpful. I cracked my friends up with those tapes. Now I was a full-grown adult of nineteen years. The time had come to pass the baton to my little brother.

I told Matt that I wanted him to sing his favorite song to Ian, the guy who wrote the song he loved. He agreed to this mission with no thought. Nothing about this was strange inside a 9-year old's mind.

Ian answered the phone. With no introduction, Matt launched into his perfectly imperfect acapella rendition of "20 Nothing." I listened in the other room, recording it, trying with all my might to not die from laughter. Ian didn't say a word the entire time Matt sang.

"That was great," Ian said.

"Is your name Ian," Matt said, suddenly full of questions.

"It is. You just sang my song," Ian said.

"What's it about?" Matt said.

"Well, I was expressing something I felt at a low point..." Ian paused, thinking.

"Oh, ok. Thanks," Matt said. He walked into my room and handed me the phone. I fumbled to hang it up. My heart raced. I pulled the cassette out of the answering machine and checked the audio on my stereo. It was all there. Brilliant. I couldn't wait to show Kevin.

Kevin's Xmas card (L-R: Paul Chavez, Nos, Kevin Dill, Shige)

Skankin' Pickle played Slim's in San Francisco a few weeks later. I sashayed into the club with a copy of the tape in hand, and sped over to the merch booth, waving it in front of Kevin.

"*Carne*, is that what I think it is?" he said. Kevin called me *Carne*, Spanish for "meat." My Last name, Carnes, is spelled just like meat *en español*, but it's pronounced like "carns" since it's Irish. I liked the nickname. I handed Kevin the tape. He looked at it, paused and said, "This rules!" We went in my car and listened. Kevin laughed hysterically. "I'm going to torture Ian with this. Tell your little brother I worship him."

Kevin wasn't lying, about the torturing part at least. When Skankin' Pickle went on the road a month later, he sat in the passenger seat and with no intro, popped the tape in and played it at full volume.

Everyone in the band cracked up, even Ian, who was embarrassed and suddenly realized, of course, Kevin was behind that random call he got a month ago.

As Kevin and I walked back to Slim's, he told me: "You need to show your brother the brilliance that is 'So Far Away.' That would be legendary."

"I've tried," I said. "He's stuck on '20 Nothing.'"

We talked about "So Far Away" all the time. It was an unreleased Skankin' Pickle song that Ian wrote. Kevin and I sang it to each other and wedged the lyrics into our conversations whenever possible. The group recorded it in their *Sing Along With* demo sessions. Mike Park gave me a copy of the demos when they were still working on the album. By the time they finished, "So Far Away" was missing in action, presumably because Kevin had so ruthlessly made fun of the song. He'd soured the band on it.

It was a good song, similar to "20 Nothing" in its influences, but faster and heavier. Lyrically, it was a very heartfelt expression about Ian missing his wife Tracy while on tour. (*"It makes no sense to me that you're so far away/ What was I thinking when I said I wouldn't stay?"*)

When Ian joined Pickle in 1993, they were already a full-time touring machine, so it was understandably hard for him to suddenly be away from his wife all the time. Nobody else in Pickle, apart from Lynette, had a significant other to miss, so those lyrics were an easy target for Kevin. He was merciless to Ian, who didn't know how to take it at first but soon caught on that for Kevin, it was a sign of affection. If he found some way to provoke you, he'd beat you over the head with it until you laughed. It was precisely why the band liked him so much. He was more than just a merch guy.

When Skankin' Pickle released *Sing Along with Skankin' Pickle*, they added Kevin's face to the cover, alongside the rest of the band. His presence on tour and at shows made everything fun. Even boring band stuff, like driving eight hours to a gig became an adventure with Kevin. He'd taunt the new bass player with a recording of a crank call some nine-year-old made.

Kevin met the band back in the late '80s. He was just some random Gilman weirdo who happened to catch one of their sets in the Bay. He liked how over-the-top insane and goofy early Pickle shows were, and, more than that, how much the super serious, suit-wearing rude boys *hated* them. He thought it was hilarious that they'd stand there, arms folded, pissed off and resenting a band for having the time of their lives.

However over-the-top the band already was, Kevin egged them on to be even crazier. When you were around Kevin, you felt empowered to go nuts. He alone decided what was cool. If a spazzy, out-of-tune high school ska band sang their hearts out on stage, he'd declare them the greatest band of all time. And you'd agreed with him. Meanwhile, he'd savagely mock a band with musical know-how if they were even the slightest bit pretentious. And you mocked them, too.

Kevin loves his mom

Pickle loved how Kevin made a joke of everything and started inviting him to all their shows—plus, he had to, because "your last name is Dill." It was airtight logic Kevin couldn't argue against. Once Pickle hit the road and started touring, Kevin naturally fell into the role of merch guy.

To me, Kevin was the funniest person ever. The first time I went to his house in Vallejo, where he lived with his mom, I was amazed by his massive library of VHS tapes, filled with obscure and weird footage. Clips ranged from silly to disturbing. He dubbed me a tape and wrote, "Japanese Funk" on the label. He'd recorded an entire episode of *CHiPS* where the actor who played Ralph Malph on *Happy Days* guest starred as a satanic metal singer named, 'Moloch.' Moloch sang a song called "Devil Take Me" and believed the devil was trying to kill him. Japanese Funk also had a clip from Corey Haim's 1989 "day in the life" documentary video *Me, Myself and I*, where Haim jammed on his Roland synthesizer, high as fuck, and deemed it, "Japanese funk."

Aside from a montage at the end of the tape of Buddhist monks repeatedly making themselves vomit, Japanese Funk was wholesome fun. Kevin shielded me from his morbid and gross clips, like *Junkyard Lesbians*, which I'd only heard about. And from what I heard involved a lot of motor oil.

After the tape of Matt crank-calling Ian went over so well, it occurred to me I should dig up my Sammy tapes for Kevin. I even added some new crank calls with Flat Planet's singer Alex Rosario doing his "Papa Don" character as Sammy's dad and my friend Bruce Landry doing his dark and disturbed "English Guy" character, which was Sammy's death-obsessed brother. I dubbed Kevin a copy and sat with him as he listened to it. He freaked out, like I'd given him a bootleg of his favorite band.

He brought the tape with him a few months later when Skankin' Pickle went on their *Sing Along with Skankin' Pickle* full US tour. The band brought Hawaiian ska-soul band Tantra Monsters with them. Kevin played the Sammy Sody tape to the Tantras constantly. They loved it, especially their drummer Johnny Swoish, and their trombonist Shige.

Kevin regaled me with endless stories about Shige. Shige was a nickname. His real name was Ryan Kunimura, but everyone called him Shige, a reference to a bit that Hawaiian comedian Rap Reiplinger used to do (*"Don't worry Shige, I have a plan"*). Kevin said Shige was a maniac, and he liked *my* Sammy Sody tape! It was a huge compliment.

Midway through the tour, in Providence Rhode Island, Pickle slide trombonist Gerry Lundquist had to leave due to a blood clot in his leg. The doctor told him that it could have been fatal if he waited much longer. Gerry was hospitalized in Providence for ten days. The band couldn't stick around; they had a tour to finish. Shige learned Gerry's parts and filled in. He brought weird, dark energy to Pickle's normally goofy set. When Mike introduced each member during the breakdown in "Larry Smith," Shige always shocked them with something from out of left field. One time, Shige appeared on the side of the stage, stark naked, but with an ice scoop covering his genitals. Rather than do a horn solo or wacky dance, he stood there for 30 seconds and stared at the crowd, unblinking.

During the long drives, Shige filmed "TV segments" that no one, aside from Kevin and his circle of friends, would ever see: *Fun with Shige*. In one episode, Shige interviewed Mr. Walrus, aka Tantra's sax player Caesar Mercado's talking butt, Ace Ventura-style. However, his butt was actually naked, with a walrus face drawn on his butt cheeks and his testicles as the walrus trunk. Shige pretend to be a silly children's show host. He never broke character as he chatted with Caesar's exposed testicles, who talked back like a goofy cartoon Walrus. The whole thing was disturbing and undeniably hilarious.

Kevin gave me constant updates on Sammy Sody's popularity. "Tantras are losing their minds over the Sammy Sody tape. They can't wait to meet you. It's all they're talking about," he said. Without thinking, I blurted out that I had a Sammy Sody song. It was forty-five seconds of me repeating one major chord on my keyboard and improvising nonsensical lyrics. Kevin paused. "You need to play that song on stage with the Tantras."

A week later, Skankin' Pickle and the Tantra Monsters performed at Palookaville in Santa Cruz, their final stop on tour. Kevin introduced me to the band, who were confused and disappointed I wasn't actually a weird kid named Sammy. Kevin thought this was so funny. Before they had a chance to process this, he announced I would be joining them on stage to perform the official Sammy Sody theme song.

I didn't expect them to invite me up for real, but sure enough, at the end of their set, Shige got on the mic and announced, "We have a very special guest in the house tonight—Sammy Sody!"

Kevin hangs out with Sammy Sody: Very Special Guest

Everyone clapped as I pushed myself up on stage. I stood behind the keyboard and looked at the room filled with transfixed eyes. I stumbled through the forty-five second song, mumbling gibberish. Fortunately, the Sammy Sody pseudo-lisp disguised every word. I looked down the whole time, embarrassed, but oddly thrilled. What the hell was I even doing?

When I finished, everyone in Tantra Monsters gave me a big hug. It was the highlight of their tour to have the one and only Sammy join them on stage. I hopped into the crowd, feeling dazed. A random woman approached me and said in her most reassuring, compassionate voice, "You did a great job! You are so brave."

But it was Kevin's reaction I wanted to see. "Sammy Sody!" he shouted. "That was the ultimate. I can finally die now."

One time in early '95, Kevin was on tour with Skankin' Pickle. He, Gerry and roadie Paul Chavez, who frequently traveled with Voodoo Glow Skulls, hopped into the elevator at their Chicago hotel after a gig.

A lanyard-wearing tour manager (or "guy with a shoestring haircut," as Kevin described it) joined them in the elevator. Kevin, Gerry and Paul started to lick the glass mirrors inside the elevator. The tour manager stood frozen, terrified. He exited quickly when the elevator got to his floor. They all laughed, but then Gerry suddenly broke down and told the others that *that* was the guy from 311 and he *hated* him. Gerry grew up in Nebraska. 311 were a Nebraska band. This was a Nebraska beef.

Kevin didn't know 311—they were just starting to crack the radio —but if Gerry hated them, then so did he. The two went back and forth, ripping on 311, despite Kevin's lack of knowledge of the band apart from the guy's douchey hairdo. When they got up to the hotel room, low and behold, like a gift from heaven, they saw 311's tour bus underneath their window. It was a sign.

He knew he had to do something, but what? The two discussed pissing on 311's bus. Before anyone whipped their dicks out, Kevin stuck his head out the window and started up a pep-band chant at the top of his lungs: "Get up, get down, 3-1-1 is a joke in this town!" Kevin threw whatever objects he could find around the hotel room at the van —empty coke cans, bath towels. "You're the fucking worst!" he taunted. Several heads turned up and saw some guy starting shit three flights up. Why? Because why not!

Kevin was also on the phone at the same time, crank-calling Gwen Stefani, who was staying in the same hotel. She just laughed it off. "Hi Kevin," she said and hung up. 311 didn't have the same sense of humor about the whole thing. They quickly figured out exactly who was mocking them: Skankin' Pickle. The next morning, as Skankin' Pickle piled into their van, the same shoeshine haircut guy stepped up to Ian, who had no idea what was going on. To Ian, he said: "What's up with the neg vibes, bro?"

Ian responded, "No neg vibes bro." The guy proceeded to lecture Ian about how they were a bunch of "peace-loving hippies" and didn't appreciate the shit-talking. No argument from Ian. Everyone drove away, a little confused. They were all heading to Minneapolis that night to play First Avenue, Prince's club. Skankin' Pickle was the opening band. No Doubt was main support. 311 were headlining. A few hours into the drive, they got a call from their booker Rick Bonde. 311 were furious with Skankin' Pickle and wanted them off the bill.

Obviously, Kevin was behind this ludicrous squabble. Pickle thought it was funny, but they still wanted the gig to happen. They asked Rick to work something out. There was much discussion, and Rick negotiated a deal with the promoter that Pickle could play the show, only if their roadies were at least a full city block away from the venue. Kevin wasn't thrilled at this. It wasn't that he cared about being banned. His problem was Pickle taking it seriously.

Later that year, Kevin was in Berkeley hanging out with Paul Chavez and friend Eric Yee. They were driving around, drinking Kool Colt 45s and basking in the ridiculousness of their mentholated alcoholic drinks, when they noticed rows of scooters in front of the nightclub Berkeley Square along with several plush suit-wearing rude boys lingering in front. There was a big traditional ska show tonight!

Kevin liked ska, but he liked making fun of rude boys more. His prime targets were always any group of people that lacked a sense of humor about themselves. Everyone in the car agreed the rude boys needed to be ruthlessly mocked. Eric flipped a U-turn and screeched in front of the club. Paul pulled his camera out and hit record. Kevin blurted out the most caustic thing he could think to say to a group of rude boys minding their own business. *"Skaaaaa! Put that rudy in his place, smash a fucking bottle in his face. Fuck you rudys. Come on, eat my ass, you fucking pieces of shit. Yeah, your mom, too."* And then, like that, they sped away, angering and confusing these rudies.

Without Kevin's knowledge, Paul showed this clip to the Voodoo Glow Skulls, who loved it and decided to put the audio version of it on their Epitaph debut album *Firme* before the song "Empty Bottles." They played Kevin the full record a few weeks before it was released, keeping a straight face the whole time. To the masses of people who heard the "Empty Bottles" intro, it was a punk rock "fuck you" to all the ska purists who were dicks to bands like Voodoo Glow Skulls. For Kevin, it was an in-joke gone viral. The funniest thing in the world.

I asked Kevin once if he ever felt like he took any of his pranks too far. He said he tear-gassed The Pacers backstage at Slim's and he regretted it. Why? I asked. Because they weren't the ska band he meant to tear-gas.

. . .

I wanted to top the weird Sammy Sody performance. A few months later, I had my shot. Flat Planet was opening for Skankin' Pickle at the same venue, Palookaville. I had an idea. It would blow Kevin's mind. We'd cover "So Far Away."

It was supposed to be a surprise, but a few weeks before the show, I couldn't resist. I told Kevin. He loved it. "You have to get Tracy to go-go dance on stage," he said. The song was about her after all.

He told everyone what we were up to, except Ian and Tracy. Lars came up to me before the show and said, "So Far Away," patting me on the back, laughing. Kevin got Tracy to blindly agree to go-go dance on stage during our final song. When she asked why, he told her it would be for something "special" for her husband. She must have known there was something unseemly attached to it, but that's the power of Kevin. You agree to do whatever he says, knowing you'll likely face embarrassment.

The venue was packed. We played thirty minutes of our typical Flat Planet set and got a positive response from the crowd. Then it was time for "So Far Away." I got on the mic: "We need Tracy to join us on stage to go-go dance!" She was on stage in seconds. She looked back, waiting for me to count the song off. Once we started, she danced like she was Goldie Hawn on *Laugh-In*. The moment I started singing, she recognized the song and almost fell over laughing, but composed herself and kept going. Like a pro.

Lars, Lynette, and Mike were on the side of the stage, clapping along, singing. Ian stood behind them, shaking his head. As soon I crashed down on the cymbals on the final beat, Ian appeared behind me and dumped a full bucket of ice-cold water over my head. I contained myself from the shock, and stumbled backstage, soaking wet. Ian was waiting with a towel. Still shaking his head, he said, "*Carne!*" laughing.

What was this like for the audience? An opening band played a punk song as a random woman danced. Then the headliner's bass player dumped a bucket of water on the drummer after they finished. What did any of it mean?

Kevin came backstage, skanking in place and singing "*It makes no sense to me that you're so far away.*" "You're the best *Carne*. I can't even put to words how much you rule right now." Kevin emanated pure joy. I don't know if I'd ever be as happy as he was in that moment. I would never be able to top "So Far Away." Kevin saw everything as a joke. His perspective on life blurred the lines between comedy and tragedy into one big, ridiculous gray mess. He intrinsically understood that to take anything serious was a waste because life was a joke, and our death was the bitter punchline. Sometimes I think that Kevin's the only person in the world that's got it all figured out.

ANIMAL PLANET

Have you ever heard a ska song on Animal Planet and wondered, who's this band and why do they sound so familiar? There's a pretty good chance it's Boston legends Bim Skala Bim.

"The Animal Planet uses our stuff a lot. Home and Garden uses it. Food Network uses us. MTV uses us a lot. *The Real World*, they have Vinnie's trombone lick for the promo," explains Bim Skala Bim bassist Mark Ferranti. "Just the other day on *Man Vs. Food*, I heard our riff being played. It's all over the place." The band also has a song in the ten-part 2008 PBS documentary *Carrier*. In the eighth episode, during the "Crew Plays in Perth" scene, some of the sailors are cheering with raised shot glasses. "When they go clink with the shot glasses, our song kicks into a long sequence of people partying to our music on the beach. That was good," Ferranti says.

Bim Skala Bim were one of the first US ska bands. They released several albums and toured the country in the '80s and '90s too many times to count. In the 2000s, they slowed down as road dogs, but their music was still out there on TV shows thanks to Getty Images, who places them wherever they can: shows, movies, and commercials. Apparently, ska is in high demand.

Background music is how a lot of people first hear ska music. When I pitched this book to agents, one replied, saying she really liked the ska music she heard on the British-French crime drama, *Death in*

Paradise. Strange response. I sent her my full proposal anyway. Big surprise, she passed. She wasn't convinced people would want to read an entire book about background music. Like this agent, many people don't realize ska is a legitimate musical genre.

In a 2002 interview with the *Boston Phoenix,* former Mighty Mighty Bosstones guitarist Nate Albert lamented on ska's relegation to mere TV music. "Every comedy show, or every commercial that's supposed to be funny, the soundtrack is ska-core. I was watching *America's Funniest Home Videos,* and it's like the whole soundtrack is ska-core. And I'm thinking, 'Is this what we gave to the world?'"

Ska music is fun and does add an instantly joyful tone to any movie or show. What's wrong with that? Besides, if ska is in high demand on shows, then more ska musicians are going to get paid to make more ska music. Win-win!

Vinnie's famous "Real World" lick

Bim Skala Bim have done well for themselves licensing ska, a nice turnaround after several bad experiences in other areas of the industry. They stopped working with record labels when things went sour with Celluloid Records in 1988. "It left a bad taste in our mouth. It just seemed like any deal with a record company meant more complications and more entanglements. You can go record the albums yourselves," Ferranti says. "We'd hear these stories of people getting these record deals, and then go spend $100,000. The last record we made was for $5,000."

Bim Skala Bim at the Ashby Mass Reggae Festival, 1984

The band's relationship with soundtracking TV shows started in 1987. They played CBGB's with the Toasters and were approached by two nervous teens, asking if they could use their music for a video they were making to try to get an MTV internship. Lead singer Dan Vitale told them they could use it for free as long as they gave them credit and didn't forgot them if they ever hit the big time. Those interns got hired at MTV and did indeed use Bim's music. On nearly half of every *Real World* and *Road Rules* episodes. Later the nervous teens formed Pump Audio, which specialized in placing indie music in TV shows, and continued to work hard for Bim. In 2007, Getty Images purchased Pump Audio for $42 million and suddenly Bim found themselves working with a huge company they never directly signed with.

The deal works well for Bim because Getty does all the work and the band gets a percentage of the fee. Getty places so much of Bim's music because they have a lot to choose from. At some point, the band handed over everything they'd ever recorded to Getty including instrumental outtakes, remixes, and any noodling that might have been captured on tape they later forgot about. "I would hear stuff on television that I thought was me, but I didn't recognize it. But it was actually me," Ferranti says. "It's not like it pays tons of money. It keeps the candles burning."

There's the added bonus that Getty has helped them go after companies that were bootlegging their albums, great considering the group has been independent since the late '80s. "We don't have a major label behind us, but we don't need them," says Vitale. Ferranti agrees. "We don't think of the music industry in any way as an ally, except Getty Images," he says. "We kind of backdoored our way in. We have people calling us up, hey I just heard you on the Food Channel or the Animal Planet."

Overall, the quantity of ska on TV has only increased, an unexpected twist for a genre deemed deader than a toad with a brick up its ass. Ska is now all over kids' shows, another fact that everyone likes to make fun of. But I think it's great. Ska finds a way to reach people, even if its vehicle is cute animal videos or silly kids' shows. If all goes according to plan, all this ska on Yo Gabba Gabba and Bo On The Go will plant a seed in these children's minds that will sprout into full on ska fanaticism in adulthood.

MY BOY LOLLIPOP

I have a confession. I don't like "My Boy Lollipop."

I've tried, I have, but it's best to be honest. I think it's an unlisten-able, squeaky pop song that feels already too long at a lean two minutes and one second.

Some of you are furious right now. I get it. I've been you before. Hopefully, we can work through this. Others of you are wondering why I'm even talking about some old '60s pop song your grandparents used to swing their hips to at the local ice cream social. Let me explain myself.

"My Boy Lollipop" is a ska song.

Get this. It's the top-selling ska song of all time. You think No Doubt, Sublime, and Reel Big Fish went mainstream. It's nothing compared to the nearly seven million copies "My Boy Lollipop" sold. For a second it looked like its singer Millie Small was going to dethrone the almighty Beatles—with a ska song. I know! I should *love* this song.

The song is a cover of Richard Spencer's mid-50s doo-wop tune. It was the third top-selling single in the UK in 1964. It peaked at #2 in the UK and the US. If you haven't heard it in a while, you probably remember it as a standard, run-of-the-mill '60s pop shuffle. But that shuffle is, in fact, upbeats, and there's a deliberately watered-down Jamaican groove, too. So there. It's ska.

A lot of ska fanatics hold "My Boy Lollipop" up as a gem (even though *I* know *they* know they don't much care for it), but what they really treasure is the sneaky history of how it—a ska song—invaded the radio in an unexpected moment of time. Mind you, these are the same folks who haven't recovered from the stroke they suffered the day Reel Big Fish ruined ska forever on MTV.

I know My Boy Lollipop isn't the worst song ever. Not even close. My band released much worse songs. But its legacy needs to be reckoned with. It fucked up ska music in the US for decades. So, let's dig into how this unlikely song blew up the charts, and what its impact has been on Jamaican music in U.S. pop culture. Then you can make an informed decision whether to continue to pretend to love this song or join me on the Lollipop Hate Train.

Millie Mania

Millie Small recorded "My Boy Lollipop" in 1964 in England and its success on the charts surprised a lot of people. Her song peaked at #2 at the height of Beatlemania in late Spring/early summer in 1964, which meant a lot of people in the media and the music industry immediately deemed her to have superpowers. During her first trip to the US in July 1964, the *New York Amsterdam News* reported that "Millie Small is the only girl who has ever been able to challenge the popularity of the Beatles." She was 16 years old. Pop stardom suited her. She had an infectious smile and joyous air about her any time she was in public, and she was always genuinely gracious, humble and charming with her fans.

The industry misinterpreted her success. They had an unhealthy obsession with the fact that the song was ska. They assumed wrongly that "My Boy Lollipop" was a canary in the coal mine, sounding the alarm for the impending ska explosion about to decimate pop culture.

Small was from Clarendon, Jamaica, from modest means. Her father worked on a sugar plantation, and her mother was a dressmaker. She had some hits in Jamaica three years prior to her success with "My Boy Lollipop." People were always impressed with her natural talent. At the age of twelve, she won the second prize of 30 shillings at a talent show at the Palladium in Montego Bay in front of two-thousand people. She cut her first record at the age of thirteen. "I never had singing lessons, my voice was just something I was born with," she told the *Express* in 2016.

Despite all this, it's strange "My Boy Lollipop" became a shining exemplar of "traditional Jamaican dance" i.e. ska or blue beat (described as "[a] sensuous undulating dance of the slow, shuffling steps" by a 1964 issue of *Jet Magazine*). The music that backed her was hardly the gritty, groove-intense, jazz-influenced genre sprung from ghettos of West Kingston. Jamaican guitarist Ernest Ranglin played on the record. The rest of the band was local white British players. Authentic ska was perfected by The Skatalites, a group of jazz-studied musicians that went through the Alpha Boys School in Kingston, and who were Jamaica's top studio band from 1963-1965. Various incarnations of the ten members of this group played on a lot of the early ska records. They recorded on primitive recording equipment at Jamaica's Studio One, because that's all the producers could afford. The imperfections were easily forgivable by the gritty, perfect upbeat performances these musicians delivered. This music was not for pop ears. Even Jamaican middle and upperclassmen wouldn't listen to the "Rastafarian" ska music as it was too low class and African sounding for them. As is the case with much of pop music, someone got the idea to market poor people music to not-so-poor people by 'cleaning it up.' That person was Island Records' owner Chris Blackwell.

In the '70s, Blackwell would do the same thing for Bob Marley, but his efforts with Marley essentially backfired. In the legendary tale of Bob Marley, it's fashionable to talk about how Blackwell made Marley a rock star when he suggested Marley soften his Jamaican elements by infusing his 1972 album *Catch A Fire* with more recognizably rock 'n' roll elements, like solos, synthesizers and a more rock-sounding guitar tone. Blackwell hired some white, mostly-unfamiliar-with-reggae-musicians to overdub these rock-ish parts onto the album to soothe delicate American ears.

But *Catch A Fire* wasn't a success. "I think Bob & Blackwell felt that the quest was a valid one, but that they didn't arrive at the right formula. The right formula turned out to be an accent on strong songs, so that the vocals were clearly out front, and the music had interesting parts in it," says Danny Holloway, Blackwell's creative assistant from 1973-1976.

Marley and reggae music eventually found an audience in the US thanks to the ongoing popularity of *The Harder They Come* and its authentic soundtrack. For post-*Catch A Fire* albums, Blackwell and Marley scrapped the watered-down approach and subsequently did much better, gaining a bigger audience with each record. Americans didn't want a rock-infused version of reggae. They wanted the real deal.

Blackwell was a wealthy and white, albeit disheveled, beach bum who could be played by Michael Caine in the movie of his life. He grew up in Jamaica while it was still under British rule. His father was incredibly wealthy from his relationship to the food and relish company, Crosse & Blackwell, and became a Major in the Jamaican Regiment. His mother sat on a fortune from her family's dealings in the sugar and rum industries in the Caribbean. In other words, Blackwell was born into colonial aristocracy.

His love of Jamaican music was genuine, and he helped a lot of Jamaican artists release music and get paid at a time when the Jamaican music industry routinely ripped artists off. I once asked a Jamaican reggae musician friend his opinion on Blackwell. He told me he doesn't appreciate what the Blackwell family did to Jamaica, but he thinks Blackwell did a lot of good for Jamaicans. Fair point. Blackwell started Island Records with Graeme Goodall and Leslie Kong in 1959 while in his early twenties and released records by Jamaican artists.

In 1962, Blackwell moved back to London and saw an untapped record-buying market in the Caribbean immigrant communities. He was on the lookout for a crossover artist from the island who could dominate popular radio. He found his star in Small, a teenage Jamaican singer with "an unusual voice." Small thought highly of Blackwell and felt he was on her side always. She trusted him. "I had a good manager in Chris, who looked after me like a father," Small told the *Express*.

Before Blackwell, Small's early Jamaican hits were mostly as part of a singing duo with Owen Gray or Roy Panton. Small was the youngest of seven children, poor but not living in poverty. When she was nine-years-old, she announced to her parents an unlikely prediction that she would one day be a movie star or singer.

Blackwell offered her a contract and flew her to England. She arrived in 1963, a young teenager. "I missed my parents and my brother, but they encouraged me to follow my dream," she told the *Express*. "It felt like I was coming home, that this was where I was meant to be." Blackwell enrolled her in classes to lessen her Jamaican accent, "refine her skills," and learn dance moves more familiar to an English audience. He bought Small some fancy new European clothes and hired a hairdresser, a dentist, and a driver for her. They recorded a few songs together prior to "My Boy Lollipop," but none did well.

Blackwell had a feeling "My Boy Lollipop" was going to be huge and worried his small operation was not set up with the proper capital and distribution channels to handle it, so he set Small up with Fontana Records, positioning himself as her manager. The song did so well that Blackwell was able to reinvest money he made into transforming Island Records into an industry force. He'd go on to work with artists like Traffic, Joe Cocker, and U2. Small, just like her nine-year-old self somehow knew, became a star.

This Is Ska

Small's success coincided with a big push from the Jamaican government to increase tourism. For much of Jamaica's history, the government and upper class were embarrassed by the music coming out of their ghettos, but the new Minister of Development and Welfare, Edward Seaga, had a different perspective. He saw a potential for Jamaican music to attract tourists to the island.

Before I talk about Seaga's impact on ska, it should be noted that his subsequent career as a politician was to push Jamaica in a conservative direction. His proponents called him a "nation builder," while critics saw him as a tyrant, allegedly using violence to gain and maintain power, and that his policies furthered economic inequities in Jamaica.

In 1959, Seaga was nominated to serve in the Jamaican Parliament. He was chummy with Reagan and Thatcher, and as a politician in the '60s -'70s and prime minister from 1980-1988, he sought to stamp out any trace of socialism, including free education, and weakening local government agencies that dealt with road construction and garbage collection and water. His aim was to deregulate and privatize. The economy in Jamaica appeared stable in the '80s but poverty, and unemployment grew. He gave tax breaks to foreign investors to Jamaica, which further diluted the island's identity and ownership. It's hard to believe Seaga actually gave a shit about the people who built the Jamaican culture and its music: the Rastas and the poor.

Seaga had a fascination with Jamaican folk music since his college years in the '50s. As part of a college project, he recorded Jamaican artists for an album by Folkways for the Smithsonian Institute. He immersed himself in the lives of these artists. He entered the Jamaica recording industry in the late '50s and became the Minister of Development and Welfare in 1962. One of his goals was to bring the music and culture he witnessed in West Kingston to the US "as a way to identify and promote the new country he was now leading." Heather Augustyn quoted him from an April 1964 *Daily Gleaner* article in her book *Operation Jump Up*: "I think the idea has terrific potential in making the outside world Jamaica-conscious."

Augustyn, a fellow ska scholar, named her book *Operation Jump Up* after the Jamaican government's initiative to promote the culture of Jamaica for the sake of tourism. In April 1964, they sent a group of hotel owners and tourism ambassadors to six major U.S. cities, along with a calypso band and slide show, to show Jamaica's natural beauty to would-be travelers. A separate group of musicians were sent to the hip Shepherd's Club in New York around the same time to showcase the "ska beat."

Getting ska recordings into American households was of critical importance to Seaga. Atlantic Records label chief Ahmet Ertegun flew down to Jamaica with his engineer Tom Dowd at the urging of Seaga. Ertegun surveyed the local talent and ended up recording several singers (Toots Hibbert, Prince Buster). Unlike "My Boy Lollipop," these releases flopped. He also released the *Jamaica Ska* LP compilation, a minor success, hitting #98 on the US charts for one week. It included Byron Lee's non-hit "Jamaica Ska," which was more like a tourist ad than a slice of Jamaican culture. Lee was not from the Kingston ghettos, and it should be noted, was a good friend of Seaga. The sudden influx of these records, along with Small's success as proof, was enough for the industry to declare a ska craze in full motion despite little indication of a craze aside from short-lived, regional interests in ska.

An article in *Billboard Magazine* on May 23, 1964 detailed the industry's response to the new "ska craze" a month-and-a-half after Millie's song started charting in the U.K. "'He was very helpful,' Ertegun reports [of Seaga]. "Increased record activity by many companies seems assured by the Jamaican government, which views the musical promotion as part of its tourism promotion. It is cooperating fully with labels and has hired its own U.S. publicists to spread the gospel of the Jamaica ska."

Some of this gospel-spreading was done via "how to dance the ska" brochures designed by Seaga. Ronnie and Jannette Phillips, the dancers photographed, were sent to the US to promote ska and teach the dance moves on television shows and at dance studios. "The Jamaican government had to find a way to get the music to catch on with the youth in America, and the best way to do that in 1964 was through their feet," Augustyn writes. Atlantic Records also created posters that illustrated the dance moves. "Bulk quantities have been sent to record distributors, dealers, and jockeys," a *Billboard Magazine* article on June 20th, 1964 reported. Seaga also promoted ska with the forty-minute black and white film *This is Ska* that posed as a documentary. Atlantic sent Lee's "Jamaica Ska" single, along with dance instructions, to roughly four-hundred Arthur Murry Dance Studios as part of this campaign.

Industry big-wigs and the Jamaican tourist ambassadors saw this young teenager, Small, make pop gold out of ska music and knew there was something there. But she wasn't a star because she was performing ska. She was just a pop singer, and it was a catchy song. There wasn't anything else to it but that. Music industry folks continued to pursue ska, missing the obvious. Small was the reason for the song's success.

Come On And Ska

The label figureheads viewed ska as a new dance craze "sweeping the nation" a la the Twist. A few years earlier, the Twist dominated the cultural landscape in a way that seems mind-blowing today. Several movies stemmed from the craze (*Hey Let's Twist, Don't Knock The Twist*) Sure enough, the "next dance craze" was shoved down everyone's throats like a block of Eagles tracks on classic rock radio.

By 1964, popular dances were getting absurd—from The Elephant Walk to Molecule-a-Go-Go—and less popular. "By 1964 people were getting tired of trying to follow these little trends as far as dances go," says Domenic Priore, author of *Pop Surf Culture: Music, Design, Film, and Fashion from the Bohemian Surf Boom*. "Watusi was maybe one of the last ones. Then it just became more freestyle dancing, like Go-Go. That was it, until the hippie dancing thing started. The dance craze thing was over. That didn't stop record companies from trying to market that kind of thing."

Treating ska as just another dance craze dislocated it from its culture. The result was one of the more embarrassing moments in ska history as several mostly white U.S. bands released "ska" songs during the summer of '64. Many bands were swept up in writing ska for the dance craze, but they, as well as the audiences dancing to it, weren't aware of its Jamaican origins.

The Marketts were one such band. They wrote a few ska songs during the summer of '64. A few years earlier, they'd landed a hit with the surf-pop song, "The Surfer's Stomp," written for the West Coast's surf dance craze. "The Surfer's Stomp" was gaining popularity when Markett's singer Michael Z. Gordon rushed home one night to write the Surfer Stomp's official theme song, a modest West Coast success. Similarly, he saw ska gaining popularity at the dances and wrote three ska songs that summer. The only one that got released was "Come See, Come Ska." It sold okay, but nothing like "The Surfer's Stomp."

Gordon gave me his recollection of the ska dance craze. There was some energy behind it, but it faded just as fast as it started to take off. And there were no hit singles from this era, hardly making it a craze, especially compared to The Twist, which overtook pop culture. "I remember it caught on really fast. It was like a whole new era of dancing. Everyone was doing it for a while. Then pretty soon nobody was doing it because there was another dance that came along. It was a few months. Almost everywhere we went for a period of time; it was popular."

Several unlistenable ska pop songs came out and flopped. One of the worse was Neil Sedaka's "Do the Jellyfish," the soundtrack for a horrible scene in the campy 1965 film *Sting of Death*. A group of teens are busy having a backyard ska dance party, while unbeknownst to them, a monster lurks in the swimming pool.

Jamaica Gleaner *teaching the kids how to dance the ska in 1964*

There was an unbelievable amount of now forgotten American ska pop songs released in this brief period in the summer of 1964. One of the better tracks is the lesser-known instrumental B-side "Slop Back" by Baby Earl and the Trini-Dads, who bucked the trend by mixing it with some R&B and dingy garage-rock flavor. Other examples include The Pussycats' swinging harmony-rich "Come On And Ska," The Rockin' Rebels' instrumental bongo-led "Bongo Blue Beat," and Mango Jones & His Orchestra Tijuana Brass-esque "Coffee Street Ska."

The worst moment of the ska craze era is Anette Funicello's cover of "Jamaica Ska." I know you saw *Back to the Beach* in 1987 where Funicello is backed by Fishbone and think "Jamaica Ska" is awesome, but you're wrong. Her first stab at "Jamaica Ska" in 1964 has no groove, and is driven by a corny, over-produced orchestral horn section. It's hardly the brilliant song it became in 1987 with Fishbone playing the music. Some people wrongly think she had something to do with ska's eventual popularity in the US. Had she not made *Back To The Beach*, no one would have linked her to ska music.

Her actual history with ska started in July 1964, when she released her movie *Bikini Beach*. Its soundtrack contained one ska song ("Jamaica Ska"). Not a hit. She performed the song on *The Bob Hope Show* the same year on November 20th. The ska craze had already died by the end of the summer a few months earlier. She was on Hope's Thanksgiving special to promote her new single "The Clyde," but did "Jamaica Ska" as a last-second add-on to fill time. There's not even mention of the song on the episode's official press release, which promoted her as "The Mouseketeer who grew up into a living doll" and as the "youngest of Bob Hope's youthful guests" for this episode.

Footage of her singing "Jamaica Ska" with Bob Hope exists on YouTube for all to watch. The clip has gathered a plethora of views because it's ridiculous, not because it's some monumental moment in music history. In the performance, Funicello even breaks ranks from the song's dance instructions and throws in some of her own freestyle moves. Hope is by her side, hamming it up, dancing like an inflatable tube man. He joins her in the chorus, arm suddenly around her shoulder proclaiming that *anybody* can do the ska.

Did "Jamaican Ska," which wasn't a single nor the primary purpose of Funicello's television appearance have any influence on popular culture? I say no. There are no recordings of her playing ska music again, not until *Back to the Beach* in 1987, which inspired her to resurrect the song for her 1990 tour. But by that point, things had changed in the US as far as ska goes.

Unlike the *Hope* appearance in '64, her Fishbone-backed rendition of "Jamaica Ska" in '87 is awesome, but that's because of Fishbone's ability to play ska, not from Funicello's masterful vocals. I asked director Lyndall Hobbs why she decided to resurrect such an obscure song from Funicello's catalog. She referred me to her brother, the film's "surf and music consultant" Geoffrey Hales, who was behind this decision. He stumbled upon Funicello's version of "Jamaica Ska" while digging through some old music and had an idea. "Ska was quite a thing in the '80s with a big resurgence in the UK [Madness, etc.] and Lyndall immediately loved the idea," Hale told me in an email.

Fishbone ska beach party, from the set of Back to the Beach

Fishbone, Hale told me, was chosen in part because he was a fan, but he also saw a lot of symbolism by having Funicello backed by a group of young black musicians. He explained: "I had seen Fishbone play at a club in LA not long before, and I loved their manic energy, plus they had the right instrumentation and played lots of ska in a very funky manner. Also, I believe there was a certain schadenfreude about taking Walt Disney's darling Annette and having her front a black band. Disney was overtly pro-Nazi and arguably a racist, and the thought of him spinning in his grave gave us a certain thrill. So, all in all, Lyndall loved the idea of Fishbone being involved.

"I will add, during the shooting of that scene, Fishbone took me aside, I mean all of them surrounded me and demanded to know how they got to be chosen for this unlikely gig—quite stern! They wanted names and motives; I told them pretty much what I've written above and after a bit more cross-questioning of my motives they accepted it. I think they were a tad embarrassed when they saw all the polka dots and gingham Lyndall had dressed everyone in!"

I ran this quote past Fishbone keyboardist Chris Dowd, and he confirmed this story as totally accurate. "We were always up for thumbing our nose to authority—what 20-year-old isn't," Dowd wrote back.

Dowd also told me they demoed an earlier version of the song that was rejected. It had a snappy Second Line New Orleans style to it. "The demo is way better. It's way more interesting," Dowd says. Leave it to Fishbone to take something like "Jamaica Ska" in an unexpected direction. I would've loved to hear that first version.

Anette Funicello and Fishbone do "Jamaica ska," from the set of Back to the Beach

It Was Over Before It Began

People treated Small as the official voice of ska, but it wasn't a role she wanted or asked for. She even participated in the 1964 World's Fair in New York, along with Byron Lee, his band, and Jimmy Cliff, another part of Seaga's tourism push. Overall, this cleaned up group wasn't exactly an accurate representation of ska's ragged culture, but in the days before Marley's superstardom, the Jamaican tourism strategy rode a fine line of downplaying its ghetto elements, while still attempting to showcase Jamaica's unique identity in a safe package.

Small didn't have another big hit after "My Boy Lollipop." She stopped recording in 1970 and moved to Singapore. "I don't miss those '60s days. I enjoyed it while it lasted and it represented a time of pure happiness, but I look to the future now that I'm older and wiser," Small told the *Express*.

Even if it wasn't their intention, we can thank Small and Blackwell for ska music's relegation to novelty in the U.S. and the U.K. in the '60s and early '70s. People heard Small's harmless, watered-down pop-ska song, and the impressions were lasting. Even if its success did inspire Lee Gopthal to start Trojan Records, which would release many brilliant ska, rocksteady and reggae records, the song still created a hurdle for the public to overcome. "My Boy" was a crossover hit as intended, but nothing else crossed over, with a few exceptions. Desmond Dekker had a surprise 1968 reggae hit, "The Israelites," which unfortunately, got viewed through the novelty lens despite being religious, politically-charged—and—overall, amazing. Artists like Dekker and labels like Trojan would eventually rectify the genre's reputation in the U.K., to a degree—it was still considered uncool by mainstream radio, but a cult audience appreciated it. In the U.S., it would take a lot longer.

Can you imagine if this little chapter of history never happened? Instead of a summer of ska in 1964, Jamaican music could have been introduced to the US a few years later when the music buying public were happy to see artists like Indian sitar player Ravi Shankar, who dazzled crowds at the Monterey Pop Festival? What if ska came not as a watered-down teenage pop song, but as the rough and dingy jazz-influenced dance music it was in Jamaica?

Maybe there'd be footage of The Wailers bringing down the house at Woodstock. Or an incredible Skatalities appearance on 1960s *Soul*

Train. If more people in the U.S. appreciated Jamaican music, The Specials might have arrived as pop stars in the U.S. in 1980, just like they were in the UK.

No, instead we got an annoying little ditty that every ska fanatic pretends to love because it's "important." At least with "Jamaica Ska," we got a Fishbone redo. But hell, it's Fishbone. They're amazing. They covered "Date Rape" in 2006 and managed to turn that piece of shit into a killer song.

CHRIS CANDY'S SECRET

When John Larroquette appeared on *The Arsenio Hall Show* in the early '90s, he leaned back in his chair and casually spoke of his hardcore Fishbone fandom like it was no big whoop. I flipped out. *The John Larroquette!* Mr. Dan Fielding himself, TV's coolest assistant district attorney!? It was one of the most validating moments of my life. We get told from mainstream society what geeks we are because we listen to ska and wear wacky shirts. Any affirmation we can get from celebrities that the music we like is not so bad is definitive proof we're not what everyone says we are.

This is why I now bring up Chris Candy—yes, that Candy, son of famous actor, John, all-around idol to an entire nation of '80s children including yours truly. Young Candy is a charmer, a talented comedic actor and a skilled musician. As a teenager, he played in a string of ska bands. One of those, The Liptones featured a young Kevin Preston, who would go on to play in the Prima Donnas and later Green Day side project Foxboro Hot Tub. Candy has been sitting on a Liptones secret his entire adult life. Are you ready?

They were unfairly handed the first-place award at his high school talent show.

He didn't know it at the time, but Candy's mom was the one and only judge. "She was just sitting there. The sound guy was like, we need someone to judge this. She said, 'I'll do it,'" Candy says. Of course, she gave her son's band the first-place award. What kind of monster wouldn't? "At the time no one knew. I was blown away. I didn't realize she was the only judge."

He's never told this story to anyone before. This *In Defense Of Ska* exclusive shows you how much Candy is willing to go to bat for ska. While we're at it, someone should go tell this story to those bands that got "beat" by The Liptones. I assume they all broke up after losing to a high school ska band.

Chris Candy flips his hat and spits some ska

Candy has been obsessed with ska his whole life, starting at age three, when he watched *Back to the Beach* with his mom. He fell in love with the Fishbone and Annette Funicello "Jamaican Ska" scene. It snowballed from there. "I remember watching that and bouncing as a kid. That scene stuck out to me," Candy says. "The rhythm of the song was so upbeat and unlike anything I have ever heard. Angelo's blue docs, and the way everyone skanked to the song. It was a once in a lifetime moment. To this day it still gets me pumped."

Candy started his first ska band, Bay Street Hooligans, in the eighth grade while living in Santa Monica. Bay Street was a spot in

Santa Monica where he used to surf with friends. He added hooligans to the name in reference to his perceived connection between "hooligan culture" and ska music. An interesting pre-teen take on "rude boys." "I had one friend in my class that was the only other person into ska. I forced the other guys to get into it," Candy says. "This band was really bad. We wrote one song, and we covered Skankin' Pickle's 'Fakin' Jamaican,' and Bruce Lee Band's 'Gilligan's Island.'"

Two decades later, Chris brings Chotto Ghetto to the Asian Man Records 15th Anniversary show

Next came the Liptones, who only pulled off two shows before transforming into Optimus Priime. The two i's were intentional, as the band was nervous about copyright infringement. Candy describes Priime as Rocket From The Crypt-style ska. "We had uniforms—black mesh jerseys. We played the Whiskey; we played the Roxy," Candy says. "We paid to play those places," he adds.

The band ended when Preston got picked up to play in the punk band The Skulls. Optimus Priime became Sleeper Hold. They got their big break opening for Dan Potthast. "That was a big deal to me!" Candy says. In those years, he was really into the Orange County ska scene. Reel Big Fish, OC Supertones, The Hippos. "Ska was cool back then. Cute girls were into it. It was a fun scene," Candy says. "I was one of those kids in LA that thought the singer of Reel Big Fish had the coolest style in the world. That's where a lot of my gross style came from. It did not look good on my overweight prepubescent body."

During the Optimus Priime years, Candy played a lot of shows in his Bel Air backyard, inviting all the punk-ska kids over, stacking the bill with eight bands. "I had a lot of energy. I was a huge kid. I think I was intimidating at the same time. But we had people moving," Candy recalls. "At one of those shows, the singer of the Dickies came because Billy Bones from The Skulls was coming to the shows. I'm so glad I spent my time doing that in my high school years instead of something else. I really am."

After high school, Candy went on to play other styles of music. His current band Chotto Ghetto blends prog-rock mania with punk rock fury, with Candy the captain leading this psychotic ship, providing lead vocals and belligerent screaming. Never once has Candy pretended to hate ska after moving on to other styles of music like bands tend to do. You know like Sam Endicott from The Bravery who essentially shouted, "FAKE NEWS" when the media outed his ska roots.

But like I said, it's important to us when celebrities stand up for their ska past. I've witnessed hundreds of ska friends share the meme of The U.K. *Office*'s Martin Freeman talking about his love for 2 Tone ska: "2 Tone was like a religion. My whole world was black-and-white checkers." Kristen Schaal once tweeted that she grew up loving Skankin' Pickle. It made Adam Davis so happy, he tagged her and Mike Park in a post, and got her to start following Park.

And speaking of celebrity's kids, Shannon Smith, son of *That 70s Show*'s Kurtwood Smith grew up with the members of Skankin' Pickle and even came up with the band name after watching Mike Park draw a dancing pickle cartoon in class. I once played drums with Shannon in a garage-punk band called The Sudsmen. We wore Pabst Blue Ribbon twelve-pack cases over our heads and pounded through sloppy '60s garage songs. Fun times!

So, yes, having a celebrity in our corner is kind of a big deal and we'll take as many as we can get until everyone finally realizes that it's not just nerds that listen to ska. Although, to be fair, Candy is kind of a nerd so forget everything I just wrote.

GARBAGE BAG MAN AND THE PEANUT BUTTER INCIDENT

When my dear friend Mike Vianelle got married some years back, he asked me to be his best man. I was nervous about one thing—the speech. I'd spent a few years shooting wedding videos in my early thirties and seen my fair share of best man speeches. They all had a similar formula: touching, emotional, funny, and just a little embarrassing. What could I talk about that checked all those boxes?

I kept coming back to Flat Planet. We were young spazzes, learning our instruments, and finding the outer edges of our identity as people. I even had the right Flat Planet moment in mind: The peanut butter incident.

We were on our second US tour in December of '94. We played an awesome skatepark in Little Rock, Arkansas. I also found out earlier that day that a show that was booked a week later was now canceled. I mentioned our dilemma to the promoter, hoping he'd refer me to a friend in the region who put on shows. As it turned out, the skatepark had an opening next week, and we were more than welcome to play it. The same venue. A week later. Sure, why not?

There was a hitch, at least amongst us. We couldn't return and play the same set to what would be probably much of the same people. It had to be fresh. And exciting. Or, at the very least, different.

Flat Planet's first big show at the Edge in Palo Alto

We continued the tour, working on some new ideas for the second Arkansas set. We had some new stage bits, like the rhythm section playing a techno rendition of Mortal Kombat while horn players Geoff and Seth would crouch at the edge of the stage facing off. Lead singer Alex would shout, "Let the fight begin," and Geoff and Seth, would wrestle to the death, or till someone tapped out. Alex would narrate the whole thing like an overly enthusiast boxing announcer, and then we would hop straight into one of our fast ska songs. We also pulled out a few songs from our catalog we never played live, like mariachi song "Scooby Doo," where Alex sang about everyone's favorite childhood cartoon, but *en Español* (*¡Ay Dios Mio!*). On the recording, Geoff's mom played the accordion, flawlessly. Live it just sounded like a ska song trying to be polka. At least we could get a good ska dance party going. Another contender was a rarely played-live song called "Act Naturally." On it, Geoff would hop on drums while Seth took over guitar duties, leaving Mike and I as free agents. Neither of them was very good at these instruments, which added more on-stage insanity. I liked to get off the drums and dance. The real question is, what would Mike do?

"Hey Alex, have you seen my trash bag?"

We showed up in Arkansas a week later, and it was cold, like twenty degrees cold. The skatepark had no heating. The toilet water was frozen, so people were peeing outside. There was a huge crowd, but even the combined body heat couldn't warm the venue. Everyone was shivering.

We had our usual, "let's take it up a notch" pep talk before the set. Mike didn't need it—he showed up ready to impress, wearing nothing but a large trash bag wrapped around his waist, like an over-sized diaper. I knew shit was about to go down.

We'd done a show earlier that year in San Francisco. Alex couldn't make it. Rather than cancel, the rest of us decided to make a spectacle of the show. I invited my older brother Brian to come dressed as Death Metal Tiki Man, a character he invented for a church talent show. Our roadie Mark Franzen came dressed as Clown. He crooned a version of "Send in the Clowns" that sent our audience of two into tears. And Mike wore a garbage bag diaper. All I can say is, at that show he was, uh, odd.

Back in Arkansas, we were all energy, no skill. We fucked up repeatedly, didn't care, and pushed through our mistakes. We thrashed like demented cheerleaders leading the audience into a full meltdown.

It was so cold that they were willing to do anything not to freeze to death. The set zipped by. We played "Techno Mortal Kombat," "Scooby Doo," and it was time to close things out with "Act Natural-ly." It was guaranteed to be our worst song yet, but with Mike, Alex and I free from the shackles of instruments, it would also be mayhem.

Punk rock soulmates

Once the song started, Mike left his normal, reserved self behind. He was now Garbage Bag Diaper Man. Diaper Man jerked erratically like an electroshock patient and screamed unannounced in the micro-phone for no reason. He pulled out a jar of peanut butter from behind his amp and stood motionless at the front of the stage. Alex and I danced harder, working the crowd into a frenzy. Diaper Man looked above the confused faces in the crowd and stared at the wall on the opposite side of the venue as if there was something profound to study. He held the peanut butter jar above his head like Mufasa holding Simba. Alex and I swirled around him in sloppy, breathless circles. Diaper Man scooped out gobs of the chunky, freezing peanut butter. It was crusty, with a hint of mold around its edges. He smeared it on his chest like an anti-social, artist-savant, brushing his deepest emotions onto the canvas. The chunkiest parts of the peanut butter clung to the scraps of Mike's chest hair which populated his body like weeds. He grinned as he applied the peanut butter, and then roared at the top of his lungs. A full-on release.

"All the sudden I had a GG Allin moment," he told me years later. "I was like, I have to pretend this peanut butter is shit, as I smeared it all over myself. I'm staring down people. I turned into a monkey. I pulled the peanut butter out, and I started flicking it at the audience. I want them to smile; I want them to be in terror, I want them to feel everything, I want them to have nightmares about it—about me. It felt so natural."

We finished our set, and up came the lights. We were exposed. There's no more uncomfortable feeling than when you transition from a space of raw performance energy back to your normal self. And the more in the moment you are, the stranger it is to be yourself again. As I contended with these awkward feelings and processed the show we'd just put on, Mike looked down at his peanut butter coated chest hair and ran to the bathroom to clean himself up.

As he ran, it hit him: *Everything is frozen.* No running water! He found a roll of paper towels and tried to wipe the peanut butter off, but it had hardened over his skin and hair. Every crevice was crusted with the stuff.

We crashed at an audience member's house, but their pipes were frozen too. It was days before we had access to running water. Mike had to live coated in now flaking peanut butter. We all had to live with the overbearing smell of old peanut butter. I don't know who had it worse.

As I finished telling this story at Mike's wedding, I glanced over at Mike's father-in-law, who seemed a little bit impressed, but mostly horrified. Some people laughed. Others shifted uncomfortably in their seats. Mike, on the other hand, was cracking up and smiling. It reminded me of how peaceful he seemed that night, covered in peanut butter, relishing the afterglow of blown minds, wanting nothing more than a hot shower to wash it all away.

You are your most authentic self when you express your craziest impulses in front of a room of strangers. The only thought in your mind is *I hope this never ends.*

BLACK COAT, WHITE SHOES, BLACK HAT

Who's the new VJ on MTV that looks like he's dressed up as The Blues Brothers for Halloween? That's Carson Daly, with his baggy black-and-white suit, uncomfortably tight pork pie hat, and Tom Cruise *Risky Business* shades. What's he doing? He's ska, obviously!

It's the summer of 1997. Daly graduated from terrestrial radio to the big leagues: MTV. One of his first gigs on the network is hosting the two-hour "SKAturday" special.

He walks toward the camera, hands folded, inside MTV's Motel California, and blathers on about New York ska band The Stubborn All Stars. On the bed next to him, a dozen snickering teenagers dance to Madness' "One Step Beyond," though they are having problems maintaining their balance. It's a hotel bed after all. The bathroom door swings opens. A girl in an oversized sweatshirt emerges on a skateboard followed by a teenage Gwen Stefani lookalike on a large handlebar bike, followed by a bored, slightly older surfer dude on a cruiser board. "The All Stars really were in the third wave of popularity for ska music," Daly explains, "which is really like the late '80s, early '90s. They were one of the first ska bands to really make the music diverse," Daly said. (Correction: The Stubborn All Stars started in 1994, though bandleader Jeff Baker has been in the ska scene in various bands since the mid-80s. The Stubborn All Stars were one of the few '90s ska bands incorporating traditional Jamaican elements, a weird way to describe them "making the music diverse"). The dancing teens smirk and sway their hips as Daly lists the different variations of the supposed third wave: "ska-R&B, ska-heavy-metal, and ska-rock."

Daly also plays some actual ska videos. He announces Schleprock's "Suburbia" with a promise to play a band who's "known for the biggest live performances—those where you're sweating and skanking—Fishbone's coming up."

No two dancers are dressed alike, but they're all ska. A guy up front wears a plaid checkered cabbie hat and a light blue suit. Behind him, a guy in a striped polo shirt and dark shades hops around like a deranged circus seal on a trampoline. A girl in a white tank top and baggie pants twists next to a girl in an oversized blouse and jean skirt. In the far back, a skinhead proudly leaps around, while a guy dressed up in a thrift store suit, peppered with torn-up patches, dances at a frenzied pace.

For anyone already a fan of ska, watching it explained back to them on MTV as something suddenly "catching on" was loathsome. Most ska fans in the underground music scene weren't cool, especially compared to the kids in the punk, hip-hop, alt-rock and metal scenes. But to a generation of kids seeing it on MTV for the first time, ska was just another trendy phase. Which meant you were absolutely going to be teased for wearing your cabbie hat to school.

"People would be like, 'Hey man, what do you think, you're ska?' Like I was trying to be cool," recalls J.T. Turret (Arrogant Sons of Bitches) about showing up ska in high school in the mid-90s with his ska-cabbie-hat. "That's crazy to think that back then, that was the in-thing to do, that someone would tell me that It was trying to be cool by dressing ska. It's quite the opposite just a few years later."

Trying to understand the ska genre also means trying to get a handle on the fashion associated with it. By 1997, it was a big confusing mess. Before ska landed on TV, the clothing and subcultures had evolved and changed, with remnants from various eras co-existing and at times in-fighting viciously, with always the debate at hand of what exactly defined this genre known as ska. It was something far too complicated for Carson Daly to explain in bite-sized segments.

Skinhead Invasion

Greg Narvas, drummer for '90s traditional ska band Hepcat, can't remember how many times he's told someone he used to be a skinhead only to get the response, "How could *you*, a Filipino-American, be a skinhead?" The short answer is somewhat confusing: there are racist skinheads *and* non-racist skinheads. This was true back in the '80s when he was a skinhead roaming L.A. It's true now.

Narvas explains: "If you look at your typical [non-racist] skinhead, they're trying to emulate late '60s England. They're listening to '60s reggae," he says. "Then you have all these other guys [racists] that are listening to white power bands, and they're beating people up and spray-painting swastikas everywhere. The media made it seem like all skinheads were like that. I grew up in a scene where all races and creeds hung out together, and there were skinheads of all colors and backgrounds. We totally outweighed the small minority of white power Neo-Nazi skinheads."

The original skinhead subculture wasn't affiliated with Nazis. They were working-class white Brits who lived near West Indian immigrant communities in the '60s (Caribbean people immigrated to England in large groups from the late '40s to the '60s and helped rebuild the country post World War II). Skinheads were a poorer offshoot of the mod subculture, adopting a less lavish outfit than the fashion-conscious mods. Skinheads wore work boots, pants, and suspenders, and they had closely cut, short hair, mostly due to hair restrictions at their factory jobs. They grew to love the music and culture of their Caribbean neighbors. Some reggae artists of the time specifically wrote songs for skinheads, like Laurel Aitken with "Skinhead Train" and "Skinhead Invasion."

In the '70s as a recession hit the U.K., the overtly racist, anti-immigrant party, the National Front, recruited a segment of these blue-collar skinheads for their racist agenda, preying on them as the factory jobs went away. The National Front promised them housing and jobs and to "put them first," always framing the culprit of their economic woes on immigrants. One former National Front member Joseph Pearce described the recruitment agenda in the film *The Story of Skinhead* as disrupting "the multicultural society, the multi-racial society, and make it unworkable." The Selecter's lead singer Pauline Black recalls this time period: "It's the same old same old. If you want to split the working-class right down the middle, pit them against each other. Racism is about the best thing you can ever use to do it."

Eric Clapton famously supported National Front candidate Enoch Powell multiple nights on his 1976 tour. One drunken, racist rant at Birmingham was documented in August 1976: "Stop Britain from becoming a black colony. Get the foreigners out. Get the wogs out. Get the coons out. Keep Britain white...[t]he black wogs and coons and Arabs and fucking Jamaicans don't belong here; we don't want them here. This is England; this is a white country; we don't want any black wogs and coons living here. We need to make clear to them they are not welcome. England is for white people." Hypocrite is too kind of a word for Clapton. His first hit single, just two years earlier, was a cover of Bob Marley's "I Shot The Sherriff" (which ironically helped reggae grow a bigger audience in Britain) and all of his songs were influenced by black music.

At the time, he wrote a hand-written apology published by *Sounds* magazine. He blamed his angry rant on booze and a "foreigner" pinching his "missus' bum." Two years later in an interview with *Melody Maker*, Clapton defended his support for Powell, and denied that Powell was a racist, saying that he was the "only bloke telling the truth, for the good of the country."

Even if Clapton's career didn't suffer from his racism, his rant did inspire the Rock Against Racism movement in late '70s England. The organization's objective was to push back on the rise of racism and specifically marginalize the National Front, sucking any influence they had in the country's politics, which had been gaining traction among "average brits" as the rhetoric became more normalized. Many punk and reggae bands joined this cause and participated in awareness and fund-raising concerts in the '70s.

In the BBC documentary *Punk Brittania*, Billy Bragg explains the National Front's clear, horrendous goals, and how the punks, immigrants, and anti-fascists were banding together to fight back. "It was broadly believed that people of color could be rounded up and sent back. That's what we were fighting. We weren't fighting to defend our multicultural society—they were building the boats."

The 2 Tone ska movement evolved at the tail end of Rock Against Racism in the late '70s and embraced anti-racism as its creed. In a lot of ways, 2 Tone ska was the natural extension of Rock Against Racism, with bands promoting anti-racism and demonstrating multiculturism in their own racially mixed bands—exactly what the National Front feared would destroy the country.

It was a tense period with growing racism and open hostility toward black British citizens. Gaps, the Selecter's toaster (Jamaican-style rapper), describes living with this terror on a regular basis. "You'd see a police car coming down the road, and they stop you for nothing. The next thing you know, one of your friends, you'd leave him at night and you don't see him the next night. What happened to him? You heard that he'd been killed in a police cell. Things like that were happening," Gaps says.

As 2 Tone bands emerged and played shows, Nazi skinheads showed up to intimidate everyone. But the bands never wavered from their anti-racist message. "In the early days, there would be a small group of people who would come ostensibly to make trouble and would start Sieg heiling us at some point during the set," says Black. "We were not some bunch of hippies sitting around saying peace and love and stuff like that. If you're going to have a perspective which is interracial and all that, trouble is going to come your way. You better be prepared for trouble."

Greg Narvas and crew looking slick at Grand Central Station, 1988.

In this atmosphere, there was also a revival of '60s reggae-loving skinheads, embracing the original British subculture that started a decade earlier. 2 Tone was about reviving old ska, rocksteady and early reggae music. '60s Skinhead culture was a part of that. The band members realized they had to make a conscious effort to squash the fascist impulses of anyone calling themselves skinheads. What better platform to do that than punking up the old-style Jamaican music?

As you can imagine, Narvas got tired of explaining the entire history of skinheads to justify his outfit. Starting in 2008, he created a series of zines called *I Was a Teenage Filipino Skinhead*. It's funny, personal and informative. It also gives a glimpse into the '80s ska and reggae subculture which would evolve and impact American ska in the '90s.

The zine details his skinhead story. Before becoming a skinhead, he was a rude boy, then a mod. All these subcultures trickled into the U.S. by way of England where they were taken very seriously, and had complex histories, some closely tied to ska, others not so much. They were extremely underground in the states.

A rude boy in the '80s was synonymous with ska fan. They wore hip, stylish retro clothes like pegged slacks, loafers and old cardigan sweaters. Rude Boys started in Jamaica in the '60s, not directly linked to the music. They were sort of well-dressed, ruffian anti-heroes. Several old ska and rocksteady songs were directed at the rude boys to get them to rein in the violence and crime, most famously "Rudy, A Message to You" by Dandy Livingstone and "Simmer Down" by Bob Marley and the Wailers. The rude boy name and fashion were revived by the 2 Tone bands and dissociated from its previous gangster affiliation.

Mods originally were a '60s subculture linked to stylish garage-rock bands like The Who and Small Faces as well as, and copious drug usage. They also loved old soul and R&B. Mods, were generally upper-class, always the best dressed. It was a similar plush look as rude boys, but with the addition of a parka. And most rode around on Vespa scooters. England enjoyed a mod revival in the late '70s because of The Who's 1979 film *Quadrophenia,* which celebrated '60s mod culture in all its amphetamine-fueled insanity.

East coast rudies, skinheads and mod posse

Mods originally were a '60s subculture linked to stylish

L.A. had the biggest mod scene of the U.S. There, mods were closely linked to ska culture because of The Untouchables, the self-proclaimed "ska-mods." The Untouchables played ska and northern soul. In the early '80s, there were hundreds of scooter rallies occurring around Southern California. Outside of L.A., the mod scene was more niche, and not so directly connected to ska.

Skinheads were working class, usually wearing steel toe work boots, braces, strait-laced jeans, and a button up shirt, with shaved heads. In the '70s and '80s, they were into old '60s reggae, rocksteady, and ska, though some were into Oi!, a rawer version of punk. The specific rules of the subgenres seemed confusing if you weren't properly schooled. These styles overlapped with the universal love of Fred Perry shirts and tapered pants. Otherwise, there were very distinct differences that were lost on people outside of these subcultures.

Are You A Skinhead?

Skinhead history is more complex than even most modern anti-racist skinheads acknowledge. There's been a bit of rewriting history that anti-racism has always been a core tenet among skinheads. While it's true that '60s skinheads didn't identify with Nazi ideology, it wouldn't be accurate to go to the opposite end of the spectrum and call them anti-racist. '60s skinheads loved Jamaican music, fashion, and culture, and they were largely friendly with their Caribbean neighbors. Asian immigrants, though, were targets of their ire. Most skinheads were tribalistic and violence was common. Many skinheads in the '60s engaged in "paki-bashing," verbally and physically attacking Pakistani and south Asian immigrants, who they viewed as not integrating into British mainstream culture.

"The one thing I tell people is that skinheads aren't angels," says Paul Williams, author of the Specials biography *You're Wondering Now*. "They had this thing called the Anti-Paki League in the '60s. A lot of skinheads belonged to that. They were always smashing up shops in the Asian community. The funny thing about it was not only were the white skinheads doing it; the Jamaican rude boys at that time were also involved in Paki-bashing. There's no denying history. All this stuff about how real skinheads aren't racist. You obviously haven't looked at your roots enough." Skinheads in the '60s were roughly the same level of racist as the average brit, which is to say not great. Gaz Mayall, friend of the 2 Tone bands in the '70s and longtime ska fanatic explains how bad the '60s were. "Racism was endemic in the whole country. There was a lot of prejudice. That was a society thing." Many of these skinheads got worse in the '70s, when the National Front encouraged them to hate every group that wasn't white and to see their fascist ideology as a call to action.

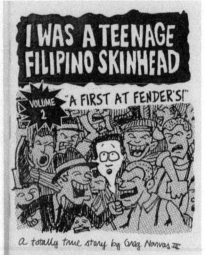

First three issues of Greg's zine "I Was a Teenage Filipino Skinhead"

When the Specials were starting out, keyboardist Jerry Dammers consciously had the band take ownership of the skinhead subculture alongside the rude boy image and recontextualize it to their audience as part of an anti-racist movement. He saw it as a necessary step in affecting change in England, especially since a lot of skinheads were becoming fans of 2 Tone ska. This is something that Williams witnessed as a young teenager that fell head-over-heels for ska in

1979. "2 Tone was definitely a catalyst [in skinheads being anti-racist] because they [the bands] were so open about being anti-racist in interviews. You knew where you stood with them," Williams says.

The anti-racist message of 2 Tone was most potent as these bands went on tour, especially in the rural parts of the country that were mostly white, and afraid of immigrants. "You get people wearing their skinhead and 2 Tone fashion [in rural England] and they have more of a fascist ideology. They had ideas about what England was supposed to be about. 2 Tone encouraged all the right things and reclaimed common sense," says Mayall.

Williams points out that the skinhead culture he came from in the late '70s as part of the 2 Tone movement made huge strides to keep the U.K. skinhead subculture anti-racist going into the '80s and beyond. "It's always seemed odd how skinheads—a complete hybrid of mixed racial influence—should have a problem with race in the first place, but primarily that early racist tendency dwindled, people moved on, and the music and fashion became the main focus of what being skinhead was all about, which is how it should be. The British Press still talks of skinheads as a racist subculture despite all steps to make it not so."

When the mod, rude boy and skinhead styles came to the U.S., they were confusing to people outside of the underground music scene. Skinheads particularly confounded average Americans. Some of the people in the US in the early '80s who adopted the skinhead look got into it because of their love for punk and Oi!; some because of their love for the 2 Tone ska revival, and like Narvas, dug backwards into the music and subculture it stemmed from. Much of the early '80s skinheads on the West Coast were "bald punks," basically hardcore kids that were more aggressive than your average punk. Some of them hung out with rude boys and realized that ska was cool, too. Some adopted Nazi ideology. While many did it for shock value; others meant it. Traditional skinheads were more common on the East Coast, but more popular in the rest of the states as the '80s progressed. The Nazi affiliation with skinheads came over mostly due to British Neo-Nazi band Skrewdriver, who played Oi! punk and were skinheads. In the late-80s, the media caught wind of Nazi skinheads in the US and started doing exposés. These had little context, no skinhead history and were highly exploitative, suggesting a coming Nazi skinhead epidemic. There was no discussion of there being anti-racist skinheads as well.

In the early '80s, Marcus Pacheco, a member of New York's ska scene was introduced to the skinhead subculture from a New York Skinhead that was well versed in its roots as an inherently apolitical subculture that celebrated Jamaican music and fashion. As Pacheco became a skinhead himself, he became aware that Nazi skinheads existed, but he never considered that people would associate skinheads with Nazi ideology since Nazi punks also existed and people didn't view punk rock as a neo-Nazi movement. But that changed, and the average US citizen started to equate the skinhead look with fascism.

In 1987, Pacheco was tired of everyone's misunderstanding of this subculture he loved and decided it was time to act. He and all his skinhead friends had adopted 2 Tone's anti-racist stance. "The best way to reject racist elements from the subculture is through an understanding of its origins in the U.K.," Pacheco says. "The skinhead subculture included immense influences from Jamaican culture expressed through a love for Jamaican music. The racist elements that infiltrated and appropriated were an aberration that was made possible because of ignorance. Do you think that some dumb racist person would be attracted to a subculture if they knew it had its roots deeply imbedded in a love for Jamaican music, fashion and style? I tend to think the numbers would be much lower."

To help educate people in the U.S. on skinheads' history, its primarily anti-racist stance in the '80s, and to dissuade more kids from becoming fascists, Pacheco formed S.H.A.R.P., which stands for Skinheads Against Racial Prejudice. Not an official organization, but rather a philosophy, Pacheco made a logo based around the American flag. Roddy Moreno of the UK Oi! band The Oppressed created his own S.H.A.R.P logo that borrowed heavily from the British ska and rocksteady record label, Trojan Records. The Trojan style logo was a clear statement that S.H.A.R.P. skinheads aligned themselves with the ska and rocksteady music and not white power bands like Skrewdriver. S.H.A.R.P.s also briefly produced a zine called "Double Barrel" that primarily discussed ska and soul music. They also rented a storefront on weekends for $100 a pop to throw ska parties, but that only lasted a few weeks.

Marcus' S.H.A.R.P. crew with Bad Manners' Buster Bloodvessel

A specific incident triggered Pacheco to start S.H.A.R.P. He and his girlfriend at the time, both skinheads, were on the subway going from the South Bronx to the Lower East Side of Manhattan. Everyone on the train besides them was black.

One guy, sitting, looked up, stood in front of him and said, "Are you a skinhead?"

"Yeah," Pacheco replied.

The man on the train said he'd seen skinheads on TV. "Why do you go around beating up black people and Jews?"

"I'm Puerto Rican and my friend here is Jewish so you need to get your facts straight," Pacheco told the man.

But the guy wasn't buying it. He went up to a group of B-Boys, tapped them on the shoulder and loudly shouted, "Those people over there go around beating up black people and Jews!"

In a strange twist, because the man had effeminate mannerisms, the group of B-Boys began pushing and shoving *him*. Pacheco and his girlfriend watched as he continued to try to rile up everyone on the bus to beat up Pacheco and his girlfriend. The B-Boys laughed at the guy and hurled homophobic slurs at him. In this commotion, the train made its next stop, and Pacheco and his girlfriend slipped out the side to avoid any potential problems, yet they felt sorry for the guy who tried to get them beat up.

"After that I realized some clarification was necessary," Pacheco says.

Pacheco kept his aim simple. "My intention was never to create an organization with leaders and followers. Politics was never a part of it either. That's why it was important to use 'Racial Prejudice' and not something specifically political. I would use the term 'member' loosely as well. We were all friends who hung out together and already had been active in pushing back against racism and bigotry. Anyone who was a skinhead who rejected racism was a skinhead against racism."

Original S.H.A.R.P. logo

Since one of the aims was to educate the larger public on the skin-head subculture, S.H.A.R.P.s agreed to do interviews, though they realized the media were willing to exploit them and didn't care about getting the truth out. Pacheco didn't watch a lot of TV, so when a producer for *Geraldo* reached out to him in 1988 and invited him to be on a panel to talk about the skinhead subculture and its various incarnations, he took it at face value. Pacheco saw this as a golden opportunity to further educate people that real skinheads believed in anti-racism.

Before the show, he and his friend Troy, a black skinhead, were told to meet the *Geraldo* security team in a nondescript building so they could be snuck in the back for their safety. He and Troy were not put on stage, but rather in the front row along with a few other non-racist skinheads. To their left, they saw an entire section in the audi-ence filled with aggressive Neo-Nazis the producers flew in from Orange County. Some were skinheads; some were just plain old Nazis.

Thirty-eight minutes into the show, John Metzger, head of the White Aryan Resistance Youth called black activist Roy Innis an "Uncle Tom." Innis jumped up and started choking Metzger. Nazi skinheads and other racists from the audience rushed the stage. Amid the dustup, Geraldo took a chair to his face and got his nose broken. "The couple of people I was with, we were busy trying to protect an infant and her father who were in the front row to the left of us because the father claimed that their family had been attacked by Neo-Nazis on a train platform. He was there to tell his story," Pacheco says. As soon as the cameras stopped rolling, Pacheco recalls watching the blood trickle down Geraldo's face. "His expression changed from distraught to extreme happiness—a smile ear to ear. He was overjoyed with what happened. He knew the potential for ratings. It was gross. That's when it all came together for me. That's when I saw we had been used as props. I'm certain they knew it was an inherently volatile situation which they exploited, and it was more than likely by design. It was a disappointment."

Pacheco never got to say anything on camera about S.H.A.R.P.s except while the credits were rolling, at his insistence to the producers during the final commercial break. By that point, no one was listening. "After that I appeared on several cable television shows. I knew what time it was when it came to their priorities, but I figured I would cautiously exploit some of those opportunities to get our message out," Pacheco says. "No matter how careful I was about who I dealt with they almost all just wanted the opportunity for a sensational ratings grabber and never seemed to have any interest or respect for us or what we were saying."

Everyone had their own idea of what it meant to be an anti-racist skinhead. For a lot of S.H.A.R.P.s, they saw their purpose as to physically oppose Nazis and prevent them from dominating public spaces. Steve Abrams, guitarist for New York ska band Skinnerbox, a skinhead briefly, recalls the early days of S.H.A.R.P.s. "They were very passionate. It was like, you're going to look like someone that the average person equates with being a fascist. That's a lot of work," Abrams says. "You got to wear a lot of patches on your jacket to convince people; I'm the good guy. It's kind of crazy but yeah, they were good guys."

In 2016, when out and proud white supremacist Richard Spencer got clocked on live TV, a heated debate emerged in liberal circles about whether it was okay to punch Nazis or not. This conversation has been going on in the punk and ska scene since the '80s. A lot of S.H.A.R.P.s were very much in the pro-punching Nazis camp. "They were walking around with baseball bats trying to find Nazis. It got crazy—the fighting," Abrams says of '80s New York.

Pacheco didn't encourage violence. He hoped he could persuade Nazi skinheads—who he never called skinheads; it was always "boneheads"—to reconsider their lifestyle choice. "My thinking is that beating them up won't change their mind about their ideology and may serve to reinforce or cement their feelings of alienation and hatred and they may seek further refuge in their ideology. My method of confrontation usually involved a discussion where I might question their involvement with fascism and Neo-Nazism," Pacheco says. "Some of these kids—we were all just kids—were flirting with ideas and not even clear in their thinking. There were times I would get them to denounce their quasi-political ideology, or their affiliation with the term 'skinhead.' You can believe whatever nonsense you want to believe but you can't call yourself a skinhead anymore."

. . .

As a mod in the '80s, Narvas was learning more about the history of ska music. He found himself enjoying the old style of Jamaican music more than the 2 Tone bands, which is why he decided to make it official and become a traditional skinhead. Narvas, his core group of friends, and others, who would eventually start Hepcat with him in 1990, fell in love with old ska, rocksteady, and '60s reggae. Trojan Records was starting to reissue a lot of the old original music, which was hard to come by. As the ska scene grew, some of the DJs got their hands on these old records and spun them between bands. Narvas and his friends would dress up in their best outfits and go to these shows, waiting through the live bands sets to have their opportunity to dance to old Jamaican tunes.

They also frequented a club called Gino's in Hollywood, an underground gay disco club in the '70s that broadened to encompass more genres in the '80s. They had weekly ska and soul dance nights for a short stint from 1986 till 1987. It was all DJing, no bands. It was the spot to be for hardcore fans, a very small, niche group at the time, which was what Narvas and his friends preferred. The DJ has one Trojan reissue and mixed in a song or two along with newer tracks. These Trojan records were just starting to come out again. In 1985, Colin Newman (the accountant, not the singer of Wire) purchased the defunct Trojan Records and led the company to focus on reissuing its extraordinary back catalog of '60s and '70s reggae and rocksteady tunes. "It was the only place you could be around people that had as much dedication to that style as you did. Everyone went to that club dressed to the nines," Narvas says. "Mods were mods. Rude boys were rude boys. And skinheads were skinheads. There was no dilution in fashion at all. You could not go if you looked half-ass. There was nobody there that went sloppily dressed."

Narvas also points out that most people who went to Gino's all decked out danced solo. You went there to show off your moves and to show your very specific threads. "It was like a show-off contest. Everyone parked their scooters in the back and drank and hung out. On the dance floor on any given time, I can't imagine more than twelve or fourteen people at the most. People loved to go there because that's where they knew the scene hung out. That's where it was guaranteed that you would be amongst your own. If you were a mod and you wanted to be around where other mods were."

When Gino's shut down, Grand Central Station opened in Long Beach. The DJs there had a couple Trojan reissues. Narvas and his friends would show up around 9pm and they would wait around, sometimes all night, for the DJs to play old ska. "Sometimes they wouldn't play any of the old stuff until midnight. We would wait all night just to do that." At that time, there were only a handful of Trojan Records' reissues that were out. Usually Narvas and his friends had to request old ska and rocksteady songs in order to get the DJs to whip out the Trojan LPs and hear songs like "Phoenix City" (Roland Alphonso and the Soul Brothers), "54-46 Was My Number" (Toots and the Maytals), "Them a Laugh and a Kiki" (The Soulmates), and "Skinhead Moonstomp" (Symarip). . "Just to play any tracks on those records would be heaven for us. We didn't mind being the only ones on the dancefloor dancing to these old songs. Everyone else would look and go, 'What is this?' Because it was such a drastic change from 2 Tone and the newer contemporary stuff. Here's this old rickety sound that's just so different. It was like we owned the music."

More people got into these specific subcultures as the '80s progressed. In his zine, Narvas recalls going to see Bad Manners and Fishbone at Fender's Ballroom in Long Beach in Feb 1986 and being shocked by the number of people all dressed up in the correct fashion but hanging out together without animosity. "Everyone was really faithful and committed to the music. This was so cool because there was unity amongst everybody," Narvas says. "You would see the whole spectrum of mods and rude boys and even skinheads. It was something that was super underground, and no one else knew about, but it was thriving. It was a life-changer right there."

No Fashion, No Identity

In the early '90s, more traditional ska bands started to emerge like Hepcat and Jump With Joey in L.A. On the East Coast, there was the Scofflaws, who formed in the mid-80s, but by the early '90s, played more traditional stuff. The Slackers formed in '91. In their early years, they were very much about old style ska. You also had the return of the Skatalites in the late '80s, who had stopped playing in 1965. They reunited for their first show in 1983 at Jamaica's Sunsplash. In 1986, they did a series of gigs at New York club, The Village Gate, joined by different guests each week: Charley Palmieri, Arthur Blythe, Monty

Alexander. The success of the Village Gate shows led to several international tours in the late '80s. And they showed people how the music was *really* played.

Simultaneously, other bands went in the opposite direction, infusing punk with ska. Those bands (as well as their fans) mostly moved away from the rude boy, skinhead and mod look, and dressed however they felt. Their apathy toward fashion and disinterest in adherence to ska's "tradition" caused a rift in the scene.

Date night with Hepcat

Ska-punk shows saw a mix of rude boys, punks, hippies, meatheads, whatever. It created tension, particularly on the coasts where interest in traditional ska was highest. "We played side by side with ska-core bands," Narvas tells me. "There was no fashion, or identity associated with it. It was just dancing and going crazy. In the meantime, you had all the skinheads and the rude boys that knew all about the roots and the origin. The skinheads would look at all these ska-core kids and be like, 'What the fuck are you guys? This isn't even ska.' The ska-core kids would look back at them and say, 'What's up your ass? Why are you so snobby?' You had two completely different attitudes and approaches to the music."

Some of the trad ska fans were so obsessed with the culture and fashion that they actively tried to stop bands from "fucking it up." Dan Potthast of the ska-punk band MU330 recalls skinheads showing up to shows for this express reason. "They'd stand in front of the stage and try to intimidate you with their arms folded to tell you that they didn't like you mixing the punk with their ska," Potthast says. "I'm pretty sure you're buying a ticket. You did that just to come tell us we're bad?"

The Mighty Mighty Bosstones got a pass from most of the purists despite how "impure" their ska was. They were slick dressers and trad ska lovers, so skinheads generally didn't fuck with them. Potthast recalls playing shows with Detroit's Gangster Fun. The skinheads hated that these guys didn't look the part and delivered a stage show that was chaotic and scary. "I remember a skinhead standing in front of Gangster Fun, arms folded because their bass player had long hair—it was really upsetting that he had long hair," Potthast says.

Karina Denike of the Dance Hall Crashers recalls dealing with skinheads and ska-purists in the early '90s in Northern California. Though her band started off by Gilman scenesters that took old school ska fashion and scooters seriously, they more and more looked like surfers and skaters and developed a faster sound. "There was a lot of fighting at shows in those days. I grew up in England in the '80s before moving to Berkeley as a teen so [I] had been around some amount of that tension with the Brixton riots and mods vs. punks and skinheads infighting at shows as a young rude girl. But still, California had a pretty rough scene," Denike says. "We started looking and sounding more like skater punks and the music went in a more in a bubbly sounding pop-punk direction. That made us outcasts of the trad scenes. A lot of people had closed minded views on what ska should be, but at least there were less fights at our shows."

Mike Park of Skankin' Pickle hated the violence and elitism in the ska scene. Skankin' Pickle got it particularly bad from the purists. He recalls one specific show back in the early '90s at the Whiskey in L.A., where every other band on the bill was ska. "All the bands looked really good. I was like, I want to look as gross as possible. I remember wearing giant yellow sweatpants, a California visor that was rainbow colored. I pulled up my sweats as high as I could and went crazy," Park says.

So many shows were battles that Skankin' Pickle decided to stop playing ska shows. Park told the promoter at Spanky's in Riverside to put Pickle on a bill with no ska bands. That show had nine speed-metal bands and Skankin' Pickle. They opened their set with "Asian Man," which begins with metal, but quickly breaks down to a slower hip-hop-rock beat.

"We are going out of our minds. The crowd is going crazy. I was like, 'we got it.' The ska scene didn't like us. We'll find people that just like weird music," Park says. "Skinheads wanted to hear 2 Tone and trad ska. If you were playing distortion, they weren't having it. We drew from the metal people, the punks, funk, hippies, and the ska people. It was just random kids who were having a good time."

This tension between skinheads, rude boys, and punk-ska bands died down by the mid-90s. A lot had to do with how much the ska-punk scene grew and built their own scene, with bands like Skankin' Pickle leading the way. The ska-punk scene encouraged bands to be adventurous with what styles they mixed with ska and downplayed a need for a specific outfit. There was rude boys, skinheads, punks; others looked as wacky as possible. A more inclusive community evolved. You could walk into a Skankin' Pickle show with zero knowledge of the music, wearing a clown outfit, and no one treated you like an outsider. "As the scene expanded to be more inclusive towards the mid-90s, it was a relief to have a real mix of people—rude boys and girls, punks, freaks—and little-to-no bullshit at the shows," Stephen Shafer, former Moon Records employee says.

The downside was that newer bands and fans knew less about the culture and history of the music. Enter MTV and a rush of major labels. Ska music had developed in the US on its own, with ska-punk being its most commercially viable version. A strange hodgepodge of culture, fashion, and band-individuality all mixed together into a big, confusing web. If you were deep in the scene, you had some context to unravel this mess, but it was too much for labels and new fans to comprehend. With only a handful of bands launching to stardom, they inadvertently became the models for the "ska style." MTV perpetuated the idea that ska bands wore plaid or Hawaiian shirt or mismatched suits. New kids digested the message and followed suit.

Skankin' Pickle's first heckler

Not Our Kind Of Ska

The MTV version of ska didn't include traditional and non-punk ska bands. When Carson Daly told everybody about the new "third wave" of ska, he wasn't including Hepcat and The Slackers.

Even The Stubborn All Stars, who Daly mentioned as being part of "the third wave of popularity," were outside of the mainstream ska explosion, and were rarely played on the network outside of the SKAturday special. The All Stars influences were closely aligned with actual Jamaican music. And they didn't have pop hits. "Ska has never been in the mainstream. What's in the mainstream is called ska, which I will call the lowercase 's' ska," says singer/trombonist Jeff Baker. In 1995, when Another Planet Records signed Stubborn All Stars, Baker told the folks at the label to manage their expectations with how big The Stubborn All Stars could get. "I said we're not a rock band, like all these other 'ska' bands. I know you can't tell the difference, but I can. The reason this isn't going to work is because it's not that. And that's not this. That's Rock. This is ska and reggae. It's not beats that Americans can relate to. If you play ska authentically, it's not going to go be pop," Baker says. "Upbeat guitar is the least distinct factors in ska music. Drum style and the bass style, is most important—it's afro-Caribbean music."

Hepcat always wanted to bring authentic ska elements to their music. In the early '90s, they toured the West Coast with The Skatalites and studied the nuances of their playing. "That's where we all started picking up what we should do and what we shouldn't do. They're the ones that pretty much made us," says co-lead singer Greg Lee. One of the biggest effects that touring with Skatalites had on Hepcat was learning the techniques of how to properly play a ska drumbeat. In the '90s, The Skatalites were still touring with original drummer Lloyd Knibb, whose playing is unmatched. "We all sat and watched as Lloyd was sound checking. [Later] Lloyd comes up [to Greg Narvas] and goes, 'Why your drum go *pop pop*, when it should go *boom boom?*' He showed Greg how to tighten up his heads and a little bit more about ska drumming. Greg, after that, was the only guy in town—in the states arguably—playing just like Lloyd Knibb."

Hepcat did okay for themselves in the '90s, but they didn't get as big as they deserved. Their 1997 album, *Right On Time* is a classic. The skinheads and rude boys idolized Hepcat, but a lot of the newer ska fans who came to the music from punk-ska bands didn't understand where Hepcat was coming from. It was a different, somewhat intimidating atmosphere, compared to the punk-ska shows. Lee recalls how some audiences, primed on ska-punk, seemed dumbfounded by them, especially once they left the coasts. "What they wanted to do was run in place for an hour and get really hot and sweaty and drunk and say what a great time they had," says Lee. "That was the antithesis of what we wanted to do. We wanted people to show up dressed nice, hopefully, come with their girlfriend or boyfriend or meet somebody there and dance. Like really dance."

When they hit the road with the Dance Hall Crashers in the mid-90s, Lee recalls seeing audiences standing in place during their set. Frustrated, after one Midwest show, Lee asked a local DJ why no one was getting into their set.

"He said, 'people love you, but they don't know how to dance to you. They know when they come see Skankin' Pickle or Let's Go Bowling or Dance Hall Crashers or Fishbone, they can go crazy and do whatever they want to. With you, it's a little more specific.'" said Lee. "From that point forward, Alex and I began doing those semi choreographed moves to show people how to dance. To kind of be the cheerleaders for the crowd."

A lot of the traditional bands saw an increase of their fanbase in the 2000s when ska-punk bands were no longer in vogue. The Slackers started out as traditional ska in the '90s, but they slowly evolved to incorporate soul and garage-rock. And they always dressed in stylish suits. Vic Ruggiero's voice is reminiscent of the broken rock 'n' roll stylings of Van Morrison and Mick Jagger.

"We played the years that there was the ska boom; it wasn't our kind of ska boom. It was happening because of The Bosstones, Goldfinger, Reel Big Fish—not our kind of ska," Ruggiero says. "We were lucky we didn't get caught up in that. When the hype died, ska was a dirty word. The people that liked us kept coming to our shows. We had a much better scene." The band was featured on NPR in 2001 when ska was supposedly dead yet drawing bigger crowds than they were a few years earlier.

Another traditional band to emerge in the 2000s was the Aggrolites, which played old school, late '60s skinhead-style reggae. The band formed in 2002, not an ideal time for ska music. Wagner saw the project as them doing for early reggae what Hepcat did for old ska. "Bring reggae back, like old school reggae, the traditional style of reggae to the mass; they call it skinhead reggae," he told me.

Since the Aggrolites weren't playing '70s roots reggae, but rather the bouncy, poppy version of the genre popular in the '60s, it wasn't the reggae crowd that was drawn to them. It was the trad-ska scene, and definitely the skinheads, as old reggae was exactly what they loved the best. One of the group's biggest moments in the mainstream was performing a cover of the classic skinhead reggae song "Banana" on *Yo Gabba Gabba* in 2007.

A lot of the fans of the Aggrolites and Hepcat to this day are still skinheads and rude boys, but it's an entirely different vibe. The skinheads and rude boys are mostly older people that have aged with these bands and have softened up their vehemence over time, but they still love the music and the fashion. Mike Park's rebellion against nicely dressed ska bands has also softened with age. Nowadays he likes to wear suits when he's playing ska, unlike his early visor-wearing days. He tells me how much he loves traditional ska and that he has fun playing it now. There aren't a lot of young ska bands dressing nice, he admits, but the right band could reignite interest. "I'm waiting for that next wave of fashion."

CRAB RANGOON

Not all ska in the '90s had a commercial sound. When ska was hitting its mainstream peak in 1997, there were hundreds of bands toiling in the underground doing their own thing. Link 80 took Madball style street hardcore and mixed it with ska. Choking Victim played ska with anarcho-punk as its musical and political base. The Blue Meanies infused ska with Mr. Bungle mayhem. The Pietasters kept their ska soulful. Siren Six played New Wave pop tunes, but with a ska beat. Mephiskapheles were almost as weird as The Blue Meanies but with more jazz.

Of all the bands grinding in the club circuit a million miles off the radar, MU330 were my personal favorite, specifically their third full length, *Crab Rangoon*, released in September 1997. *Crab Rangoon* is an out-of-place album: ska, but with alt-rock elements, particularly taking influence from Weezer's now beloved sophomore album *Pinkerton*, a critical and commercial flop upon its release in 1996. Rolling Stones readers voted *Pinkerton* the third worst album of the year. Later in the 2000s, several *Pitchfork* bands cited *Pinkerton* as a huge influence on their sound, causing a lot of people to reconsider its artistic merits. In 1997, no critics cared MU330 had embraced the record.

Like *Pinkerton*, *Crab Rangoon* is an album of pain, as the ordinarily upbeat lead singer/guitarist Dan Potthast wrote the album in the thralls of a breakup. "*Pinkerton* hit me at a time where I was ready for it," Potthast tells me. "We toured so much. That inevitably led to that breakup. That's going to happen to anybody that's dedicated their life to touring."

Much of the record inspects his post break-up emotional state from multiple points of view, like on "Understand" from his ex's perspective ("*You wouldn't understand/Cause you've never been in love like me/Someday you'll understand/When you really fall in love with yourself*") and "Fragile" ("*I'd like you to think I'm not so soft/you see right through it, my hopeless act/and it all comes down you see right through me*").

It's a strange record, with mid-tempo Weezer licks, aggressive 2 Tone upbeats, and eerie horn lines. The trombone line on "Ireland" is a bizarre see-saw, hopping between notes. Potthast's frayed voice barely conceals his anger. His melodies on *Chumps on Parade*, the previous record, leaned in on crazy circus music. MU330 referred to themselves as "psycho ska," a fitting descriptor for that era. On *Crab Rangoon*, Potthast expands into Elvis Costello and Peter Gabriel territory, with hints of his carnival barker "rock 'n' roll" voice, used to funnel raw emotion with a smirk.

Shortly before recording *Crab Rangoon*, things came to a grinding halt for the band. In the span of a few months, they lost their lead singer Jason Nelson, saxophonist Traygen Bilsland, and trumpet player Nick Baur for various personal reasons. MU330 were left with the core rhythm section and lone trombone player, Rob Bell. The leftover MU330 snatched trombonist Gerry Lundquist from the recently broken up Skankin' Pickle, making their horn section two slide trombones and nothing else, an odd timbre. Bell and Lundquist created a powerful and haunting force of trombones.

Potthast wrote most of the band's music in the past, but now with *Crab*, he took over as lead singer. Suddenly he cared more about the content of the lyrics. No more songs about toes ("Didgits") or stealing money ("Stuff"). He wanted to express himself sincerely. The lightbulb moment for him was reading lyrics for Fishbone's "Unyielding Conditioning," a gorgeous ska song that meditates on the world's lack of compassion, and the bravery it takes to be different. "I needed to try harder," Potthast says. "I started realizing I could put more of myself into these songs."

Potthast has proven to be a diverse and underrated songwriter, using melodic hooks that transcend genre. More MU330 albums followed, as did countless Potthast solo albums and side projects. He continued to write meaningful lyrics. One of his most emotionally impactful song is "Melbourne" from his 2012 solo album *Around the Word*. He sings about his brother Tom joining the Army and buying a guitar with one of his first paychecks. Training in the army fucked Tom's back up permanently. However, a young Dan snuck into his brother's room and secretly played the guitar while his brother was away. In "Melbourne," Dan dedicates his entire music career to his brother and his unfortunate injury. He never would've traveled the world if his brother didn't join the Army and buy a guitar "that he paid so dearly for."

MU330: still ska

When MU330 released *Crab Rangoon*, no major labels came knocking. They had a loyal fanbase but struggled to pack clubs. "We were watching people around us be courted by major labels. The common knowledge was you signed to a bigger label and moved on. We just wanted to tour and play music," Potthast says. Ska elements hindered the record's success. It wasn't right for the mainstream ska crowd and too ska for indie-rock kids. If you mix the horns out, replace the upbeats with distorted power chords and show it to any random hipster roaming the street, they'd wonder, *what great lost indie rock album have you found?* But the album as is, they'd tune out the second they heard upbeats.

The experimental philosophy behind *Crab Rangoon* was very much part and parcel to the time period. That's the whole point. Ska was an ingredient that musicians were mixing with everything else, and it yielded many interesting results. The true greats could even take a specific Weezer album and use it as the basis for a great, original record.

Now, over two decades since its release, the fact that *Crab Rangoon* is a ska record is part of its charm. I encourage all to rediscover it. It's an unexpected melding of worlds. MU330 took distinct influences and constructed an incredible album ignored at a time when all eyes were on ska.

NANCY REAGAN

My name is Nancy Reagan; my husband's name is Ron. He rules the nation. All my clothes are from the best designers. All my china is a perfect match.

-Blue Riddum Band, "Nancy Reagan"

"Nancy Reagan," one of the best, most subversive anti-Reagan songs of the '80s is a laid-back, horn-driven reggae revelation that should have been a hit but instead treaded water in obscurity.

It's a shame because it's unbelievably catchy with a melody like a lullaby. The simple repetitious phrase and feel-good, upbeat tone encapsulate the endorphin-fueled greed and willful ignorance of the Reagan administration, who turned a blind eye to the AIDS epidemic and growing homelessness crisis. Not to mention the "trickle-down" economics conservative scam he was the figurehead for, a tax theory that favored tax cuts for the rich. The promise was that the wealth would trickle down to the poor. Instead it helped kill America's middle class.

The song was released in 1982 by underrated Kansas City reggae band the Blue Riddim Band, who tirelessly toured the country in the late '70s and early '80s to little acclaim. Roger Steffens, co-host of a ska and reggae-focused radio program in the '80s, told me they "should have been America's UB40. They were authentic. They just blew people away."

Blue Riddim Band tirelessly touring in their van, Somewhere, USA

Anti-Reagan songs of the early '80s were pretty much the lifeblood of American hardcore, with subtlety not being a priority. Anarcho-punk band Reagan Youth formed in 1980 seemingly with the sole intent of protesting Reagan and the conservative movement, which they compared to the Nazi Youth in 1930s Germany. '80s American ska bands had plenty to say about Reagan as well. The album cover for Portland-based Crazy 8's debut record *Law and Order*, is a Jack Ohman satirical cartoon, depicting old Ronnie in his sheriff outfit, getting ready to draw his weapons. Instead of pistols, he's drawing nuclear missiles from his holster. Some radio stations refused to play the album because of the provocative cover.

"Nancy Reagan" is a different kind of protest song. It isn't angry or provocative, and it doesn't cite specific corrupt policies. Instead it comments on the toxic, mindless materialism of the time.

I had a chance to chat with drummer and founding member Steven "Duck" McLane about "Nancy Reagan," and I was surprised to learn it was never intended to be a protest song at all. McLane told me the song was a lighthearted jab; he even floated the word *novelty*, a word most musicians shun. "It doesn't have a blunt political edge. I never really thought that much about it. It just seemed like at the time, if you were going to sing about Nancy Reagan, what are you going to sing about? You can talk about clothes being from designers. It's just the way she was," said McLane. The song was birthed in late 1980 by trumpet player Scott Korchak; they played it frequently at rehearsals. Korchak envisioned it as an Ethiopian-style instrumental. One day, McLane started improvising lyrics over it about Nancy Reagan. "She was on TV so much," McLane says. "It went on for a half an hour. Everyone started laughing. We started writing shit down." Korchak protested, but it was too late, the song was now "Nancy Reagan."

They recorded the song the following year with Jack Number at a New York studio while they were in town to play some shows. They self-released it, along with three other songs as a twelve-inch single on their label "A Major Label." They called it that because they'd been told by several friends that if *only* they could get "on a major label," they would get huge. "That's too fucking easy. We'll print up a record and we'll put 'a major label' on it," McLane says. It was also a little bit of a jab, as the group, a few years earlier had recorded some demos for Island Records and were rejected. Chris Blackwell told them it wouldn't work out. "What he said was, 'It would cost me way too much money to create an identity for you guys. I can get any band from Jamaica I want for $4,000 and do an album and put it out. You guys would be a major investment of my money to make it worthwhile," McLane says, explaining Blackwell was thinking about how the cost of producers, studios and marketing in the States would be a lot more than in Jamaica. Besides, those guys were the real deal.

We gotta get our van to Jamaica

The group printed up copies of "Nancy Reagan" and sold them at shows and took them to college stations, and that was that. I couldn't contend with why the band viewed this brilliant song as novelty. Whether it was intended to be political or not, it certainly made a statement. Maybe it's because "Nancy Reagan" diverges from the band's usual vibe. The rest of their catalog is not only serious but attempts Jamaican music with the highest level of authenticity. And it was written during the early '80s when most Americans understood very little about Jamaican music.

Blue Riddim played hard-rocking '70s style reggae songs with a robust American R&B component. It wasn't one single reggae groove. They knew the ins and outs of decades of Jamaican music and incorporated it all. "We said 'reggae' because that was a catch-all phrase," McLane tells me. "Rocksteady, ska, reggae, we think in terms of them being separate music styles, but these styles melted into one another. There's an evolution of the music."

McLane and Blue Riddum guitarist Bob Zohn, a childhood friend of Jaco Pastorius, started playing together in the early '70s in several short-lived soul bands in New York and Florida. They discovered reggae from Ken Williams reggae show on WLIB, New York City's first black owned radio station. Later they discovered Lister Hewan-Lowe's reggae show "Saturday's A Party" on WUSB-FM. They eventually met the Jamaican-born Hewan-Lowe in person. He continued their Jamaican music education off air as a friend and mentor. Zohn and McLane loved the music so much, they vowed to start a reggae band as soon as they could.

Hewan-Lowe encouraged them to go to Kingston if they were serious about playing reggae music. Once there, they needed to track down Soul Syndicate, the backing band that played on nearly every record coming out of the island from 1972 till 1978. They took his advice and flew down to Jamaica in 1973. They found Soul Syndicate gigging at a nightclub called the Turntable Club. McLane described their first introduction with Soul Syndicate like Wayne and Garth meeting Aerosmith. ("We're not worthy!"). The members of Soul Syndicate not only taught them about the nuances of the music but let them hang out with them. "We started rolling with them. We'd go to the recording studios; we'd go to where they ate. They just took us in and took us on a ride of a lifetime," McLane says.

McLane and Zohn moved back to Kansas City and set out to start a reggae band. First, they named it Rhythm Funkshun, then Pat's Blue Riddim Band (which they named right before their first gig after looking down at a bunch of empty Pabst Blue Ribbon cases in their band house. Get it?), and finally as the Blue Riddim Band in late 1977, with the addition of a horn section. "Most people said you're out of your fucking mind if you think you're going to have a reggae band out of Kansas City," laughs McLane.

Since that original 1973 trip to the island, McLane and Zohn journeyed back to Jamaica at least once a year. One thing they learned going back to Jamaica over and over again was the other genres Jamaican musicians were influenced by: jazz, rhythm & blues, calypso. It gave them a common language to understand each other, and the ability for the Blue Riddim to grasp the nuances of reggae. In 1981, when Blue Riddim's first album *Restless Spirit* was released, Zohn's wife Janice suggested McLane take a crate of LPs with him on their next trip. He drove to both radio stations in Jamaica, telling them his band had a record. At the first station, RJR, the security guard wouldn't let him inside, but he agreed to personally take the record up to the DJ. As McLane drove to the other station, JBC, he heard his music on the air. He got so excited, he recorded the sound of his music being played on Jamaican radio on a portable tape deck. "You got the engine noise going while the song is playing. I must have played that for I don't know how many people," he says. The DJ at JBC played Blue Riddim Band a few days later. After a few months passed, Janice called the booker for the Jamaican Sunsplash Festival and asked if they'd be willing to book the American reggae band that the radio stations had been playing. They said yes, as long as the band flew themselves to the island on their own dime.

They were booked at 5:00 a.m. and introduced as the "All white Blue Riddim Band" to an understandably skeptical Jamaican audience. The band opened their set with a Skatalites-style ska rendition of "Chariots of Fire," which caught the audience off guard. "It blew people away that we knew what ska was and that we were able to play it correctly," says McLane. "We did a really believable, authentic job of playing their music. People jumped up and danced and went completely crazy." The Skatalites' saxophonist Tommy McCook was at this show. He later thanked McLane for that set. He told him that he decided to put the Skatalites back together for Sunsplash the next year after watching Blue Riddim Band and seeing how excited the audience got when the group played ska.

The Blue Riddim Band released a live recording of their Sunsplash performance in 1984, calling it *Alive in Jamaica*. This, their second album was historic, as The Blue Riddim Band were the first American band to ever to play Jamaica's famous Sunsplash reggae festival.

In the mid-80s, they had a few near misses. Grateful Dead were interested in taking them on the road but didn't say so outright. Blue Riddim showed up to play a gig in Berkeley and someone was setting up microphones and recording equipment on the stage. The band, unclear what was going on—and a little paranoid by how secretive the sound people were being—told the person to take the recording equipment down. The band later learned The Dead set this up; they wanted to get a recording of the band to see if they were the kind of group they wanted to take on the road with them. And they did not since they didn't have said recording. Later, CBS took an interest in the group and asked them to make some demos, but tried to make them sound like Boy George, who was popular at the time. Those didn't go anywhere either. One of the weirdest coulda-beens came from a lawyer in LA they worked with to help broker deals. He told them there was a rumor that Paul Simon wanted to make a ska album. Blue Riddim submitted material and were considered. But obviously, it never happened. A few years later, Simon made the World Beat-infused *Graceland*, which was unfortunately ska-free.

In 1986, the band stopped using the name Blue Riddim Band because their management presented them with a bill they couldn't pay. In those days, few indie bands toured. The Blue Riddim Band were on the front lines of reggae in the US, hitting bars across the country where no other reggae band had previously been. Management was paying for Ryder trucks so they could haul gear. The band was barely making enough to gas up the vehicle and get some food in their bellies. They became SDI (Strategic Dance Initiative) and would back a diverse pool of bands including Dr. John, Junior Reid and Rufus Thomas. But they were Blue Riddim Band no more.

The Blue Riddim Band had all the ingredients for an '80s breakout band, especially as reggae's popularity continued to grow in the US, but they were never able to break through. McLane attributed it to being on the road too much, rendering them unable to record much material. "We were road warriors. We'd go out for two-to-three months at a time," McLane said. "We had a frickin' van and a Ryder truck with our equipment. We did what we did as long as we could."

Yankee Reggae

Blue Riddim Band are among a small group of mostly forgotten early US reggae and ska bands that started in the '70s and included Terrorists, Jack Miller, Rebel Rockers, and Babylon Warriors, all LA bands, except for Terrorists, who hailed from New York. These bands all took Jamaican music seriously and tried to master the subtleties of the grooves. It was a generation before US reggae became synonymous with "frat-reggae," a style removed from the culture and politics of reggae, with a heavy emphasis on "good vibes."

As pioneering as they were, none of those early bands were the U.S.' first reggae band. That title belongs to Berkeley band The Shakers who built an impressive reggae scene at a tiny club called The Longbranch during the early to mid-70s. The band was the brainchild of drummer Ron Rhoades, a reggae fanatic who'd been collecting imports since the late '60s and wanted to start his own band. He was in love with the distinct way Jamaican artists played the drums. At that time, most folks in the US thought reggae sounded like a weird backwards rhythm. "I would play a King Tubby single for one of my friends, and he would look at me like I was from outer space," Rhoades tells me.

He finally formed a reggae band in 1973 called The Titans. He asked Malcom Williams Jr., the owner of The Longbranch, if he could have the typically dead Sundays to try to build something up. This first partnership only lasted a few months. Rhoades was never able to draw much of crowd, despite promoting it tirelessly. In the summer of 1974, Rhoades joined the rock band, Cold Feet, who headed to Alaska for the summer for some steady paying music gigs.

Not long after the move, the leaders of Cold Feet, a married couple, got in a fight and took off, stranding the rest of the band with no money, no set, and several contracted gigs still needing to be played. Rhoades taught the other two musicians a bunch of reggae songs from his personal collection, which he brought with him to Alaska. It went surprisingly well.

Yankee reggae stars The Shakers

They stayed up there the remainder of the summer, playing gigs and working a day job at the nearby crab factory. They worked as 'shakers,' which meant standing at a conveyor belt, shaking meat out of the legs to be packed into a can and sold to the public. When they scrounged up enough money to get back to Berkeley, he and the guys started a new reggae band, The Shakers, and got Sundays back at The Longbranch.

Things had changed since his first run at The Longbranch. Jamaican film *The Harder They Come* had made the rounds and was becoming a cult classic. The film starred a young Jimmy Cliff and had a fantastic soundtrack full of mostly '60s ska, rocksteady, and bouncy early reggae. *The Harder They Come* presented Jamaican life in its authentic harsh reality, not the tourist version the government had been pushing on the international community for decades. The music was what Jamaican people were listening to, straight off the streets of Kingston, not fancy Jamaican hotel sanitized Calypso. Suddenly a market opened for Jamaican music in the U.S., made up of college kids and hippies. The Shakers built a scene around them.

A pivotal moment for Rhoades in his quest to play authentic music was seeing the Wailers in late 1973 at The Matrix, a small rock club in San Francisco. The band played four nights in October 1973. Rhoades saw three of them. He studied everything he could. Not just the grooves, but what instruments they played and how they tuned their amps to get that perfect sound. "On one of the breaks, I went up to the stage and looked at the drums and realized that Carlton Barrett didn't have a drumhead on the bottom. They were all muted, so all the heads were dead. I looked at the bass cabinet. The bass up to ten. Treble all the way up to ten. Mid-range to zero," Rhoades says.

Rhoades wanted to turn the success of the Sunday nights at The Longbranch into a career. The band recorded demos and sent them to every label they could think of. The only one that replied was Trojan, which they had to turn down because they couldn't afford to move to England.

Eventually, they got a deal with Elektra-Asylum and were signed by David Geffen himself. The Shakers were the last band Geffen signed before abruptly leaving the label. In hindsight, it was a big mistake to go with Elektra-Asylum. "At the time, we didn't know," Rhoades says. The producer, Chuck Plotkin, knew nothing about Jamaican music and had a clear vision of turning them into a pop-singles band, which was not what the band signed on for, and not at all what they wanted.

"It was devastating. They took away all the rough edges and King Tubby dubs we were doing. He tried to turn us into a nice shiny Bubblegum pop version of reggae that he knew nothing about," Rhoades says. For their lead single, Plotkin demanded the band do a reggae-cover of the Persuaders' 1973 R&B track, "Some Guys Have All The Luck." Rhoades was furious, but eventually relented.

"It pissed me off so much I had a tantrum in the hotel room. I threw everything in the swimming pool. I just went crazy. I did not want to do that song." The track got decent radio-play but wouldn't become a massive hit until Rod Stewart recorded a not-reggae version of it in 1984.

Yankee Reggae (1976) is the result of a major tug-a-war between the band and the record company and doesn't capture what the band was about. The title was an affectionate name given to them by reggae icon Toots Hibbert, but within the context of a watered-down, major label record by a white band playing reggae, "Yankee Reggae" felt disrespectful to the culture of which they felt reverential. Rhoades says they got viewed by people as "stealing" from Jamaicans, which was the opposite of his intention. Rhoades intended to honor the music and was never looking to get rich off of it. He even spent his own money to keep things afloat. Geffen left while The Shakers were on tour promoting *Yankee Reggae*. The new CEO, Joe Smith, immediately pulled the plug on tour funding. Rhoades sold his publishing rights for $25,000 just so the band could finish the tour.

They hoped the label would let them record a second album and do it right this time. They even had interest from Bob Marley to produce it—someone that knew a thing or two about Jamaican music. Marley liked the idea, but only if The Shakers covered a few of his songs. Marley saw an opportunity for the record to promote his own music, and reggae in general. Rhoades was happy with this arrangement and pleaded his case. "Joe Smith said, 'How many singles does this Marley guy have?'" Rhoades recalls. Smith clearly wasn't impressed by Bob Marley or his notion of "authenticity."

By 1977, just as the Blue Riddim Band was getting going, The Shakers were done. They lost too much steam from dealing with Elektra-Asylum, and members were receiving offers for other opportunities. Rhoades' biggest regret was that they didn't sign to Trojan when they had the chance. "That's one of the highlights of my career, was getting that letter [from Trojan]," Rhoades says. "One of the worst moments was I couldn't figure out a way to get over there. They weren't in America at the time. So, that was the end of that." Rhoades next band, The Fabulous Titans, had the distinction of being the first US band to tour Cuba back in 1981.

By the late-70s, Marley was making headway in towns like San Francisco and Boston with primarily a white audience. He was disappointed he couldn't gain interest from Black Americans. His second to last gig, opening for The Commodores, was done almost exclusively to grow his Black American fanbase. The response that night was underwhelming. "It was the great disappointment of his life. 'Why aren't my people listening to me?'" says Steffens. Reggae was a cult form of music with Marley a modest figure in the '70s. Reggae would crossover into the mainstream in the mid-80s. Marely gained megastar status at the release of his retrospective, *Legend*, in 1984, three years after his death.

A Fringe Thing

Reggae slowly seeped into American culture through the '70s and multiple attempts ensued to popularize the genre. Island Records employee and Chris Blackwell's creative assistant Danny Holloway tells me that in 1976, they did a big roll out of reggae music with albums by Burning Spear, Toots and The Maytals, and The Heptones. "It started out being a fringe thing. As the years went on, a guy in some city in LA or Boston would start a radio show devoted to just reggae. Reggae music never 100% broke out during that period. Even in terms of where Bob [Marley] played. He never played a big gig in LA. He played The Roxy, which was four-hundred people. Jamaican music is now considered far more important."

Even though reggae has grown in popularity in the states, bands and audiences seem disinterested in its history, just wanting feel-good grooves to dance to without thinking beyond the beat. It's hard to view bands like The Blue Riddim Band and The Shakers in the prism of their time, which prioritized honor and respect for the Jamaican pioneers, and the culture reggae was created in. They were a big part of introducing the music to people all over the country and giving lots of folks their first opportunity to hear it performed live. That increased interest paved the way for many Jamaican musicians to be able to fly to the States, play gigs, and make some money.

Considering McLane's words, I can see why it's a little odd The Blue Riddim's biggest song was "Nancy Reagan." As great as it was, it didn't represent what the band was about. But the group likes the song. McLane tried to get a copy to Mrs. Reagan herself. "Somebody on her staff probably opened it up and saw what it was. They probably didn't give it to Reagan."

In 1985, rocker and reggae-lover David Lindley remixed "Nancy Reagan" with newly recorded vocals by The English Beat's Rankin' Roger. The single was issued with a new cover: Nancy Reagan smiling, holding a handful of jellybeans while ignoring the starving African children next to her. Clearly, I wasn't the only person that heard "Nancy Reagan" as a grandiose political statement.

The Blue Riddim Band weren't happy with Lindley's cover. "It wasn't like it was anything so bad that anyone was upset. We looked at it and went, 'What the fuck?' Just because it wouldn't have been anything we would have put on the cover," McLane says. If there was any lasting message they wanted to leave behind with people, it was spoken through their music, and how meticulously they studied the grooves. There's magic in those Jamaican beats. The Blue Riddim Band and The Shakers spent their whole lives trying to understand that magic.

NUMBER ONE FAN

In the five years Flat Planet existed, we only received a few fan letters. My favorite came in the summer of '94 after Flat Planet got back from our first tour. Someone named Jesus Portillo saw us play in El Paso, Texas. He said he listened to our tape every morning in the shower and that we were awesome because we wrote so many songs about food. We also thought we were awesome for writing about food. We had one song about our undying love for *mashin' taters*. Then there was the one about the joys of all-you-can-eat buffets. *Gives me more, till my stomach gets real stuffed.* If there was one thing Flat Planet was, it was obsessed with food.

Jesus included a phone number in his letter, so I gave him a buzz. He was surprised but delighted to hear from me and invited Flat Planet to open for his band Fla Fla Flunkies next time we came through El Paso. He offered to let us crash on his parents' living room floor. The following winter, we took him up on the offer.

It was a long drive from our gig in Albuquerque and we hung out at a rest stop for a few hours along the way, shooting movies on camcorders and singing Snoop Dogg songs. The next day, instead of getting much-needed sleep, Alex and I meandered across the border to Mexico. As we crossed back to the US, we were grilled by the border agent about what business we had in El Paso. "We're playing a show tonight with our band," Alex said. "Do you play country or western," the border agent responded to Alex, who had a spikey mohawk and a Misfits shirt. I had bleached blonde hair and wore a red thrift store shirt that said #1 Dad. "Ska," I said.

We were barely awake by the time we got to Jesus' house, but his mom greeted us with a delicious Mexican breakfast and Jesus showed us his potato gun in the backyard. Fun times.

A few letters rolled in after we broke up. "I heard your song on *Misfits of Ska II*. Will you be playing Glendale on your next tour?" one said. "I bought your tape at your show in Littlerock a few years ago. I love your song 'Papa Smurf.' Is that about someone you know?" said another. The song *was* about someone we knew: a semi-homeless man who hung out with us every time we went to the Golden West diner for post-practice curly fries and sodas. The letters dried up. Then, in 2015, to my complete shock, I received a Facebook message from a German guy in his thirties named Marcel Windrath, a Flat Planet fan!

What an unexpected treat, though odd, since we'd never played Europe, and we were small potatoes compared to the millions of other '90s ska bands. As it turned out, Marcel was an avid collector of '90s ska-punk and punk rock demo cassettes. He heard our song, "Mr. Goodbuddy" on the *Misfits of Ska II* Compilation, as well as our five songs on the Tomato Head Records' *Bay Area Ska* compilation, the extent of our "nationally distributed" content, and wanted more.

Marcel tracked me down from Pete Rice, guitarist for San Jose ska-punk band Janitors Against Apartheid. Those guys were on a whole other level of insanity, and only reached a slightly higher level of fame than Flat Planet. They played brutally fast ska-punk. The singer MC Loaf screamed through their songs like Pee Wee Herman getting beaten with a club. He sang about his obsession with Punky Brewster, his tattooed penis, and a desire to gobble up all breakfast pastries. Obviously, we played several shows together—us singing about extra-large burritos and them responding with pastry anthems. Anytime we played with Janitors, Alex, usually, in one of his semi-ripped Metallica shirts, leapt around the front of the stage so hard, the audience assumed he was in the band too.

Marcel and all the '90s ska-punk cassettes

MC Loaf was a tall, lanky guy who worked at an arcade making change for kids, just like Paul Reuben' character in the 1980 cinematic masterpiece *Midnight Madness*. When he sang, his body spasmed like a violently shaken Muppet. His performances hypnotized me. The music was secondary to what felt like watching an exorcism.

After he quit Janitors, he did a hard one-eighty and went full-on hipster. I ran into him at a Tortoise show in Santa Cruz years later, and he gave me a sideways cool guy nod. All I could picture was him singing about his penis in his puberty-breaking voice: "I got a girl-friend named Doooooaaaannnnnyyyyy." I had to resist all urges to sing Janitors' songs to his face.

Marcel loved the Janitors Against Apartheid. They were his number one favorite ska band. He told me the singer sounded like Kermit the Frog and Mr. Bungle. An excellent observation. Marcel and I talked a lot about '90s ska, punk rock and other weird, distinctly '90s bands, like funk-punk Nuclear Rabbit and ultra-sarcastic punkers Your Mother. His '90s demo tape collection was massive, and he shared much of it with me. His extensive knowledge came from piecing bits of history together via those cassettes, which were, for the most part, the lowly, obscure bands of the era, not what most people think of when they imagine '90s ska.

He'd email me MP3s of bands he digitized from these tapes. Most of them I'd never heard of—snotty punk vocals, sloppy upbeats, shitty distorted guitars. Sometimes the bands were raw skate-punk or heavy funk, but a lot were ska-punk. None were traditional ska. That wasn't his thing. He sent me bands like Splurge, Crankshaft, Wet Nap, Agent Twenty-Three, The Pee Tanks. All excellent time capsules from the era.

Marcel sent me these relics and ended his emails with: "Hope these songs will make your day a little bit brighter 😃."

Eventually, I dug through my memorabilia box in the garage and found the original Flat Planet demo *La Venganza Del Muerte* (The Revenge of Death!) as well as a live recording we made a dozen copies of called A *Message To Rudy*. I sent them to him. He liked them, and eventually digitized them for me. "Hey! I heard your tape👍👍Its great, no fillers, all winners. Some tracks I knew from comps but here are rawer and I prefer that," Marcel wrote.

One song confused him. "Who is Joey Lawrence?" he asked me. I had written a song called "I Want to be Joey Lawrence" as a tribute to the '80s child star turned '90s pop star. (*Joey Lawrence! You were the mack on Gimme a Break!*). Neither *Blossom* reruns nor Lawrence's hit single, "There's Nothing My Love Can't Fix" reached Germany, so I gave Marcel a full detailed history lesson on Joey Lawrence, with a link to his music, and a jumbled explanation of why it was funny that I pretended to like him. He replied: "Typical '90s stuff, a boy with a bad haircut who is a checker for the chicks 😊. Doesn't he look like that one guy from *Full House* the comedy series?"

In one message, Marcel casually referenced a three-way split cassette he scored that included Flat Planet. And had questions for me about it. I had no idea what he was talking about. He sent me a photo of the cover and liner notes. The tape had tracks by Janitors, Midwest band Stinkfish and Flat Planet. A bootleg!

Someone bootlegged my band! Someone felt like they could profit off Flat Planet! My band! Me! We were important!

Super valuable bootleg

Marcel and I have been chatting online for years now. At first, he asked me a lot of questions about Flat Planet and ska-punk bands, but he's probably educated me a lot more on '90s ska than the other way around. I'm surprised at the number of bands that were actively touring and recording, right under my nose, and how good they all were. Maybe it's just nostalgia. All those angst-filled teens, just learning to play their instruments, cranking out fun, sloppy jams and throwing out their craziest oddball ideas whenever they felt like it. It pleases my ears. They were the energy driving the scene—not the popular bands.

Marcel asked me once to describe my favorite Janitors Against Apartheid show. He only knew them from their tapes. How strange to know them only from their lo-fi cassette recordings. To me, bands like Janitors were all about their live shows. I don't know if I'd ever listened to their recordings.

I told him about a show at Foothill College, just outside of San Jose. Twenty people were in attendance, including me and my friend Nate. Janitors brought a big bucket of stuffed animals and some Big Wheels. They devoted their entire set to ripping the stuffed animals into tiny shreds and riding their Big Wheels around in the guts. I think they played a few songs too. The show organizers were too nervous to stop them. Marcel loved it: "The chaotic nonsense thing they did fits perfect to their music☺."

I thought back to that show. A million miles away from the mainstream, there was a crazy fringe ska scene that overlapped with the weirder side of punk rock. Bands like Janitors and One Eye Open were taking ska into a bizarre and unsettling direction; a window into the minds of disturbed '90s outcasts and weirdos. What would I think now if I saw that Janitors show as an adult? I want to think I'd ask for their autograph and buy all their merch.

A few days later, Marcel sent me some MP3s of more obscure '90s ska-punk bands. His supply was endless. He asked me if I had any more Flat Planet tapes lying around in my garage. I didn't quite understand why he liked my band so much. We weren't full of angst or even that weird, at least compared to the bands he loved, yet he wanted to own everything we ever recorded. How could I say no to that? I told him there was an even older, more embarrassing demo, probably lying around somewhere called *Back To Botswana*. There was also an entire full-length album we recorded that was never released. He couldn't wait. It would be Christmas for him.

SKA IS DEAD

1...2...3...4...!!!

The guitars and drums barrel into a barely stitched-together blast of punk rock, tripping right into jerky ska. The horns kick in immediately with a staccato, robotic pep-band horn line. Lead singer Jeff Rosenstock spits out incomprehensible gibberish at auctioneer's pace over the hyper ska verse and double-time hardcore bridge. It all crashes together into an unexpected, straight-forward, and supremely catchy pop-punk, gang-vocal chorus: *"Everything is always falling apart!"*

Long Island's Arrogant Sons of Bitches small but loyal fanbase went crazy for this depression anthem, "So Let's Go! Nowhere," released in 2003. "It's the ultimate embracing negative song," says Rosenstock. "When we were playing shows, people were all singing it together. It made people feel better." He wrote the song after watching the Twin Towers come down from his dorm room on 9/11. It was a bleak moment for most Americans. It left Rosenstock speechless. He later processed the black hole of darkness of that moment with "So Let's Go! Nowhere" (*"Fuck the world/Everything is breaking and changing/And everything inside of me is breaking and changing/Why can't I ever let it go/I concentrate real hard, and I might not ever even know"*).

Earlier ASOB songs were more juvenile. Songs like "I Just Want to Have Sex With You," "American Penis," and "I Pissed In Your Mountain Dew." Post 9/11, he wrote several new songs that stemmed from the tragedy, which would end up on the band's 2003 EP, *All The Little Ones Are Rotting*, though none of them explicitly referenced the towers. Rosenstock never intended people to picture 9/11 when they listened to these songs.

Jeff Rosenstock going nowhere

Many of the tracks ended up more optimistic than the pissed-off insanity of early ASOB. "So Let's Go! Nowhere" was dark, but it had a glimmer of hope. At the time, Rosenstock was getting treatment for depression and anxiety. "I wanted whoever to hear it [to] connect to the feeling that death is imminent and shit's hopeless. What are you going to do to make your situation better right now?"

Since the band formed in 1995, "So Let's Go! Nowhere" was the first song fans connected to on such a passionate level. It melted inhibitions and created an anti-kumbaya effect. People related to the dreariness and felt like they weren't alone. "It's an amazing feeling to hear that many people singing your song at the top of their lungs—scream it until they lose their voice," says ASOB keyboardist J.T. Turret. "Things in your life are shitty. Raise your fists and say, 'Everything is always falling apart' in the happiest, catchiest, most melodic way possible."

It's that sense of dread that gave Rosenstock a new perspective on life. Music had been important to him and yet his prior attempts to pursue it were wishy-washy. He vowed to give ASOB a real shot. They started hitting the greater region hard, and by 2003, they were booking full US tours and trying to get labels to release their music. But as emo-punk gained traction in the mid-2000s, there was little chance for "So Let's Go! Nowhere." Ska was dead.

In the 2000s, ska, and the people who loved ska were banished to dimly lit clubs and spaces far away from popular culture. Mustard Plug singer David Kirchgessner created the *Ska Is Dead* tour package in 2003 to ironically embrace this depreciative tone and surprise some folks of its continued underground popularity even as everyone else was actively hating it. "We wanted to prove to promoters and media people that it was still really strong," says Kirchgessner. The shows did well, but people outside of the ska scene were blissfully unaware.

David Hillyard from The Slackers, another group that continued playing ska into the post-90s years, saw a lot of people running from the music. He says there was a particularly insecure way ska musicians distanced themselves from the music. "I'm not saying that people can't play other music. If you want to go play other music, go play other music," he says. "It's just sad that you have to diss ska to do that. People in ska have this musical inferiority complex. It's not real music. It's kiddy music. I don't really got time for that."

Several bands broke up or tweaked their sound to try to wash the ska stink from themselves. One of the most popular ska bands in the 2000s, Streetlight Manifesto, actively downplayed their association with ska. "We're not really that influenced by ska music. We're not even necessarily huge fans of ska," lead singer Tomas Kalnoky said in a 2008 *AP Radio* interview. "We try to do a mixture of different genres. One of the main ingredients happens to be ska."

The big crowds at Kirchgessner's *Ska Is Dead* tour blew some minds, and the success of The Slackers 2001 *Wasted Days* album also surprised a few folks. But no one was embracing ska as aggressively as ASOB. They were on a mission to pummel anyone's ska shame into oblivion and take a stand for the music they loved. "I saw bands that were adamantly like 'We're not ska. We're rock with horns,'" Rosenstock says. "I never want to say that to somebody. I can't think of any other genre where people have come up to me and said, 'I like you guys, but I don't like ska, so I don't listen to your band.' That's like your uncle saying, 'I like all music but country and hip-hop.' That's fucking insane."

Mysterious drunken Skankin' Pickle shirt

The Arrogant Sons of Bitches broke up in 2004 but played scattered shows until 2006, their official end. Rosenstock became an indie legend in subsequent years. His schizophrenic cult punk band Bomb The Music Industry! (2004-2014) gave away music online over a year before Radiohead was praised for revolutionizing the music industry with their "pay what you want" release of *In Rainbows*. By 2018, Rosenstock became a *Pitchfork* darling, thanks to a handful of phenomenal indie-punk records capturing the anxiety, fury, and sorrow of the Trump era. In spite of all his success, he's never written a single song that shot so clearly above the rest the way "So Let's Go! Nowhere" did for ASOB. "That's the quintessential song," says John DeDomenici, bassist for Bomb, Jeff solo albums, and various instruments with ASOB. "I think Bomb has records. Never the one standout song."

It was the hit single that never was, in a time when ska wasn't allowed to have a hit single. Even if they knew on some level that they didn't stand a chance, ASOB gave it their all. If ska was dead, fine; they'd be the fucking zombies prepared to eat humanity alive.

Built To Fail

Arrogant Sons of Bitches formed in 1995 by Rosenstock and his friend Joe Werfelman, both thirteen-years-old. Ska popularity was on the rise, and Long Island had an incredible scene with local bands galore. "There was a good twenty-to-thirty ska bands in Long Island alone," says ASOB drummer Mike Costa, who joined in 1998. "There was this one venue in Long Island, Deja One, that would have a show every Friday. You would just go. You didn't give a fuck who was playing. Spring-heeled Jack used to play there; The Pilfers played there." The Long Island ska scene continued to stay active through the '90s and even into the very early part of the 2000s.

There was an ever-rotating cast of players in ASOB, and a live show like a train wreck you couldn't tear your eyes from. The first time Costa saw the band, he recalls bassist Chris Baltrus smashing his instrument against a pillar in the venue mid-set for no reason. "It was a wild live show. I was like 'Fuck it, I'm in,'" Costa says. "We were definitely not good. When we first started, we had no idea what we are doing." The first two records *Built to Fail* (1998) and *Pornocracy* (2000) were sloppy, lo-fi, and full of teen-angst. The band broke up in the summer of 2000 on what was supposed to be their first three-day tour. One of the band members' dads rented them a Winnebago to tour in. He had them sign a contract making them financially responsible for it if they wrecked it. Some of the people in the band were so upset by this, they quit. There wasn't enough of a band to tour with. "We just sat in the Winnebago in front of my parents' house for a few days," says Rosenstock.

Then the towers came down. The band was asked to play a show with World/Inferno Friendship Society, a band they loved. It seemed like a good reason as any to play together again. By that point, they missed hanging out, they'd all become better players, and Rosenstock was writing more personal, emotionally piercing songs. The band was now connecting on a new level—still with train wreck-energy, but much more in sync. "We knew what the next song was without a setlist," Costa says. "Jeff would turn around and look at you, and I was like, 'that song.' We vibed off each other."

They ventured outside of Long Island in the early 2000s and weren't always greeted well. They were a ska-punk band playing shows primarily with punk, emo, and indie bands. The smell of anti-ska was in the air.

"When it started being a thing that people were talking shit about, and seemed to be embarrassed about, it bummed me out, because that was everything to me," Rosenstock says. "Music is supposed to make people feel happy. If it's a good ska band, there will be some fun shit going on." But the more ska was dissed, the harder ASOB dug in their heels.

Their stubbornness about ska created a bombastic live show even more intense than the angsty early ASOB years. As they got better, it created a platform to deal with their personal issues rather than screaming about juvenile stuff. "People would see us and wonder if someone was going to be seriously fucking hurt at the end of the show," Rosenstock says. "Dave, our trombone player, he's smoking cigarettes, turning bright red while playing the glockenspiel as hard as he can. I'd have Christmas lights wrapped around my guitar cables, just running around everywhere and buying $100 guitars and just smashing them all over the place. People were like 'What the fuck is this?' I would just go into the audience and drink people's beers while we were playing because I thought it was funny. I was in a dark place in my life. I wanted somebody to fucking kick my ass. I pushed it further and further and further."

Live And Uninvited

The group headed out to the West Coast in 2003, ready to show the world the best ska show they'd ever seen. But their record label forgot to book tour dates to get home, leaving ASOB stranded on the opposite end of the country with almost no cash and a nearly maxed out credit card. Desperate to make money to get back home, they meandered over to Boise, Idaho where the Warped Tour was stationed for the day. Rosenstock contacted Arielle Bilelak from 1-800-SUICIDE "The Hopeline" and asked if they could work as volunteers. He and Turret took turns passing out suicide prevention pamphlets. When Turret wasn't working, he looked up Warped Tour founder Kevin Lyman, who he'd met a few years earlier when his other band Sprout played the festival. He asked Lyman if ASOB could play in the parking lot and sell a couple CDs. ASOB even had a generator and speakers ready to go for a parking lot show. Lyman told him to knock themselves out, but that they "didn't hear it from him." The band printed out flyers that read "Performing Live and Uninvited On the 2003 Vans Warped Tour" and prepared for their first Warped Tour show.

In the early evening, Dropkick Murphys, or it might have been AFI, were on the main stage and pulled off mid-set due to a tornado warning. The audience was told to go home and find somewhere safe. In the parking lot, ASOB blasted through "So Let's Go! Nowhere" as people streamed from the event and ran for their cars.

"We were jumping off of shit, stealing people's hats, running around and being a really intense punk band in a tornado. We had a really good time," Rosenstock says. The next day they received offers to play at multiple tents inside the festival, including the Subway tent and the Backseat Conception Tent (friends of Turret's, who were making a movie called *Punk Rock Holocaust*...Rosenstock and Turret both had a small part in the movie). They continued to play Warped Tour for a few weeks as official uninvited guests, even getting to play on a real stage a few times to fill in for bands that dropped off.

Eventually ASOB needed to stop back home to return the trailer they'd been borrowing from Big D and The Kids Table. When they returned, they discovered they'd been disinvited. Other bands had been reading ASOB's blog, which detailed how they snuck into the Warped Tour, and now were trying to do the same. Their Warped Tour stint was over.

ASOB crashes Warped Tour

Last Show?

In the heavy touring years of 2003 and 2004, a division formed in the band related to how they should deal with money. It grew more divided, the more they toured. Trombonist Dave Renz and Turret focused on keeping the band financially sustainable by investing a lot of money into merchandise. They even purchased a new trailer because they had so many shirts.

The whole thing got on Rosenstock's nerves. "The reason I started going to punk shows was because I didn't want to go to the fucking mall," Rosenstock said in Bomb The Music Industry! documentary *Never Get Tired*. The problem might've been solved if they'd had label support, but no one was interested in signing a ska band. "People didn't want a band with an obscene name that played ska with horns," says Turret. So, Renz and Turret pushed hard to sustain tours through heavy merch sales. Since the shows were so small, they were going into debt rather than making their money back.

While the band was in Stockton, California, disagreements boiled over and a fight ensued. Rosenstock said he didn't want to dump the $1,000 they'd made from tour into buying more merch. He wanted to use it to record music. They hadn't released a new album in ages. But other members didn't see how it was possible to continue touring without getting more merch. The two sides were firm in their position. They had a long, uncomfortable drive home.

Once home, they played two shows at Mr. Beery's and advertised it as "Last show?" They couldn't totally break up because they were in so much debt. They owed $2,000 to Turret's Home Depot credit card for the trailer, and over $2,000 to screen printer Tommy Rockstar, who fronted them merch, as well as $3,500 they'd ran up on Rosenstock's credit card. ASOB played roughly ten shows over the next year to pay off their debts, and three more shows in 2006 to celebrate the release of their final album.

During this time, creative energy was slowly diverted elsewhere. In 2004, just after the final tour, Rosenstock began working on his new project, Bomb The Music Industry!, a band that went so far in the other direction, they gave all their music away for free. If anybody wanted a Bomb The Music Industry! shirt, the members would spray-paint the band's name on their shirt free of charge. Turret started to play solo under his name. Other members joined Bomb with Rosenstock. Renz left music and went back to school. "I was thankful that we weren't doomed to self-destruct and burn our lives out on this band," Rosenstock says.

Album Minus Band

Bomb the Music Industry! incorporated a broader range of musical influences than the primarily ska-core sound of Arrogant Sons of Bitches. In the early 2000s, as Rosenstock's songwriting improved, he was recording better demos. He'd always heard songs in their complete form and demoed them on Cakewalk using MIDI. In college he used a computer compatible with real instruments to record demos that sounded even closer to the songs as he imagined them.

Rosenstock began recording full Bomb the Music Indusry! albums on his own. Since he wasn't writing for a band, he could create non-stop, unrelated changes in the songs, and layer them with ridiculous amounts of instruments and vocals if he so desired (and often did!) Songs were mixed with synth-pop, ska, drum machines, and sad piano noodling, then abruptly into noisy, distorted acoustic guitars with gang vocals galore. Styles that didn't belong together were mashed into one song. "I didn't have to worry about how we are going to do this live because I thought we were never going to do it live. I think that let it expand naturally," Rosenstock says. He released his first record, *Album Minus Band* in 2005.

Bomb did eventually become a live band, initially with people coming and going as a "collective," and then a solid lineup. Ska always remained a component even as Rosenstock broadened his influences. On the group's brilliant *Scrambles* record from 2009, occasional ska parts wedged in nicely between scatterbrain synth sections and carousal punk breakdowns—entirely spontaneous and done when *no one* was playing ska on their albums. "It's like putting the section of music that isn't popular, no one wants, and you're not good at because you don't do it, but here it is," DeDomenici explains.

Some amount of ska appeared on every Bomb The Music Industry! record except for 2011's *Vacation*, the group's final album, a much more straight-forward indie-punk release. Regardless, Rosenstock never forgot his headstrong commitment from those ASOB days to proudly represent ska. If anyone wanted to call Bomb a ska band, he encouraged it, even when it wasn't true. "The last Bomb record [*Vacation*], it's ska. There's no ska on that record. That's fine. You can call it that if you want to," Rosenstock says. "You can't shake it no matter what. I don't think it's something you should shake."

In 2011, Bomb the Music Industry! went on tour with The Slackers. The Bomb members felt like big awkward losers compared to how cool and laid back The Slackers seemed. Bomb decided to prepare a ska song for all The Slackers' fans, but it had to be a Pavement song the audience no doubt would hate. "What's the most annoying thing we can do? Let's cover a song that these people probably don't want to hear because they think Pavement is *Pitchfork* bullshit and let's make it a traditional ska song so that anybody that does like Pavement is like, this is ska bullshit," Rosenstock says. The song they chose was "Gold Soundz." They got ready for the animosity to roll in. Instead, everyone loved it, because, duh, ska sounds good even when it's Pavement. The Slackers and Bomb became good friends because The Slackers are not as cool as they let on. They're punk weirdos, too.

Three Cheers For Disappointment

Back in Arrogant Sons of Bitches earlier years, they wrote two songs about ska. The first one, "Go Ska," mocked all the bands hopping on the ska bandwagon in '97 ("*Shaved off my Mohawk. I got a* bald head and a tattoo that says 'I'll skank till I'm dead'") In the early 2000s, they released its spiritual sequel, "Abandon Ship," about everyone running for the hills to distance themselves from ska ("*Trade in this uncool punk/ska, make it rock with horns. The kids don't like it, it's not Limp Bizkit.*")

"Go Ska" became popular in the Napster years. Kids who knew nothing about ska dipped their feet in the waters by searching the word "Ska." As guilty as ska bands were with over-using ska-puns in their band names, there weren't many ska songs with the word "Ska" in the title. ASOB had "Go Ska." I Voted For Kodos had "She Hates Ska." There wasn't a whole lot besides that.

It's a shame it wasn't "Abandon Ship" that everyone found and downloaded, because if there's a single song that summarized how the band stuck up for ska, this was it. "I was frustrated seeing people in our vibrant ska/punk scene in Long Island—which got me through my teenage years and helped me feel less alone in my depression—start turning their backs on ska/punk. As if it was a blemish on their reputation to play upstrokes," says Rosenstock. They weren't necessarily saying they alone were the ones holding the ska flag. It was more of a fuck you to the bands playing watered down punk and switching their horns for synths, just to look cool.

Three Cheers for Disappointment was released in 2006. It was ASOB's third and best full-length. It took several years and multiple attempts to get right. The band broke up before they could enjoy its success. It stands as one of the best ska-punk albums from the 2000s. At the first of three release shows, Rosenstock wore a shirt that said "ASOB Broke Up." For most of ASOB's life, they struggled to find a fanbase. They were finally able to pack local venues, but now it was a drag to be in the band. Signing posters after the final release show, when they just wanted to hang out, curbed any urge to keep things going.

A few months later, booked at the Knoxville Ska Weekend but uninterested in performing, Bomb The Music Industry! took to the stage instead, with Turret joining the band for 3 final ASOB songs at the end. They passed out notes saying, "The role of The Arrogant Sons Of Bitches Will Be Played By Bomb The Music Industry!"

ASOB booked two reunion shows in September 2007, which sold out. They closed with an extra-long version of "That's What Friends Are For," while the sound guy yelled at them and DeDomenici drunkenly fell off the stage. "Yeah, that seems about right," Rosenstock wrote on a *Punknews* post wrap-up of the show.

In 2012, the group decided to play another reunion show, one they'd take more seriously. The show they booked at New York's Warsaw (one-thousand capacity) sold out in less than twenty-four hours. In shock, they added two more shows, one at Webster Hall in Manhattan and another at Heirloom Arts in Connecticut. This crazy out-of-time, out-of-place ska band meant a lot to so many people. The band members didn't know how to wrap their minds around any of this, other than to try to soak in how many people they affected by waving the ska flag so proudly.

Those final shows in 2012 were incredible, but a far cry from the scrappy, desperate shows of the old days. "A real ASOB show is a tiny room with about one-hundred kids, screaming their lungs out, and sweating on each other while skanking," says Turret. "I love it, and I'll always remember it."

I KNOW WHAT RUDE BOYS LIKE

Most people know The Waitresses for their sassy "I Know What Boys Like" and the festive "Christmas Wrapping," a song still so popular, British filmmaker Steve Thompson filmed *Couldn't Miss This*, a 2019 documentary about the song's enduring success in the UK. But did you know that The Waitresses have several ska songs?

I learned about The Waitresses' ska proclivity in 2017 when I got a surprise Facebook message from guitarist Christopher Butler. I'd never met or spoken with Butler before. The message wasn't completely out of the blue. I'd just written "The 10 Best New Wave Albums to Own On Vinyl" for the website *Vinyl Me Please*, and included The Waitresses' fantastic *Wasn't Tomorrow Wonderful*. Butler read my list and wanted to send me a little "thank you." As he searched my name, ska came up. He immediately jumped into a long monologue about ska, which he assumed (correctly) would be the best icebreaker.

He began by telling me about his first exposure to ska in late 1979 at the Hurrah Nightclub in New York, where he saw Madness perform on their first US tour. He guessed I wouldn't consider Madness the "real deal," but for him it opened the door. "I went to Bleecker Bob's the next day and got The Skatalites and several compilations. I was hooked." The experience of seeing Madness completely changed his perspective on music. He loved the energy and the upbeat rhythm which was unlike anything he'd ever heard.

Butler was communicating more than just *I am a ska fan*. He was acknowledging ska as an important yet rarely written-about influence on The Waitresses. There's secret ska hidden in other pockets of '80s US pop music. How many people remember the watered-down ska rhythms in Julian Lennon's 1984 single "Too Late For Goodbyes"? How about Philadelphia New Wave band, The Hooters, who most people know for their power-popping "And We Danced" and "All Your Zombies"? They started out, in the early '80s, playing ska and reggae influenced songs. The Police, Elvis Costello, Joe Jackson, all artists scoring hits in the US that had ska songs on their records.

Let's not forget, Oingo Boingo, who will always be remembered for their 1985 dance tune "Dead Man's Party." They deserve credit as one of the first American bands to experiment with ska. Even in their non-ska songs, the group retained hints of ska and would go on to influence bands like No Doubt, Reel Big Fish and Skankin' Pickle. No Doubt were such big Boingo fans, they tried to get guitarist Steve Bartek to produce *Tragic Kingdom*. Interscope rejected No Doubt's request. They didn't know who Bartek was. Boingo Bassist John Avila, who would go on to produce dozens of '90s ska albums, agrees with me about his band's ska origins "We had a couple songs that were full-on ska tunes," Avila tells me, adding that Danny Elfman was a big Madness fan. "Danny Elfman composed some very intricate and interesting melodies using the ska genre."

I wanted to know more about Butler's ska past, so he and I spoke on the phone a year-and-a half after he messaged me to go further go down the ska rabbit-hole. "Ska saves trombone players from starvation," he told me at the front of the interview, as his own defense of ska —a good one, too.

"It's one of those genres that is so eclectic. It can be political; it can be for parties, it's so versatile and has such a unique rhythm," Butler said. "I grew up playing in blues and R&B bands. You fall into this very short list of beats, shuffles and here's something completely new— everything on the upbeat. Even the moodier ballad stuff, it still has a lift to it."

Ska wove itself into The Waitresses' music immediately, adding to the band's already unusual history. The Waitresses started as a light-hearted side-project. Butler wrote and recorded "I Know What Boys Like" with some friends while playing in the Akron, Ohio rock band Tin Huey in 1978. It sat in the can until he moved to New York in 1979. Interest grew from Island Records for the song. They made a deal to release it as a single, but it needed a B-side, so Butler and Patty Donahue (the vocalist on "I Know What Boys Like") recorded the ska-tinged "No Guilt."

"I Know What Boys Like" became an underground hit. Success inspired Butler and Donahue to form a proper band for future projects, keeping The Waitresses' name. Their debut LP, *Wasn't Tomorrow Wonderful?* (1982) has ska all over it, but no one noticed, because few people in the US pop market knew what ska was.

One of the biggest struggles ska bands had in the U.S. in the '80s was that ska was viewed as alternative/college rock. In the U.K., ska was pop music. They hit the Top 40 immediately and stayed there until the public moved on to something else.

The ska revival was brief. As the decade progressed, these bands morphed into non-ska pop or broke up and formed New Wave groups. They had more success in the US in the non-ska years. Madness' biggest stateside hit was the 1983 pop tune "Our House." English Beat's most successful album, *Special Beat Service*, had slight Jamaican grooves on it but mostly steered towards pop. And look at some of the bands who rose like phoenixes from the ashes of The Specials and English Beat: Fun Boy Three, General Public, Fine Young Cannibals. All New Wave. And all bigger stateside than the ska bands they came from.

Ska became pop music in the US in the mid-90s. No Doubt, despite only hinting at ska, were most responsible for this sea change. The long and meandering journey ska took in the US kept the 2 Tone bands in the cult category. In 1990, when English Beat members played as The International Beat at The International Ska Festival & Earth Day Celebration at the Greek Theater to eight-thousand people, the members were shocked. Rankin' Roger didn't realize this audience existed. He went back to England and formed The Special Beat.

Let's Go Bowling play to thousands at the Earth Day Ska Festival in Berkeley

Special Beat featured Roger, as well as Specials members Neville Staples, John Bradbury, and Horace Panter. The group's setlist combined Specials and English Beat songs. In a 1990 interview with the *Chicago Tribune*, Roger explained "We want to be successful this time around." They played big shows, but remained cult artists. Word was out that there was an audience for ska in the US. The Selecter reformed in 1991. Madness reformed in 1992. The Specials reformed in 1994. The Specials lead guitarist Roddy Radiation reflects on this time. "I was amazed at the ska scene in the states. We played packed venues—large halls of about 2000-4000 capacity, and festivals. We went down a storm everywhere," he says. "[In the '80s] Only the hip places on the East and West Coast got what we were doing, as punk rock—let alone ska—had hardly made an impression in the U.S. at the time," says Radiation.

Remember, Judge Roughneck will not tolerate any disobedience in his courtroom

All the 2 Tone bands did well, but fans hardly got a glimpse of the groups at their peak. Besides, none of these bands were writing new material that held water to their early albums. The new crop of ska-influenced bands like No Doubt, Sublime and Reel Big Fish were different because their music made sense to the US pop market, as more American rock and pop elements seeped into the mix. So, when we think about ska's popularity in the '90s, let's raise a glass to the forgotten pioneers on US soil that that helped bridge the gap between 2 Tone and the '90s Third Wave. Three Cheers for Oingo Boingo, The Waitresses, and all the other secret '80s ska bands who are rarely ever recognized for their part in bringing ska to the US audience.

MISFITS

It was 1995. I was in Minneapolis at First Avenue, Prince's nightclub, acting as a roadie for Skankin' Pickle's two-week Midwest tour. You could close your eyes and imagine Morris Day and the Time right there on this stage. Skankin' Pickle played several large, packed venues already, but this one, at a fifteen-hundred capacity, impressed me. I looked out at the sea of faces, amazed at how many people were there to see Skankin' Pickle. Back at home, it was five-hundred people at Slims. Here it was fifteen-hundred. Sold out in advance. People had to be turned away.

Chicago ska-core outfit Slapstick opened the show, with posi-hard-core legends 7 Seconds as main support. Once they finished their closing song, "In Your Face," I ran to the stage and helped drummer Troy Mowat cart his drums off the stage as quickly as possible, then built Skankin' Pickle drummer Chuck Phelps' drum set up. A few days into the tour, I'd lost his drum mat, which had all the exact spots for each drum and cymbal stand taped out. Chuck was furious for a couple of days but ended up forgiving me. I'd been focusing hard on getting his drums set up right without the mat as a *mea culpa*. When he got on stage, he made a few minor adjustments and seemed happy. I felt relieved.

I helped move a few amps forward to their rightful place. Guitarist Lynette Knackstedt gave me a sideways high five. "Thanks, *Carne*."

Everyone called me *Carne*, except for Gerry, who called me Sammy—
he loved the Sammy tapes almost as much as the Tantras Monsters did
—and Mike Park, who called me *Carnitas*.

Mike Park: future Ska Dad

I stood off to the side, next to Gerry and Lars. They blew quietly
into their trombones. I crouched, waiting for the show to start. Gerry
looked over at me. "Hi, I'm Sammy, do you have any *shodies?*" His
impression wasn't great, but his enthusiasm was spot on. It was weird
to have all this talk of Sammy with Kevin no longer around. He didn't
do merch anymore. Legendary Stockton/Modesto promoter Middagh
Goodwin the tour's merch guy. If you asked Middagh, he'd tell
you I was a terrible roadie. I disagree. Although the drum mat incident
proves his point. Ian Miller wasn't in the band either. Now it was Jay
Vance, formerly of The Blue Meanies. He played an upright electric
bass on stage and hopped around like an evil gnome. Jay had a

constant reservoir of manic energy. I thought he was funny. Several times on tour I'd declared him my best friend. He offered me his baked potato at Arby's in exchange for no longer being his best friend. I couldn't tell if he was joking.

First Avenue had a smaller 250 capacity venue attached called 7th Avenue, which had a separate show that night. All metal bands. It was packed in there, too. One of the opening bands saw Pickle sound check and got a glimpse of Lars' metal scream. This guy was a gruff, long-haired, muscular guy with a jean jacket and no shirt. He insisted that short-haired, clean-cut Lars hop on stage during their set and give the audience his best scream and devil horns. Lars agreed, showed the skeptical metal crowd what a real vicious metal screech sounded like and got an uproarious applause.

Back on stage, Gerry and Lars were fidgeting. Mike paced while Lynette looked down at her distortion pedal. Jay hopped up and down in anticipation of the show. The only thing left was for the club announcer to say their name. Those couple of moments felt like an hour. I stared down at the fifteen-hundred eager people crammed in that venue like an eight-piece ska band in a mini-van. They were from all walks of life, all ages, waiting in anticipation for Skankin' Pickle, just like I had done as often as possible the past three years. What other ska band was touring currently, drawing these kinds of numbers other than The Mighty Mighty Bosstones? My favorite band was on the verge of stardom.

Things fell apart for Skankin' Pickle not long after. I was supposed to roadie for them on a weekend trip to Santa Barbara, and they forgot to pick me up. I later found out they'd had a heavy band conversation before leaving. Mike was tired of touring. He wanted to slow down and focus on Dill Records. The rest of the band wanted to continue to tour hard. He gave them the option to pull back with him or go on without him. They went on without him. Those were his last shows. They played with Much, a band featuring Dustin Diamond, TV's Screech from Saved By The Bell. A strange ending.

The rest of the band did a few more tours, including their first ever trip to Europe, but then called it quits in 1996. Gerry joined MU330. Lars and Lynette started The 78 RPMs. Chuck, I heard, got into acting and Jay created Captured By Robots. Ian was playing in hardcore band Redemption 87. And Mike had started Asian Man Records. Rumor was, Kevin Dill was now Guttermouth's roadie. I could only imagine the shenanigans there.

"I'm Hulk Hogan, I'm losing all my hair!"

I saw Gerry every once in a while because I loved MU330, even more with him in it. We ran into each other at iMusicast in Oakland in 2005 while Mike and Dan Potthast were doing a West Coast Plea For Peace solo tour by way of bicycle, from Olympia, Washington to San Diego. At that show, Adam Davis' post-Link 80 not-ska band Desa were also on the bill. RX Bandits headlined. Gerry was driving behind Mike, Dan and a handful of friends. He brought gear and was available if anyone needed to stop riding their bike. He saw me before the show. I was outside smoking a cigarette. He was amazed. "Let's get a drink," he shouted, and carted me across the street, filling my pint glass as quickly as I could consume it. "Sammy likes beer," he announced, like a proud father.

Mike and I stayed good friends. I lived with him briefly in the late '90s. In 2013, he released my (and Adam's) band Gnarboots' debut full-length *A.L.B.U.M.* For our hidden track, we snuck in a cover of "Song #3," an old, fifty-two second Skankin' Pickle ska song where Mike laments about how hard it is to be a touring musician. Mike discovered it only after it was too late.

The whole reason Mike released *A.L.B.U.M.* was because we were friends, not because he thought he'd make a dime off us. Mike did that sometimes. He lost money on bands he was friends with because that's what friends do. He'd also reminded us at every step that he was losing money on us. His ruthless teasing turned into a bet where, if we broke even, he'd treat us to dinner at Sizzler. It was game on. Adam and I hustled hard and won. We went out for a fantastically mediocre Sizzler dinner and brought a professional photographer, Geoff Smith, to cover this important event in music history (Geoff even wore a laminated press badge!). When it was over, and it was time to pay, Mike couldn't believe how expensive Sizzler had gotten— we might as well have gone to a real steakhouse. Well, at least the salad was all-you-can-eat.

I didn't see anyone else from Skankin' Pickle after the band broke up, even Kevin. I'm not sure why we lost track. I bumped into him in 2010 at a WWF event in San Jose. I was walking toward the restroom and heard *"Carne!"* I turned around and saw Kevin pretending to look the other way. We briefly chatted before he ran off to scream at wrestlers.

I recently tracked Kevin down to discuss facets of this book. We interviewed for a couple hours at an arcade/gaming venue called Epicenter in Santa Rosa. After we chatted, we played a 3D circus zombie game and did a walk-through of the arcade. Kevin pointed out all the games Sammy Sody would like, like the Minions wack-a-mole and the Wizard of Oz air hockey table.

We passed by a big wall of flashing lights. Kevin urged me to play. "How?" I asked. He told me to jump as high as I could as soon as the game counted me off. So, I did. Nothing happened. He kept egging me on. "Jump, *Carne!* Jump! Jump as high as you can!" I got a few jumps in before I realized jumping wasn't the objective. You were supposed to hit the flashing lights as they lit up. Kevin fell over laughing. He'd tricked me. It was one of his most wholesome pranks.

Sweethearts: Mike Vianelle and Lynette Knackstedt

Someone told me that after the band broke up, Lynette moved to Gilroy, the nothing-town where I grew up. I also heard she worked as a mechanic. She died of a drug overdose in 2007.

My friend Mike Vianelle had a crush on Lynette in her Skankin' Pickle days. He talked about her in a lovesick, smitten way. He knew she was gay, but no matter, he had it bad for her. I told Kevin, who passed this message on to Lynette. She was delighted. She took several cute pictures with Mike, which made him blush *hard*. Mike then handed her his senior prom photo with her face pasted over his date's, something a serial killer would do. Lynette held it tight and hugged Mike. "I'm going to put this on my fridge." A few months later, Lynette's girlfriend approached Mike at a Pickle show, and frowned. "You...you're the guy in the photo."

Back then, when I went to see Skankin' Pickle as often as possible and hung out with the band, I never thought much about Lynette's sexual orientation. I now realize she was an LGBTQ pioneer when a large percentage of the country was uncomfortable with homosexuality. Ellen Degeneres came out on TV in 1997. Lynette was out in the late-80s. She was out and proud to the hundreds of people who saw Skankin' Pickle every night. "She was fearless," Lars told me recently. "She fought for it. Just getting out there and making sure everyone knows that it's cool to be gay. Look at me. You too, can do this kind of thing."

Lynette was a trailblazer, just like Mike, an Asian-American singing lead vocal in a band at a time when there wasn't any representation at all. It wasn't just a gimmick for him to call Asian-American people on stage while he sang "Asian Man." He was sending a message, that they could break away from society's stereotypes and expectations of who Asians were supposed to be. For a lot of kids, it was a powerful message. "I would bring them on stage because there were so few of us," Mike told me. "I wanted to make a point in singling them out. That was super important from day one. I wanted people to know." For many people, Mike was the first Asian-American they saw on stage playing in a crazy punk band, and it inspired them.

After Pickle, he started a side project, The Chinkees, an all-Asian ska-punk band. In 2017, an all-Asian band from Portland called The Slants made a lot of press for recontextualizing a slur for their band name. Mike did it in 1998.

I couldn't help but think about Lynette and how she never got the accolades she deserved. The world she lived in during Skankin' Pickle wasn't friendly to open lesbians. She never hid herself. She wore rainbows. She talked about "cute girls" on stage. After playing in 78 RPMs for a brief time, she left the spotlight just as more musicians and celebrities were coming out and receiving praise as LGBTQ heroes.

Skankin' Pickle never had a reunion. There was too much post-band tension. Mike played a Bruce Lee Band show in 2014 at Bottom of the Hill, perhaps the closest thing there would ever be. He brought Lars and Gerry to join him on stage, along with Dan Potthast, Jeff Rosenstock, Kevin Higuchi, and John DeDomenici. They played songs all over Mike's catalog, including Pickle songs.

I was at the show that night. At first, I pushed as close to the front of the stage as I could, to make Mike laugh with my over-the-top dance moves. But when I heard the old Skankin' Pickle songs, the urge to goof around melted away. I just wanted to dance my heart out to my favorite band.

Gerry closed out the set with "Hulk Hogan." He's a big strong beast of a nerd and does a killer impression of Hulk Hogan. He was so winded, he spit out lyrics that were mostly gibberish. Lars put on his wrestling mask and somewhat cautiously wrestled Gerry. Mike got in and did a roundhouse kick to Gerry's chest, which left a bruise. Near the end, Gerry did what he always did during the song, and ripped his shirt off. The crowd cheered wildly. It was a satisfying gimmick we all knew was coming and couldn't wait to see.

The world missed out on Skankin' Pickle. When I asked Mike about Pickle's legacy recently, he told me they could've been the Fugazi of ska. Maybe that's true, but we'll never know. Would they have been swept up in the MTV ska craze too? I doubt it. Real misfits stay misfits.

LAND OF SKA

Alex and I walk around a large football field in Oaxaca, Mexico. There's a stage on either side and a makeshift sound system. A group called Los Rude Boys are dressed in their nicest suits and hippest sunglasses, skanking back and forth on Stage One as they play a bouncy 2 Tone style ska song. They shout *"Sin policia"* ("no police") and *"derribar el capitalismo"* ("tear down capitalism") between upbeats. The crowd of teenagers and early twenty-somethings vehemently shout along to what sounds like a call to action. After their set, we wander to Stage Two where plain-t-shirt-wearing slackers Royal Club play a grimy surf-punk ska song that sounds vaguely familiar. It hits me. They're covering Mephiskapheles' silly '90s ska classic "Bumble Bee Tuna," but in Spanish. When the chorus comes up, instead of singing about how Bumble Bee Tuna is yum yum yum, they forego words altogether, singing: "La la la la la la la la la la." The crowd enthusiastically skank-dances in a tight mosh-pit-circle.

There's food, beer, and t-shirt vendors sprinkled along the fence, and several large wooden planks randomly sprouting up in the football field, spray-painted with different wacky cartoon characters: an orange-blue fox with Tom Cruise shades and a sleek porkpie hat, a pink octopus with lighting beams shooting from its piercing eyeballs, and a shirtless muscle man with an oversized sombrero and pink tentacle beard. Each sign has the name of this ska festival painted in large boxy letters: "Skatlón."

Alex and I met at the Oaxacan airport a few days ago. We haven't seen each other in over a decade, ever since he moved to Michigan. For the past couple of years, we've talked about doing a Flat Planet reunion. I left the band in '95. Alex kept it going a little longer, but then it came to its natural end. We can't get all the old members to commit to a proper reunion, so it hasn't happened. Now here Alex and I are in Mexico, skanking to ska bands, and eating as much food as we possibly can. It feels like the Flat Planet reunion that coulda/shoulda/woulda been, even if it's just the two of us. Especially yesterday, when we roamed the streets of Oaxaca, doing nothing but eating, and talking about tour memories. But now the food is better.

That first morning, Alex asked a street vendor in the town center where the best food was. The vendor didn't hesitate. "*Paseo De Carne*," and pointed a few blocks over. Alex and I looked at each other in shock. *Pathway of the Meat?* This was our walkabout!

We found *Paseo De Carne* with a little exploring. Pounds of uncooked meat dangling from dozens of vendor carts. We chose the savoriest cuts and sat at a cramped booth with strangers, all of us waiting for baskets filled with juicy asada, tortillas, and salsas. We dug in like two *cochinas*. A woman stared at us gorging and Alex exclaimed, "*Tenemos mucho hambre porque nuestras esposas no nos alimentan!*" (We are hungry because our wives don't feed us!) She laughed, shaking her head.

Oaxacan food was amazing. However, we noticed an assortment of hamburger stands all over downtown. Alex pulled a vendor aside and pointed at the kiosk. "*Para los gringos?*" The guy laughed but didn't answer. Here at Skatlón, we see yet another burger stand and no *gringos* but us. Alex can't resist. "I have to try one of these burgers." We watch as a thin, frozen, cafeteria patty sizzles on the grill, and then gets placed on a bun with three slices of deli ham. Ham? What's going on, Oaxaca? Alex takes two bites and throws it away. I don't even want to try it.

It's early afternoon, and there's a few thousand people walking around. Later, as the sun begins to set, and Mexico City ska band Nana Pancha takes the stage, there will be roughly ten-thousand people all skanking along as Nana Pancha blasts through their Less

Than Jake inspired punk-ska songs. We munch on Oaxacan tamales and contemplate the skanking force of a ten-thousand ska show.

Our fixer for the day is a middle-aged rocker named Chava Rock, who I later learn runs a ska-heavy YouTube channel. When we met him, he was surprised to hear we wanted to interview Mexican ska bands. He said, *"En Mexico, El ska no es una tendencia; es un estilo de vida."* ("Ska isn't a trend in Mexico. It's a lifestyle.")

Skacore Invasion, 2018

When Nana Pancha lead singer Abraham Torres takes the stage, he looks out at the crowd. Clouds are forming after a long, hot, humid day. Torres shouts, *"Si llueve, no vas a dejar de bailar, ¿Verdad?"* (If it rains, you're not going to stop dancing, right?) They roar back, a verbal agreement to dance no matter what Mother Nature throws their way. Rain interrupts the set twenty minutes later, but the audience keeps their word.

Torres wears a thick jacket and remains stationary as he monot-ones like The Specials' Terry Hall. The horn players and bassist dance with crazy energy. Guitarist Chilly Willy swoops his arms around like he's surfing the largest wave of his life with a continuously shocked expression. People in the crowd call out to him repeatedly: "Chilly Willy! Chilly Willy!"

14

After midnight, headliners Sekta Core stand at the side of the stage, ready to perform. Over the sound system, Ministry's "Stigmata" blasts through the speakers. A film projected on a flimsy screen dangling behind the drums plays a collage of disturbing imagery: a still beating heart pulled out of someone's chest, gory Looney Tunes parodies, flash-cuts of '80s era Satanic rituals, sped up footage of animal carcasses decaying. The band enters the stage in Druid cloaks and demonic makeup. They begin with doom metal with mid-tempo ska breaks and brutal blast beats. Co-lead singer Jorge Salcedo removes his cloak. His body is saturated in tattoos. A large Satanic emblem covers his back. Etched on his stomach are the words: *"Ska-core o Muerte"* (Ska-core or death).

Chava Rock is with us backstage, contemplating the success of the day's festival. He comments that this 10K sized festival is small, but *okay* for Oaxaca's first attempt at a ska festival. Ones in Mexico City draw twenty-five thousand people and more. I don't recall ska festivals in the US bringing these kinds of crowds, even during the '90s.

Here we are in 2019, almost twenty-five years after many of these bands formed: Nana Pancha, Tremenda Korte, Salón Victoria, and Sekta Core. Mexico's two biggest ska bands, Inspector and Panteón Rococó, are on their own tours at the moment, but Skatlón are still selling their shirts. Ska is the biggest it's ever been here in Mexico, probably the biggest ska scene in the world.

A friend of mine, Rick Maciel, an artist and musician from Querétaro, Mexico that goes by the name Halo Between, once told me, "Mexico is the land of ska." After tonight, I believe him.

We Don't Do Spanish Rock Here

A few years earlier, in 2015, I drove down to Lincoln Park in East LA to see the Los Angeles "SkaWars" festival. I was on assignment with *Playboy*, covering LA's Latino ska scene. I got a tip about it from Voodoo Glow Skull guitarist Eddie Casillas. Once I saw it, I was amazed. It was sold out with three-thousand kids in a park, dancing to ska. People had to be turned away!

Lincoln Park is in the heart of East L.A., surrounded by taquerias and markets. I showed up at noon and looked around the tranquil park. Families picnicked. Children played on the swing set. Teenagers rode their skateboards. After walking around a few minutes, I spotted the outdoor community center La Plaza De La Raza where the concert was taking place. It was the most DIY festival I'd ever seen. Two stages; one traditional and the other barely propped off the ground in the back corner in true punk rock fashion. Most of the audience were between sixteen-to-twenty-five, with folks in their thirties and forties showing up later in the evening. The younger audience members mashed up hodgepodge styles as their own: a girl with a bright pink mohawk, 2 Tone suspenders and pale goth makeup. A dude with shaggy, dark hair reaching down to his lower back, pointy metal bracelets, stoned eyes and a Sublime shirt.

The only vendors I saw were a local ma 'n' pa Taqueria, one I drove by earlier that day, that had a line looped around the Plaza, a Thrasher booth and a couple guys in the back selling random band t-shirts: Operation Ivy, Bad Brains, Slayer, System of a Down, Wu Tang Clan. And my favorite, one that said simply, "I Love Ska."

The audience was primarily Latino, though random white, Black and Asian kids were around. The audience members came from the nearby East LA, South Gate, South Central, Boyle Heights, Inglewood and Lynwood neighborhoods, and well as Santa Ana, Inland Empire, and the San Fernando Valley. Kids skanked in a circle while singing along to the bands, in English and Spanish. These were local bands mostly. La Resistencia, South Central Skankers, The Delirians, Steady 45s, and Viernes 13. The bands played everything from '60s style Jamaican ska and rocksteady to brutal punk-ska and ska-pop-rock to offbeat prog-math-rock-inspired-ska. One interesting component was the prevalence of metal. You'd hear a band playing 2 Tone ska with Lamb of God blast beats wedged in the middle, something I've never seen outside of these bands.

At the center of it all is Clemente Ruiz, a short unassuming guy ten years younger than me. Under the banner Evoekore Media, he booked this festival. In 2015, the festival had been happening just under a decade. He also books a similar, punkier, festival known as "LA Skacore Invasion." He puts on several non-festival ska shows all year long. He's the drummer of La Resistencia, and when he's not involved with LA's ska scene, he's riding along with artists like Deftones, Blink 182, Post-Malone and Pepe Aguilar, working in the creative fields and mixing music. What's happening in LA is more than just a genre of music or a regional take on ska; it's its own distinct subculture that pulls from Mexico and the U.S., mixing it up and creating something new. "I grew up listening to bands like Voodoo Glow Skulls, Madness, The Specials, Reel Big Fish, Less Than Jake," Ruiz says. "But I also grew up listening to Sekta Core, Panteón Rococó, Maldita Vecindad, and Nana Pancha. I absorbed both worlds."

It's about more than just the music, which is why it's so alive and continues to grow. It is truly the best of L.A. in a nutshell. "People dress a certain way. They dance together. Most of them are bilingual, but you see all ethnicities: African-American punk-rockers, straight up Mexican people that don't speak English or even Mexican kids that don't speak any Spanish. It's a clash of many different ethnicities and languages. That's something that makes us very different."

It's also the byproduct of many years of evolution. Ska seeped into LA's Latino communities in the early '90s. It was a component of the growing *Rock en Espanol* scene that kicked off at Hong Kong Low, an '80s punk rock venue in LA's Chinatown. Some of the bands included Los Olvidados and Las 15 Letras. Bands played a variety of styles, with ska being one component. These bands took influence from the rock bands from Mexico that toured through LA. Some of them like La Maldita Vencidad and Tijuana No fused ska in their music. "All of Latin America was discovering that we could play rock in Spanish," says Martin Sanchez of Las 15 Letras. "Because of the few ska songs that we have, people considered us a ska band. They always counted the disco songs as ska as well because they could dance around and skank the same way."

By the mid-90s, ska was gaining interest all over the Spanish-speaking world. Chris Acosta from New York band N.Y. Citizens, who also worked at Moon Records, took notice of this trend after visiting relatives in Barcelona. He curated two compilations for Moon called *100% Latin Ska*. Prior to these comps, ska kids in the US were completely unaware of ska's ascension in the Spanish world. "There's bands from Italy, Argentina, Venezuela, and New York," Acosta says of the bands he assembled for his comps. "I thought it was interesting that this was a parallel universe going on." Tijuana No! made a stab at the US market in the mid-90s. "We see ourselves as an extension of the voice for the poor and the disadvantaged," percussionist Teca Garcia told the *LA Times* in 1997. It didn't resonate with the US audience.

Acosta also got Moon to release Puerto Rican ska band Los Pies

Negros, who formed in 1991. Their name, translated to "Those Black Feet" refers to "the black feet that are freed from the chains of slavery, and racial discrimination from having a different skin color," bassist and founder Werner Rodriguez tells me. Rodriguez discovered ska by way of The Specials and Bad Manners by sharing tapes with friends in other countries. "I was really impacted by the sound," he says. Acosta brought the group up to the Skavoovee Festival at S.O.B.s in 1994 alongside Toasters, Scofflaws, and King Chango—their first show ever. They also played in Connecticut with Spring Heeled Jack. The group got a great response, but their 1994 album *Moviendo Los Pies* and the two *100% Latin* comps didn't sell well. Moon's primarily English-speaking ska audience didn't connect with it.

Meanwhile, an actual ska scene was growing in Latino neighborhoods in LA in the late-90s, one completely undetected by the rest of the country. Ruiz's band La Resistencia was one of these early bands. Ska was hot in Orange County and Hollywood, but the Latino bands got brushed off by the bigger venues. "The established promoters in LA would never look at us. When we went to the House of Blues, the talent buyer at the time automatically assumed it was *Rock en Español*. He told us, 'We don't do Spanish rock here.' He would blow us off like that," says Ruiz. "I'm like, 'We're not Spanish rock. We can play with bands like Reel Big Fish.' They wouldn't even look at us."

Ruiz and the other bands built their own scene. It started in back-yards, alongside punk and metal. At first, they would be one ska band among five metal groups. "The metalheads would clown us. They would say 'The marching band is here.' It was never in a negative way. Metalheads are always clowns." Soon there was enough ska bands that they'd put on stacked backyard shows with six-to-seven bands per bill, two-dollar ticket and three-hundred kids squeezed in someone's back-yard, hanging out, drinking 40s and moshing. "It was always a bunch of high school friends getting together to enjoy their weekend," says Angel Salgado of The Delirians, a group from this scene that has mastered old school Jamaican grooves better than anyone else. "The cops would show up and shut it down."

In the early 2000s, while still in high school, Ruiz was booking as many shows in backyards and random spaces as he could. It was take-what-you-can-get as far as the spaces went. Then in 2001, a friend told him about a coffee shop in Lynwood called Our House. The owner, an older guy in his sixties named John Riley (who co-owned the space with his wife Corey Shoemaker), initially held acoustic shows there. Once he decided to allow electric shows there, he invited Ruiz to throw shows, but with some restrictions. Shows needed to be over by 8 p.m. and only thirteen-to-seventeen-year-olds were allowed. Attendance for the shows grew and gradually Riley let Ruiz and the other promoters go past 8 p.m., play louder and have people eighteen or older. Ruiz did sound, even when it wasn't his shows. Other people that booked at Our House included One Shot Records, Jorge Leal, and Warning Productions. In late 2001, the City shut the venue down because it had gotten so popular. Kids from out of the area would show up and drink on the street before and after the show. Never inside the venue. Alcohol wasn't permitted.

In late 2002, Riley and Shoemaker bought an old movie theater in Southgate called Allen Theater with the express purpose of putting on all-ages live shows, and with Ruiz doing live sound. He let a similar batch of promoters book the shows. Jorge Leal did ska and some Spanish rock. He was able to pull in bands from Mexico. Roland Mora booked metal shows. One Shot Records booked punk hardcore, psychobilly and ska music. Ruiz booked most of the ska shows. The first Allen Theater show was well attended, but no one was allowed to dance—they learned that they needed a dancing permit, which Riley quickly took care of after that show. The Allen Theater lasted until early 2007 with no alcohol sales and five-hundred-person capacity. It stayed alive with people from these different scenes all supporting it. In his time, Ruiz promoted shows for bands like Mighty Mighty Bosstones and Sekta Core. They played two consecutive sold-out shows. "It survived solely on door sales, which is hard to do," Ruiz says. "Lighting, sound, was all ok. There wasn't many venues, so a lot of people came out. Shows were a reason to come together and socialize. A lot of people came just because they liked the music and community."

The Allen Theater, 2003

As this scene was building at the Allen Theater, Ruiz thought to put on festivals with the same DIY spirit as the backyard shows. He created the annual Skacore Invasion in 2005. A few years later, he started SkaWars. "It just hit me. We need to put together an all-day event. It had to be outdoors. The roots of our music are well-connected to the backyard scene. There's just something that's different than playing inside a venue," Ruiz says.

Ruiz connected with bands from Mexico first rather than the U.S., since they were more open to this scene. Eventually, he was able to convince some bookers that these shows were going to be better than anything they'd book in Orange County. Leftover Crack, Mustard Plug, Buck-o-Nine and The Toasters have all played Ruiz's shows. The Voodoo Glow Skulls, though technically outsiders, were honorary members of this scene and have played a bunch of the show as far back as the Allen Theater days. In the '90s, they were one of the only mainstream US ska bands featuring mostly Latino members. "When I heard Voodoo, I was like, this is the best of both worlds. It's punk rock with horns and the drums are driven. For a lot of LA people, Voodoo was a band that was a major influence," Ruiz says. The Voodoo Glow Skulls weren't aware of what was happening in East L.A. until Ruiz promoted them at The Allen Theater, but it made sense. "Los Angeles might as well be the sister city to Mexico City. There's a lot of Latinos in LA. That's why that scene is so huge," says Casillas. "You get more immigrants that come from Mexico. Then you get the influence of Voodoo Glow Skulls and Sekta Core, and you end up with that scene. I'm not surprised that it turned into that. It seems to be thriving. I was waiting for it to die out, but there's always new bands."

A Funny Sound

In 2019, backstage at Skatlón, Nana Pancha singer Abraham Torres and bass player Arturo Salinas sit with Alex and I over traditional Oaxacan *tlayudas* and discuss the band's formation in 1996. Their name "Nana Pancha" comes from a song in the popular 1954 film *Escuela De Vagabundos*. In the '90s, they were teenagers living in a poor Mexico City neighborhood. Their one respite from the violence and starvation around them was watching MTV on a stolen cable box. The music videos that grabbed their attention were the punk-ska bands blowing up in the US. "It was a funny sound. This upbeat music got our attention," Salinas tells us. "For Nana Pancha to even exist, MTV was very important. Without MTV we wouldn't have gotten influences like Rancid, Voodoo Glow Skulls, Suicide Machines, Less Than Jake, The Specials, No Doubt."

I'm not one for talk of waves in ska, but if people are going to insist there's a Fourth Wave, it's Mexican ska, or MexSka as it is commonly known. The MexSka bands that formed in the mid-90s, like Nana Pancha, were largely influenced by '90s Third Wave. And they took that and created their own distinct culture from it. When I tell people that ska is huge in Mexico, they assume it's somehow related to the country's proximity to Jamaica and their interest in dance rhythms like cumbia. That's not the case. MexSka is the natural of extension of the US's '90s ska. And because of MTV and Third Wave's influence, most MexSka bands dress in a style more reminiscent of '90s grunge than snappy suit wearing Jamaican rude boys.

Ska had been around Mexico for a while, but never as an organized and exciting scene the way Torres and Salinas witnessed on MTV—certainly never one that was identified as "ska." There were Mexican musicians that date back to the '60s that played ska, like Toño Quirazco y Su Grupo, who plays, arguably, the best version of "Jamaica Ska," in Spanish of course, over a bouncy orchestra. The forefathers of modern Mexican ska are La Maldita Vecindad y los Hijos del Quinto Patio, a group who formed in Mexico City in 1985 and embraced pachuco clothing (Mexican-American style of the '50s). For La Maldita, ska was one ingredient of many, an ingredient they themselves knew little about, though they did gather bits of the culture from the occasional 2 Tone song that trickled into Mexico; Maldita saw their music as a fusion of sounds that happened during their creative process. Few people in Mexico referred to Maldita as a ska band. They were part of Mexico's *Rock en Espanol* surge alongside groups like Maná and El Tri, who were recontextualizing rock music using Mexican elements, singing in Spanish, and addressing issues important to their culture. Yet, Maldita influenced a lot of bands that came after them to experiment with ska rhythms when playing rock.

Ska, as an ingredient, grew in Mexico and Latin America in the late '80s and early '90s with groups like Tijuana No! (Tijuana) and Los Fabulosos Cadillacs (Buenos Aires). The MexSka bands came next but they were much more of an underground thing. They might have forever been lost in obscurity were it not for Pepe Lobo ("El Padre del MexSka"), a soft-spoken, plainly dressed man who championed the music. He was one of the few rude boys in Mexico in the '80s that had extensive knowledge about ska music from trading tapes with people in other countries. Another important figure was Miguel Tajobase, an '80s punk rocker who fell in love with ska after catching La Maldita in concert and hearing a recording of Madness' "One Step Beyond" (or "Un Paso Adelante" as Madness' Chas Smith recorded several version of his vocals in foreign languages in 1980).

Pepe Lobo originally edited and sold books and cassettes at "La Lagunilla," a Sunday market in Mexico City. As the '90s progressed he moved towards selling tapes and focused on ska music. Tajobase started selling crust punk tapes in 1990, usually whatever he could get his hands on from overseas. In the mid-90s, both men had gotten booths to sell tapes at the popular Saturday flea market "El Chopo," a curious place where swaths of punks, goths, metalheads, hippies and rude boys co-mingled. At El Chopo, you could purchase obscure bootlegs, fanzines, and patches for all your favorite weirdo bands. For mid-90s ska fans, it was *the* place to find music and merch. Once Tajobase was selling tapes at El Chopo, his inventory included more ska tapes than crust punk. He would write directly to US ska bands and record labels he read about in *Maximum Rocknroll* with the help of his guitarist in his group Revuelta Propia, who spoke good English. Less Than Jake, Skankin' Pickle, Let's Go Bowling, Hepcat, Dance Hall Crashers, etc. Lobo on the other hand focused on finding Mexico's homegrown bands, recording them and selling their cassettes directly to their audience.

Most of these MexSka bands, like Nana Pancha, were just forming in the mid-90s, though a few had started as early as 1992. When Acosta was putting together the *100% Latin* comps, he didn't feature a single Mexican band on either one since these bands were still new and playing underground spaces. A third *100% Latin Ska* comp was planned for 1998 and was supposed to include a Revuelta Propia track, but Acosta's house burnt down and with it all of Volume 3's contributions.

These mid-90s MexSka bands separated themselves from the few '80s Mexican ska bands with a couple important distinctions: their musical diversity, their scrappy attitude and their punk rock approach to playing instruments with no prior experience. With the MexSka bands there was almost no hint of traditional ska even though they were the first Mexican bands to promote themselves as "ska." The fans gravitated to this label as well. They referred to themselves as skaceros and skatos, many of whom were skateboarding kids that wore small backpacks, and baggy pants. Within this subculture, some of the kids brought their Elmo dolls into the pit with them. It symbolized "lost childhood" since they spent their formative years on the streets.

By early 1996, the MexSka shows were small, with a handful of bands on every lineup, and the same few promoters putting on shows at bars, parties and alternative spaces. One of the first ska festivals in Mexico happened in 1996 at Alicia Cultural Multiforo in Mexico City, a co-production by the venue and the bands. It was called "Skalicia." It drew thousands of people and solidified this collection of ska bands as a movement. In 1997, Jesus Arriaga from ska band Inspector organized his own festival in Monterrey. "At the time, ska was not known in Monterrey. I invited bands from Mexico City so people could learn about them. People responded really well," Arriaga says. It drew ten-thousand people. Despite this and several more festivals that occurred in Mexico City with huge numbers, Mexico's recording industry was uninterested in ska. "The bands of those times, all aspired to sign to a label, and there was no label for this genre, nor interest from producers," Tajobase says.

The term "MexSka" was coined by several of the bands during a meeting in mid-1998 prior to "ReSkatando V.I.H.das," a Mexico City festival that drew a whopping fifteen-thousand people. At least one member of each popular band was in attendance. The term "MexSka" played off of "MexSide," a label for the North Mexican hip-hop subgenre.

The bands by this point had gelled into a full-on scene with a rabid audience. MexSka bands mostly retained the joyous, infectious sound of Third Wave ska, which Torres describes as "festive," but lyrically it was a different story. The groups weren't singing odes to their favorite foods and screaming about suburban isolation; Mexican ska bands spoke about the harsh realities of their lives, income inequality and the evils of the Mexican government—they took a stand more so than bands in other Mexican scenes. "Ska became popular in poor neighborhoods because we sing about the problematic system they live in. Mainstream radio doesn't represent how life really is in Mexico," Torres says. "We were raised in a rough neighborhood. There's a lot of delinquencies, a lot of assassinations, drug usage, prostitution, and social unrest. There's people that have nothing to eat. We talk about social issues because no one else will."

Many of the MexSka bands, as well as some punk and alternative bands, held concerts in support of the Zapatistas, who were protesting government policies negatively impacting Mexico's indigenous population. These concerts raised money for food and supplies to help the Zapatistas as they fought and brought awareness to the movement. Maldita Vecindad formed the organization "Paz, Baile y Resistencia" in support of the Zapatista's goals. Other bands that were involved included Sekta Core, Nana Pancha, Salón Victoria, Los de Abajo, Royal Club, and Panteón Rococó. MTV recorded and aired some of these concerts. "We did a lot for the movement. Together Sekta Core and the Zapatista movement grew with each other," says Sekta Core singer Jorge Salcedo. "It was a hard fight. Mexico at the time was very mixed up politically and with that carried a lot of problems."

It's no coincidence that MexSka became so political. It came up in the mid-90s as the country was in turmoil. "There was a high unemployment among the youth. The value of our currency depreciated, and the rise of the Zapatistas occurred in the highlands of Chiapas. This injected rage to the youth of society. In that environment, the MexSka bands began," Tajobase says. "There were practically no bands in the rock world that addressed this, or would criticize society, as practically all the bands of the MexSka movement did."

Where Is The Quinceañera Going To Be?

Pepe Lobo first approached Sekta Core in 1996 about making their cassette, *Terrorismo Kasero*. No one else was interested. Immediately, it sold like hot cakes. After that, he produced Le Tremenda Korte's *Orden En La Sala*, Pateon Rococo's *Toloache Pa' mi Negra* and Nana Pancha's *Nana Pancha*. Lobo recorded these tapes with Juan Carlos Hernández ("El Loco") as the producer. Every tape sold surprisingly well. Lobo only expected to sell three-hundred copies of Nana Pancha's debut tape but sold twelve-thousand after it got some unexpected radio play.

Arriaga recalls meeting Lobo when Inspector came to Mexico City in 1997 to play "Alicia." The band was so broke, they didn't have enough money to return to Monterrey. Lobo offered to buy their tickets home in exchange for recording the show that night, and turning it into one-thousand cassettes, calling it *Ska Live!* The band agreed to these terms.

In 1998, word spread to a lot more people about MexSka through Pepe Lobo's first *Skuela De Baile* CD compilation. That first volume had amazing tracks by Nana Pancha, Salon Victoria, Revuelta Propia and Inspector.

Lobo captured the raw energy of the MexSka groups, still mostly teenagers, and largely living in poverty. Of them, Sekta Core was the most musically intense, and one of the most outspoken of the oppressive government. "Our main message is we are against stupidity in all places—and the government is the biggest player in stupidity," Salcedo tells me. Sekta Core formed in 1994, originally calling themselves Sekta. Later they heard about The Mighty Mighty Bosstones' album *Ska-Core, the Devil, and More*. Without hearing it, they connected to the idea of "ska-core." They added "core" to their name and embraced the ska-core genre description. "We started to play a harder version of ska," Salcedo says. "Since the music is a lot harder, the message comes out harder."

Early Sekta Core was less political with mostly fictitious stories the members imagined. But they realized that the real world where they lived was more compelling than anything they could fabricate. Drummer Miguel Rizo told *Vice* in 2019, "Some of our songs could have been written by our neighbors. We are the reflection of everything that happens. That is why I feel that many people identify with what we say."

Los Pies Negro were unaware of the MexSka scene happening, and that they were beloved by its fans. The first time they played Mexico was in 1999 at the first "Latin America Ska Festival" in Deportivo Leandro Valle in Mexico City. Los Pies may have done fine when they visited the US, but in Mexico they were stars, which surprised them. "Mexico is the place we have more fans, more friends; when we play in Mexico, we feel we are home. We feel comfortable," Rodriguez says.

At the first "Latin America Ska Festival," Los Pies met Lobo. He was hanging out with the bassist of La Tremenda Korte and approached them. They talked at length about ska and Lobo offered to distribute Los Pies Negros music in Mexico. The next year, Rodriguez returned and gave Lobo the masters to Los Pies Negros first two albums and Lobo began to distribute them, which increased the band's popularity in Mexico exponentially.

Sekta Core was the first MexSka band to sign to a major. "Pepe Lobo found us playing in clubs. We went from cassette straight to Sony," says Salcedo. That album, 1997's *Morbos Club* is a monster of an album. The title refers to how violent and gory the TV stations and newspapers were at the time, so much that it desensitizes you. The record is an urban chronicle of Mexico City, commenting on the murder and corruption. Rizo recalls eating dinner and watching a story on the news about a missing man that was found days later after already decomposing beyond recognition. "It didn't matter if you found a dead person in the street. We were used to seeing it in the newspaper. It's still very normal today. That is why *Morbos Club* represents everything that was happening at that time," Rizo told *Vice*. The second album they recorded with Sony, *Infierno*, was even bigger and produced by Oingo Boingo bassist John Avila.

On the other end of the spectrum was Inspector. More personal than political, they were one of the few bands to embrace the 2 Tone sound and rude boy fashion, something that MexSka fans understood very little about. "When we went out to play, wearing dark suits, with a tie or suspenders, the most common comment was 'Where is the *quinceañera* going to be?' Obviously, it was not known that it had to do with the musical genre," Inspector keyboardist Homer Ontiveros wrote in a *La Zona Sucia* piece in 2017. The group's 1998 album *Black and White,* released by Lobo, is a benchmark for 2 tone style ska in Mexico, a critical album for Mexico's small scene of skinheads and rude boys. It greatly increased Inspector's fanbase. It also earned them a record deal with Universal.

In 1999, Panteón Rococó's *A la Izquierda de la Tierra* was a huge hit, and the first ska album to cross-over into the pop realm, particularly the lovesick "La Dosis Perfecta" which earned them a record deal with BMG Mexico. They quickly became pop stars. Nana Pancha were offered a record deal but didn't take it because the contract stated that the label would literally own the music "in all the world and the galaxy and the galaxies that will be discovered." To this day, they are glad they didn't sign that contact.

Inspector hit big in 2001 with *Alma en Fuego,* particularly the song "Amnesia," which featured Roco of Maldita Vencidad and Ruben of Café Tacuba on vocals. Following "Amnesia," the next single "Amargo Adios" hit hard. It became a phenomenon. To this day, you can hear mariachi bands all over covering the song and Inspector's original is often blasted in soccer stadiums.

Many rock fans and critics didn't find MexSka worthy of their praise, referring to it as "pachangueras" meaning trashy, neighborhood party music. The thought was that since the ska beat was more closely associated with traditional rhythms like cumbia, salsa, or merengue, it wasn't as modern, cultured and exciting as rock. In 2003, Mexican rap-rock band Molotov famously put ska down as less sophisticated music, saying that rock is *cultura* and ska is *agricultura.*

As the rich and middle-class kids mocked ska, the genre continued to maintain a close alignment with politics and the struggle of the poor. "The upper-class people like saying that people that listen to ska are a bunch of idiots and have no class. But ska is one of the few genres that brings social awareness and a social consciousness through music." Ska music stands in stark contrast to much of the culture in Mexico. "In Mexico, people are very ashamed to speak their minds.

They've been taught to not rock the boat. Ska is a political tool," says Salinas. "Our message is to not be embarrassed."

Many hip-hop artists come from the same poor neighborhoods as these ska bands, and plenty of them rap about the harsh realities of their environment. But rap often encouraged a culture of status, and as many rappers gained fame, they embraced money and flaunted their rich lifestyle in their music. With ska bands, many continued to live in the neighborhoods they grew up in, putting money back into the community instead of into purchasing fancy cars. "Ska artists have a different ideology in how they carry themselves in public," Torres says. "We would rather spend our money helping the kids in our neighborhoods get educated. Better jobs. That's the real difference between rappers and ska bands."

Not Just The Rude Boys

Skatlon Festival, 2019

After the first few major ska festivals in Mexico City, promoters got in on the action and put on bigger festivals, drawing sometimes twenty-thousand people, more than other "popular" genres. Meanwhile, most of the MexSka bands only had DIY tapes out on Pepe Lobo Rekords. The promoters of these festivals were ripping the bands off. Torres says they played massive festivals and received the equivalent of $5-$25 US dollars per band. Most were too young and naïve to know better.

Bands eventually grew tired of being taken advantage of and stopped working with exploitive promoters. They decided to put on their own shows, even if that meant playing smaller venues. Ska music dipped in popularity in the mid-2000s. Many of the bands lost their deals and were back to either small labels or self-releasing music, but they still played live as often as possible. These shows got bigger each year, until, by the early 2010s, the festivals returned. The bands were either putting them on themselves or working with promoters that paid a decent fee.

Flat Planet "reunion," Oaxaca, Mexico,

In the past five years, ska has gotten bigger in Mexico than it's *ever* been, even compared to the early 2000s when the bands were all over the radio. Huge international ska festivals cropped up. Non-Stop Ska began in 2016 specifically to attract the top tier international bands like Skatalites and The Specials. Co-creator José Luis Olan 'Deals' came up as a kid helping Pepe Lobo pack records and would practice his trumpet at his "El Chopo" booth. He aimed to make Non-Stop Ska the biggest ska festival in the world. And it's worked. Tajobase puts it best: "Mexico City has become the ska capital of the world." Ska is so ubiquitous in Mexico that you hear it everywhere. There are ska fanatics, and then there's just people that like the music and know nothing about it. "A lot of people in Mexico are fans of Inspector but they don't know ska," says Arriaga. "Ska music is for all people, not just the rude boys and skinheads. Grandmothers, kids, all the family members like Inspector."

Panteón Rococó and Inspector have gotten so big that they are in the top ten bands of all Mexican rock. In 2015, Panteón Rococó became the first Latin American rock band to fill Arena de la Ciudad de México, one of the largest stadiums in Mexico City with twenty-five thousand people, as they celebrated their twentieth anniversary as a band. As to why ska is so huge in Mexico, Deals gives his thoughts to *Vice.* "There is no clear definition of ska. People who go to Non-Stop Ska are people who really like rhythm."

In some ways, ska took a similar path in Mexico as it did in the US. It started out as a vibrant underground scene that shot up to the mainstream where it was loved by its fans and mocked by the "cool" people. Then it fell back underground and continued to be supported by hardcore fans. But where it diverged from the US, is that it returned bigger than ever, and has become a fundamental part of the fabric of modern Mexican music. Ska has gained a place in nearly every Spanish-speaking country and in Latino communities in the US. It's a part of their culture now. Lots of people have offered me their theory as to why this is the case. But it really boils down to a willingness to love music that moves you, and to not care about what other people think.

"One of the problems with the Anglo scene is they're into fads," says Martin Sanchez of LA band Las 15 Letras. "When it comes to Latinos, we have that thing where we like something because we like it. We hold it to our hearts. Metal is still huge in Latin America. Metal fans have been metal fans forever. Everything becomes fads here [in the US]. That's why in Latin America, you still have a huge ska scene. In Mexico it is still strong. It continues to be strong."

2 Tone Army

Ska cuts through all cultures. At the Skatlón festival, I watch a band, Memoria Insuficiente, one of the few bands that are from outside of Mexico—Colombia to be exact. They're covering "2 Tone Army" by The Toasters, but in Spanish. In this moment I realize how complex culture is and how it's all captured in this style of music I love. I am listening to a song written by a New York band that references a British record label that revived Jamaican music. It's being played by a Columbian band and enjoyed by Mexican teenagers who are singing along joyfully. I can't even wrap my head around the incredible journey encased in this one song.

Everyone who loves ska has an opinion on what ska is supposed to be, and what makes something real ska or not. It can be fast, slow, politically potent, silly, cathartic. None of that matters in the face of this show where ten-thousand people embrace ska as part of their identity, and dance just like Alex and I did when we were their age. Everything else is just noise.

This beat that originated in Jamaica in the '50s has carried over decade after decade, from country to country, and blended with every other genre, and no matter how many people mocked it, it's more popular now than it's ever been. The proof is right here in Mexico, where they've completely taken ownership of the music. I don't know whose it'll be next, but I'm excited to find out. It contains the same power it did twenty years ago, thirty years ago. Why do we love it so much? Why do we defend it? It's more than upbeats. It has a special place in our hearts because it so intrinsically captured us at a time when we were young, unpretentious and vulnerable. We loved ska wholly. We didn't care if anyone made fun of us. We laughed at them for missing out on this pure joy we were experiencing.

What got me the most about Mexico wasn't how the music evolved with their culture; it was how much it was the same. The suits. The horns. The dancing. The upbeats. The sheer happiness of the music. How much it means to them. How much it means to me. How we are all connected by this beat— this simple, beautiful beat.

BIBLIOGRAPHY

Books

Apter, Jeff. *Gwen Stefani & No Doubt: A Simple Kind of Life.* Omnibus Press, 2008

Augustyn, Heather. *Operation Jump Up: Jamaica's Campaign for a National Sound.* Half Pint Press, 2018

Augustyn, Heather. *Ska: An Oral History.* McFarland & Company Publisher, 2010

Augustyn, Heather. *Ska: The Rhythm of Liberation.* Scarecrow Press, 2013

Augustyn, Heather. *Songbirds: Pioneering Women in Jamaican Music.* Half Pint Press, 2014

Barnes, Richard. *Mods!* Plexus Books, 1979

Black, Pauline. *Black by Design: A 2-Tone Memoir.* Profile Books, 2011

Blush, Steven. *American Hardcore: A Tribal History.* Feral Housae, 2010

Bradley, Lloyd. *Bass Culture: When Reggae was King.* Penguin Books, 2001

Change, Jeff. *Can't Stop Won't Stop: A History of the Hip-Hop Generation.* St. Martin's Press, 2005

Costello, Elvis. *Unfaithful Music & Disappearing Ink.* Blue Rider Press, 2016

Edwards, Terry. *One Step Beyond...* Bloomsbury Publishing, 2009

Hebdige, Dick. *Cut 'n' Mix: Culture, Identity and Caribbean Music.* Routledge, 1987

Jensen, Keith Lowell. *Punching Nazis and other good ideas: Rants, Rages, and Reflections on Nazis and Punk Rock.* Skyhorse Publishing, 2018

Katz, David. *People Funny Boy: The Genius of Lee Scratch Perry.* Omnibus Press, 2006

Marshall, George. *The Two Tone Story.* S.T. Publishing, 1990

Narvas, Greg. *I Was a Teenage Filipino Skinhead,* Lefty Limbo, 2007

Panter, Horace. *Ska'd For Life: A Personal Journey with The Specials.* Pan Books, 2008

Potash, Chris. *Reggae, Rasta, Revolution: Jamaican Music from ska to dub.* Schirmer Books,

1997

Rachel, Daniel. *Walls Come Tumbling Down: Rock Against Racism, 2 Tone, Red Wedge.*

Picador, 2017

Reed, John. *House of Fun: The Story of Madness,* Omnibus Press, 2010

Staple, Neville. *Original Rude Boy: From Borstal to the Specials.* Aurum Press, 2010

Suggs. *That Close.* Quercus Editions Ltd, 2013

Walker, Klive. *Dubwise: Reasoning from the Reggae Underground,* Idiomatic, 2006

Williams, Paul. *You're Wondering Now: The Specials from Conception to Reunion.* Cherry Red

Books, 2010

Magazine, Newspapers & Online Magazines

Ali, Lorraine. "'Date Rape,' The Song, Stirs Much Debate," *LA Times,* April 22, 1995

Ali, Lorraine. "Fishbone: Give a Monkey a Brain and..." *LA Times,* May 30, 1993

Ali, Reyan. "Q&A: The Arrogant Sons of Bitches' Jeff Rosenstock on the Joys and Stigmas of

Ska, CBGB Misery and Pranky Vibes," *Village Voice,* May 25, 2012

Alvarez, Jimmy. "How The Untouchables Became SoCal Ska's Original Rude Boys," *OC*

Weekly, January 18, 2018

Alvarez, Jimmy. "Suburban Legends and Goldfinger are Still Riding High on Ska's 4th Wave,"

OC Weekly, August 31, 2018

Anthony, David. "Green Day got its Cred back, is no Longer Banned from 924 Gilman Street,"

AV Club, May 18, 2015

Arbuckle, Alex Q. "1970-1990 British Skinhead Portraits," *Mashable,* March 29, 2016

Argyrakis, Andy. "The Plea for Peace," *Phantom Tollbooth,* June 27, 2000

Aron, Nina Renata. "This 'White Power' Band has been the Soundtrack of Racist Punk for 40

Years," *Timeline,* August 23, 2017

Augusto, Troy J. "Lollapalooza '93," *Variety,* August 10, 1993

Baker, Jeff and Ruskin, Jessica. "Toaster," Rude Awakenings, Date Unknown

Bessman, Jim. "Relativity Goes After Higher Profile," *Billboard,* August 15, 1992

Bezer, Terry. "Modern Classics: Green Day – Insomniac," *One Louder,* July 25, 2014

Boilen, Bob. "Dan Deacon in Concert," *NPR,* May 17, 2009

Brown, Jake. "Ska is Dead," *Glorious Noise,* August 2, 2005

Clarke, S.P. "Hot Rock Erupts in Portland Under Volcanic Fallout of Mt. St. Helens," *Billboard,*

February 15, 1986

Cocking, Lauren. "Meet Mexico's Zapatista Rebels Fighting for Indigenous Rights," *Culture*

Trip, July 20, 2017

Colter, Aaron. "Can Pay-What-You-Want Downloads Save the Music Industry," *Digital Trends,*

March 14, 2012

Cowan, Peter. "The Jamaican 'Wailers': Fresh and Fun Sound," *Oakland Tribune,* October 20,

1973

Dawson, Mike. "Rasta Man Loves to Run," *Times Herald-Record,* June 12, 2005

De la Peza, Carmen. "Panteon Rococo: Mexican Ska and Collective Memory," *University of*

Rhode Island, March 9, 2010

Denselow, Robin. "Los de Abajo: Living la Vida Mexico," *Independent,* October 7, 2005

Dingerdissen, Matt. "Keeping Ska Alive on the Ska is Dead Tour," *Miami Hurricane,* March 2,

2004

Ferrara, Louis. "Interview: Mike Park of Asian Man Records and the Plea for Peace

Foundation," *Verbicide,* November 10, 2004

Fiasco, Lance. "Punk Bands Rock Out to Plea for Peace," *Idobi,* August 3, 2001

Fricke, David. "Chris Blackwell Remembers," *Rolling Stone,* March 10, 2005

Fricke, David. "Fishbone: Black and Bruised," *Rolling Stone,* October 31, 1991

Gamboa, Ana. "Panteon Rococo Celebrates 20 Years of Mexican Ska in Philly," *Al Dia,* October

12, 2015

Gibson, Caitlin. "A Disturbing New Glimpse at the Reagan Administration's Indiffference to

AIDS," *Washington Post,* December 1, 2015

Goldberg, Michael Alan. "Plea for Peace Tour 2004," *Phoenix New Times,* June 3, 2004

Green, Andrew James. "Activist Musicianship Sound, the 'Other Campaign,' and the Limits of

Public Space in Mexico City," *University of Glasgow,* March 30, 2018

Greenblatt, Leah. "Reaching for the Ska," *Entertainment Weekly,* April 2005

Hassan, Marcos. "This Instagram is an Archive of Rock en Espanol's Golden Years in Los

Angeles," *Remezcla,* May 9, 2018

Heath, Chris. "No Doubt: Inside the Tragic Kingdom," *Rolling Stone,* May 1997

Heim, Chris. "Special Beat: Out to Put Ska on the Map Again," *Chicago Tribune,* December 7,

1990

Heller, Jason. "From Discord to Lookout, Punk Record Labels Sparked Change in the '90s," *AV*

Club, March 11, 2014

Ibarra, Javier. "8 Discos Clasicos de Ska Mexa," *Vice,* November 5, 2018

Ibarra, Javier. "25 Anos de Ser Fuertes con la Sekta Core," *Vice,* February 20, 2019

Ibarra, Javier. "Inspector: Sus Nuevas Paginas en Blanco Dentro del Ska Mexicano," *Vice,*

January 25, 2018

Ibarra, Javier. "Non Stop Ska: Una Charla Sobre la Fiesta Mas Importante de Este Estilo Musical

en LATAM," *Vice,* February 13, 2018

Ibarra, Javier. Skins a la Mexicana," *Vice,* November 7, 2017

Ibarra, Javier. "Una Charla de Punk y Ska con Miguel Tajobase," *Vice,* January 15, 2019

Gold, Jonathan. "Fishbone's New Line: The Eclectic L.A. Funk Band Never Had Trouble

'Crossing Over' to a White Audience, but Now it Wants to Cross Back," *LA Times,* April

7, 1991

James, Ewin. "Edward Seaga – The Man Who Could Have Been Great," *Jamaica Observer,*

June 2, 2019

Jones, J.R. "Ska's Lost Cause," *Chicago Reader,* July 23, 1998

Katz, David. "Lloyd Brevett: Bassist with the Skatalites, Originators of Ska," *Independent,* May

4, 2012

Large, Victoria. "Ska's Third Wave," *Perfect Sound Forever,* September 2006

Lavin, Enrique. "Will Mainstream Say Si to Tijuana No?" *LA Times,* August 2, 1997

Lefebvre, Sam. "Did Punk Break? Green Day Played Gilman Last Night," *East Bay Express,*

May 18, 2015

Letts, Don. "Dem Crazy Baldheads are my Mates," *The Guardian,* October 23, 2001

Lieb, Kristin. "Hunt for 'Next Big Thing' Unearths Ska Underground," *Billboard,* January 15, 1994

Lin, Tao. "An Interview with Stza Crack of Leftover Crack & SFH," *Thought Catalog,* October

9, 2011

Lopez, Paco. "La Tremenda Korte Celebra 21 Anos de Mex-Ska," *Radial* 3.14, July 9, 2015

Majd, Hooman. "Chris Blackwell," *Interview*, March 17, 2009

Marks, Craig. "An American Family," *Spin*, December 1995

Marras, Vasiliki. "Plea for Peace Calls for Music Activism," *Daily Bruin*, May 19, 2004

Marsh, Ian & Frey, Jamie. "Latino Punk and Revolution: Skarroneros," *Brooklyn Rail*, February

2016

Martin, Michel. "Former PM Edward Seaga Heralds Jamaica's Music," *NPR*, December 27,

2012

Mason, Peter. "Edward Seaga Obituary," *Guardian*, May 28, 2019

McClean II, Dudley C. "History Will Judge Edward Seaga," *Jamaica Observer*, June 30, 2019

McCormick, Moira. "Chicago Retailers Have a lot of Jazz In-Store," *Billboard*, November 6,

1982

McDonough, Jack. "The Shakers," *Billboard*, August 9, 1975

Mighty Mighty Bosstones, "Mainstream Success and the Big Rig Records (1993-2001)," *Mighty*

Mighty Bosstones Official Website, Date unknown

Montgomery, James. "Killers' To-Do List: Lawsuit, Long-Form Video, Beef with The Bravery,"

MTV.com, March 28, 2005

Montgomery, James. "Ska-letons in the Closet," *Spin*, June 2005

Morris, Chris. "Black Crowes Uncover Their Roots," *Billboard*, June 15, 1996

Navarro, Eric. "Opinion: Streetlight Manifesto isn't Ska—They're Good," *Hard Times*,

November 12, 2018

Navarro, Eric. "The Term Skanking is Problematic and That's Not Even One of the Top 5

Reasons Ska is Dead," *Hard Times*, October 11, 2016

O'Conghaile, Niall, "Eric Clapton's Disgusting Racist Tirade," *Dangerous Minds*, July 3, 2011

Ontiveros, Homero. "El Ska: El Patito Feo de la Escena Nacional," *La Zona Sucia*, February 12,

2019

Ontiveros, Homero. "El Ska es Agricultura," *La Zona Sucia,* November 14, 2017

Ostrow, Adam. "Getty Images Acquires Pump Audio," Mashable, June 20, 2007

Ozzi, Dan. "Bomb The Music Industry is Dead (Probably, They're Not Sure but Yeah Whatever,

Probably), *Vice,* January 20, 2014

Ozzi, Dan. "Kill Cops: Leftover Crack's Scott Sturgeon and the 11-Year Itch," *Vice,* September

15, 2016

Padman, Tony. "Where Are They Now...? My Boy Lollipop Singer Millie Small," *Express,*

August 20, 2016

Palopoli, Steve. "Oingo Boingo Former Members Reunite for Dead Band's Party," Good Times,

September 24, 2019

Pareles, Jon. "Critics' Choices," *New York Times,* August 3, 1986

Partridge, Kenneth. "Remembering the Real Lessons of 2 Tone Ska," *Pitchfork,* August 27, 2015

Phillips, Ian. "How Oscar Isaac went from being a Ska Musician in Florida to a lead in 'Star

Wars: The Force Awakens,'" *Business Insider,* December 22, 2015

Popson, Tom. "Ska in the '90s: Is Something Going on out There?" *Chicago Tribune,* March 9,

1990

Preira Matt, "Leftover Crack's Stza on School Shootings: 'Our Government is Directly

Responsible for Worse,'" *Miami New Times,* December 28, 2012

Ramirez, Gloria Munoz. "Panteon Rococo: Somos un Reflejo de la Lucha Zapatista," *Des

Informemonos,* April 1, 2010

Reiss, Randy. "Ska Against Racism Tour Highlights Ska's Roots," *MTV.com,* April 1, 1998

Reyes, Don Rastone. "El Chopo y el Ska," *Planisferio,* October 11, 2016

Riccardi, Nicholas & Cardenas, Jose. "Freeway Slaying Victim was 'Caring, Dedicated,'" *LA

Times, October 22, 1997

Roberts, Chris. "The Great Eliminator: How Ronald Reagan Made Homelessness Permanent,"

SF Weekly, June 29, 2016

Rohter, Larry. "Rock en Espanol is Approaching its Final Border," *New York Times,* August 6,

2000

Rosen, Craig. "MCA Links With Green Day Mgrs. For (510) Label," *Billboard,* March 11, 1995

Rosenstock, Jeff. "The Arrogant Songs of Bitches," biography on *Punknews,* Date unknown

Rossignol, Derrick. "Star Wars' Oscar Isaac was in a Ska Band in the '90s," *Nerdist,* December

15, 2015

Sarachaga, Bertha Borrego. "Conferencia de Prensa: Non Stop Ska! Music Festival," *Melo*

Magazine, July 9, 2016

Schruers, Fred. "A Man of Wealth & Taste," *Rolling Stone,* February 18, 1999

Seelye, Katharine Q. "Edward Seaga, Who Led Jamaica on a Conservative Path, Dies at 89,"

New York Times, May 29, 2019

Selvin, Joel. "Ska's Roots in Jamaica," *SF Gate,* April 26, 1998

Shafer, Steve. "Duff Guide to Ska Fast Takes: The Toasters 'Ska-boom!' Reissue," *Duff Guide to*

Ska, January 5, 2017

Shafer, Steve. "Know Your Product: The Interrupters," *Duff Guide To Ska,* August 25, 2014

Shafer, Steve. "Let's Go Bowling's 'Music To Bowl By' Revisited," *Duff Guide to Ska,* March

22, 2017

Shafer, Steve. "Sean 'Cavo' Dinsmore of Unity 2," Unpublished interview for *Duff Guide to Ska,*

January 28, 2018

Shafer, Steve. "Shots in the Dark: The Toasters' 'New York Fever,'" *Duff Guide to Ska,* June 12,

2013

Shafer, Steve. "Ska in 365 Degrees," *Duff Guide to Ska,* March 5, 2010

Shafer, Steve. "Ska News," *Moon Records Skazette,* March 1995

Shafer, Steve. "What is Skavoovee?" *Moon Records Skazette,* October 1994

Shepard, Wade. "El Chopo Punk Market in Mexico City," *Vagabond Journey,* March 3, 2011

Siuta, Kris. "Interview: Fishbone," *The Pier,* January 18, 2012

Sokol, Tony. "Don Letts Talks Israelites, Trojan and the Roots of Reggae," *Den of Geeks,* July
10, 2018

Staff Writers. "10 Questions with Leftover Crack," *Riot Fest Website,* August 30, 2016

Staff Writers. "Atlantic Label Releases Hot on Jamaica Ska Discs," *Billboard,* May 23, 1964

Staff Writers. "Big Apple Blow Out," *Zoot,* 1990

Staff Writers. "How Skinheads Transformed From Inclusive Youth Into Racist Hate Group," *All
That's Interesting,* March 7, 2017

Staff Writers. "Man on the Moon?" *Skinhead Times,* August, 1993

Staff Writers. "Mr. Frightside," *NME,* April 6, 2005

Staff Writers. "Nurse Shot to Death on 60 Freeway," *LA Times,* October 21, 1997

Staff Writers. "Quienes Son los Skatos?" *Capital Mexico,* August 13, 2017

Staff Writers. "Ska Starts To Jump," *Billboard,* June 20, 1964

Staff Writers. "The 100 Best Songs of 2007," *Pitchfork,* December 17, 2007

Staff Writers. "The Top 200 Tracks of the 2000s," *Pitchfork,* August 21, 2009

Steinhoff, Jessica. "Dan Deacon is a Nerd's Nerd," *Isthmus,* May 1, 2009

Steininger, Alex. "Ska Against Racism," *In Music We Trust,* April 1998

Stewart, Shannon. "Turn the Beat Around: Youth, Art and Activism at 924 Gilman," *The Nation,*
November 2007

Stosuy, Brandon. "Dan Deacon's Old Ska Band," *Stereogum,* April 6, 2009

Strauss, Neil. "The Sound of New York: Ska. Ska? Yes, Ska," *New York Times,* October 27,
1995

Sykes, Tom. "Eric Clapton Apologizes for Racist Past. 'I Sabotaged Everything,'" *Daily Beast,*
January 12, 2018

Trinh, Jean. "Are SoCal Ska Legends Reel Big Fish and Save Ferris Opening the Door for a Ska
Revival?" *Thrillist,* January 11, 2017

Tucker, Maria Luisa & Rayman Graham. "The Police and the Punk Band Leftover Crack,"
Village Voice, September 17, 2008

Vare, Ethan Ann. "L.A's Untouchables Do it Themselves," *Billboard,* September 21, 1985

Vielma, Bob. "Never Say Goodbye: Joyce Manor's Barry Johnson Branches Out but Doesn't
Forget his Roots," *Phat 'n' Phunky,* January 16, 2019

Vineyard, Jennifer. "Ska Tour Fumbles Message," *LA Times,* April 7, 1998

Ward, Ed. "Doowop to the Reggae: True Love, Dope and Revolution," *Village Voice,* March 15,
1976

Warren, Mike. "Blue Riddim Band," *The Pitch,* August 29, 2002

Wasserman, Marc. "Ranking Roger & Blue Riddim Band Collaborate on 'Nancy Reagan' – The
Story Behind an Overlooked Protest Song of the '80s," *Rootfire,* March 7, 2016

Wasserman, Marc. "NYC Ska Live – American 'Dance Craze' Captures the NYC Ska Scene at
the Dawn of the '90s," *Marco on the Bass,* November 22, 2009

Wasserman, Marc. "Rob 'Bucket' Hingley of The Toasters Reflects on the Beginnings of the
NYC Ska Scene and the N.Y. Beat: Hit & Run Compilation," *Marco on the Bass,* March
12, 2010

Wasserman, Marc. "Terrorists – Late '70s New York City-based Punky Reggae Pre-dates 2-
Tone Explosion in the UK," *Marco on the Bass,* February 19, 2009

Wawzenek, Bryan. "25 Years Ago: No Doubt Go Against the Trends on Their Debut," *Diffuser*,
March 17, 2017
White, Timothy. "Higher Learning," *Billboard*, September 29, 2001
Williams, Wes. "This Chart Shows How Reaganomics Has Destroyed the Middle Class," *Daily Banter*, August 8, 2017
Wing, Eliza. "Small-Time Rockers on a Roll," *Rolling Stone*, September 26, 1985
Wolfe, A. "You Can't Ever Singer 'Don't Stop Believing' at Karaoke Because of This guy,"
Vice, October 16, 2012

Movies, TV, Radio and Podcasts

Abraham, Damian. *Turned Out a Punk*, "Episode 167 with Jesse Michaels," May 6, 2018
Abraham, Damian. *Turned Out a Punk*, "Episode 28 with Chris Hannah," May 20, 2015
Capaldi, Peter. *Punk Britannia*, BBC, 2012
Crow, Sara. *Never Get Tired: The Bomb The Music Industry Story*, No Future Films, 2015
Davies, Nicolas Jack. *Rudeboy: The Story of Trojan Records*, Pulse Films, 2018
Dunn, Geoffrey & Horne, Michael. *Calypso Dreams*, Major and Minor Productions, 2008
Hall, Gregory. *Impact: Songs That Changed the World. Bob Marley: I Shot the Sheriff*, Standing Room Only, 2007
Henzell, Perry. *The Harder They Come* (With Behind The Scenes Features), Syndctd Entertainment, 1972
Letts, Don. *The Don Letts Subculture Films – The Unique Story of British Music & Street Style*,
Hiphoper.com, 2013
Mann, Ron. *Twist*, Sphinx, 1992

Marre, Jeremy. *Classic Albums: Bob Marley and The Wailers 'Catch a Fire,'* Image

Entertainment, 2000

Metzler, Chris. *Everyday Sunshine: The Story of Fishbone,* Grindstone Media, 2011

Morden, Taylor. *Pick it Up! Ska in the '90s,* Popmotion Pictures 2019

Pettigrew, Jason. *Tomas Kalnoky Interviewed,* AP Show, 2008

Redford, Corbett. *Turn It Around: The Story of East Bay Punk* (Including unreleased scenes),

Abramorama, 2017

Turner, Ruby. *Reggae Britannia,* BBC, 2011

Uricky, Mark. *NPR Morning Edition,* "Couldn't Miss This One: Behind 'Christmas Wrapping,'"

2014

Winter, Sam. *Under The Influence: 2 Tone Ska,* Vice, 2015

IN DEFENSE OF SKA PHOTO DETAILS

Dedication page: Flat Planet unused press photo at Taco Bravo in Campbell, CA, 1996, courtesy of Aaron Carnes

Page xii: Flat Planet in the practice room in Gilroy, CA, 1994, photo credit: Aaron Carnes

Page xiii: Flat Planet at a show, somewhere in Texas, 1995, courtesy of Seth Blankenship

Page 2: The Selecter being interviewed backstage at the Lanchester Polytechnic in Coventry, UK, 1980, courtesy of Pauline Black

Page 3: The Specials' Lynval Golding on the 2 Tone tour at the Top Rank Club in Sheffield, 1979, photo credit: John Coles

Page 12: Graduate press photo at Kingswood school in Bath, UK, 1979, courtesy of John Baker

Page 13: Graduate press photo in a photograph studio in Bath, UK, 1979, courtesy of John Baker

Page 14: Barry Johnson's high school yearbook photo, 1998, courtesy of Barry Johnson

Page 18: Skankin Pickle is a Colorado ski lodge, photo credit: Kevin Dill

Page 20: Skankin Pickle in Lake Tahoe, 1994, photo credit: Kevin Dill

Page 21: Fan letter that Aaron Carnes sent Skankin Pickle in

1992, courtesy of Aaron Carnes

Page 22: Skankin' Pickle logo circa 1990

Page 24: Voodoo Glow Skulls on the Sno-Core tour, 1999, photo credit: Rick Bonde

Page 27: Old 924 Gilman flyer

Page 31: Skatune Network full band set at Fest at Downtown Fats, 2019, photo credit: Carolyn Ambriano

Page 32: We Are The Union meme circa 2019

Page 38: Flat Planet, somewhere in Truth Or Consequences, New Mexico, 1995, photo credit: Aaron Carnes

Page 40: Alex Rosario (Flat Planet) with Paul McKenzie (The Real McKenzies) in Albuquerque, New Mexico, 1995, photo credit: Aaron Carnes

Page 41: Rudy Sermeno (Flat Planet) in dented tour van, after hitting a deer somewhere in Texas, 1996, photo credit Aaron Carnes

Page 42: Flat Planet at a show, somewhere in Texas, 1995, courtesy of Seth Blankenship

Page 43: Flat Planet at a show, somewhere in Texas, 1995, courtesy of Seth Blankenship

Page 44: Old drawing of Flat Planet mascot "Junior." Drawing by Alex Rosario, 1994, courtesy of Aaron Carnes

Page 47: Flat Planet newsletter photo collage, 1995, courtesy of Aaron Carnes

Page 49: The Specials' Jerry Dammers on the 2 Tone Tour at the Top Rank Club in Sheffield, 1979, photo credit: John Coles

Page 53: Old flyer from 924 Gilman

Page 54: Operation Ivy at 924 Gilman in Berkeley, CA, 1988, photo credit Murray Bowles

Page 55: Operation Ivy at Barrington Hall in Berkeley, CA, 1989, photo credit: Murray Bowles

Page 63: Skankin' Pickle, courtesy of Mike Park

Page 65: Kamala Lynn Park in Oakland, CA, 1992, photo credit: Murray Bowles

Page 80: Reel Big Fish at Galaxy Theater in Santa Ana, CA, Turn The Radio Off release party, 1996, G. Scott Barrett

Page 81: Old Meal Ticket/Reel Big Fish flyer at the Nile in Mesa

Page 84: Gwen Stefani (No Doubt) hanging with Mike Mattingly (Skankin Pickle) in Anaheim, CA, 1991, photo credit: Kevin Dill

Page 88: Reel Big Fish on tour with Let's Go Bowling and Cherry Poppin Daddies, 1996, photo credit: G Scott Barrett

Page 91: Audience shot during a Less Than Jake show in Hawaii, 1999, photo credit: Rick Bonde

Page 95: The Aquabats, photo credit: Rick Bonde

Page 98: Old Let's Go Bowling for a show at Boston's in Tempe, AZ

Page 100: Let's Go Bowling "Rude 69" cover shot, behind '80s strip mall bowling lane, Rodeo Lanes in Clovis, CA, 1988, courtesy of Mark Michel

Page 103: Crazy 8s press photo, 1986, courtesy of Marc Baker, photo credit: Karen Moskowitz

Page 110: Early Uptones press photo, 1982, courtesy of Eric Din, photo credit: Rick Portis

Page 114: The Untouchables at The Roxy in Los Angeles, 1981, photo credit: Larissa Collins

Page 115: Chuck Askerneese and Jerry Miller of the Untouchables outside of Tower Records on the Sunset Strip at The Jam record signing, 1982, courtesy of The Untouchables

Page 121: Flyer for the Skalapolooza show in New York, 1993

Page 128: Old Fishbone photo, courtesy of Chris Dowd

Page 142: Slow Gherkin, during the *Run Screaming* recording sessions in Grizzly Studios in Peteluma, CA, 2002, courtesy of Slow Gherkin

Page 143: Slow Gherkin on tour in Japan, 2003, photo credit: Philip Boutelle

Page 147: Whole Lotta Milka, photo shoot for their album Al's Diner, 1999, courtesy of Greg Crowe, photo credit Rick Magnuson

Page 148: Whole Lotta Milka at Toronto, 1997, courtesy of Greg Crowe, photo credit: Lindsay Towns

Page 155: Heavy Manners press photo, 1982, courtesy of Kate Fagan Burgun

Page 158: Gangster Fun backstage at St. Andrews in Detroit, MI, 1990, photo credit: Stephen Rinaldi

Page 162: Blue Meanies photo taken for *Full Throttle*, 1997, courtesy of Michael Linde, photo credit: Erich Zander

Page 167: (L-R) Paul Chavez, Nos, Kevin Dill, Ryan "Shige" Kunimura, photo credit: Heather Lake

Page 169: Kevin Dill and his mom at the Trocedero in San Francisco, CA, 1994, photo credit: Aaron Carnes

Page 172: Kevin Dill, Aaron Carnes and Brian Carnes, 1995, courtesy of Aaron Carnes

Page 178: Bim Skala Bim at The Paradise in Boston, MA, record release show for *Live At The Paradise*, 1993, courtesy of Bim Skala Bim, photo credit: Lynette Estes

Page 179: Bim Skala Bim at the Ashby Mass Reggae Festival, 1984, courtesy of Bim Skala Bim, photo credit: Terri Vitale

Page 189: *Jamaica Gleaner* ad on how to do the ska, 1964, courtesy of *Jamaica Gleaner*

Page 191: Fishbone from the set of *Back to the Beach*, photo credit: Geoffrey Hales

Page 192: Fishbone on the set of *Back to the Beach*, photo credit: Geoffrey Hales

Page 196: One of Chris Candy's ska bands playing at a party in Los Angeles, 2003, photo credit: Rose Candy

Page 197: Chotto Ghetto at Bottom of the Hill at the Asian Man Records 15th anniversary show, 2011, photo credit: Leslie Hampton

Page 200: Flat Planet at the Edge in Palo Alto, CA, 1994, courtesy of Aaron Carnes

Page 201: Flat Planet on tour, 1995, photo credit: Aaron Carnes

Page 202: Mike Vianelle (Flat Planet) in Texas with random guy from punk show, 1995, photo credit: Aaron Carnes

Page 208: Greg Narvas and friend at Grand Central Station in Long Beach, CA, 1988, photo credit: Rich Carlstedt

Page 210: Philadelphia's rudies, skinheads and mod posse, photo credit: Mary Anne Powers

Page 210: More of Philadelphia's rudies, skinheads mod posse, photo credit: Mary Anne Powers

Page 212: First three issues of Greg Narvas' zine *I Was a Teenage Filipino Skinhead*, photo credit: Aaron Carnes

Page 215: Marcus Pacheco (bottom right) and the S.H.A.R.P. crew with Buster Bloodvessel after a Bad Manners show in New York City, 1989, courtesy of Marcus Pacheco

Page 216: Original S.H.A.R.P. logo, photo credit: Marcus Pacheco

Page 221: Hepcat in a Subway station on Hollywood Blvd, Los, Angeles, CA, 1993, photo credit: Piper Ferguson

Page 224: Skankin' Pickle in Lake Tahoe, photo credit: Kevin Dill

Page 230: MU330 at the Lambert International Airport in St. Louis, MO, 1999, photo credit: J.S. Carenza III

Page 233: Blue Riddim Band in the back of their Dodge Kary van somewhere in the Midwest, 1981, photo credit: John Andrew Myers

Page 235: Blue Riddim Band in an alley in Lawrence, Kansas, 1979, courtesy of Steve McClane

Page 239: The Shakers on the front steps at Elektra Sound Recorders in Hollywood during the *Yankee Reggae* recording sessions, 1975, photo credit: John Cuniberti

Page 246: Marcel Windrath and his massive 90s ska-punk collection, 2019, photo credit: Marcel Windrath

Page 248: 90s ska bootleg tape with Flat Planet songs on it, 2017, photo credit: Marcel Windrath

Page 251: Jeff Rosenstock and Arrogant Sons of Bitches heading to a show in West Virginia, 1999, photo credit: Mike Costa

Page 253: Jeff Rosenstock singing with Arrogant Sons of Bitches, 1998, courtesy of Mike Costa

Page 257: Arrogant Sons of Bitches playing outside the Truth bus on Warped Tour in St. Louis, MO, 2003, photo credit: Mike Costa

Page 265: Let's Go Bowling playing the Earth Day Ska Festival in Berkeley, CA, 1990, photo credit: Dion Garcia

Page 266: The Specials' Neville Staple on the 2 Tone tour at the Top Rank Club in Sheffield, 1979, photo credit: John Coles

Page 268: Mike Park (Skankin' Pickle), courtesy of Mike Park

Page 270: Skankin' Pickle, courtesy of Mike Park

Page 272: Mike Vianelle (Flat Planet) and Lynette Knackstedt (Skankin' Pickle), 1994, photo credit: Aaron Carnes

Page 277: Skacore Invasion in Los Angeles, CA, 2018, Photo credit Clemente Ruiz

Page 283: The Allen Theater, 2003, photo credit: Clemente Ruiz

Page 287: Flyer for big ska festival in Mexico in the 90s

Page 292: Skatlon Festival, 2019, photo credit: Aaron Carnes

Page 293: Alex Rosario and Aaron Carnes in Oaxaca Mexico, 2019, photo credit: Aaron Carnes

ACKNOWLEDGMENTS

It wouldn't have been possible to write *In Defense of Ska* without the help of the hundreds of people that donated their time in the form of interviews, information and honest—not always flattering—feedback. At the top of the list is my wife, Amy Bee, who edited the book for me twice in 2019, even canceling a backpacking trip on one occasion to help me unravel this gargantuan task of defending ska. And she doesn't even like ska! This is the greatest sacrifice she's made in the two decades we've been married.

I can't thank Christoph and Leza at CLASH enough for taking a chance on my weird hybrid piece of creative non-fiction. They also hate ska (I'm sensing a theme here). Yet they took a morbid interest in me defending this "indefensible" genre. In the end, they hate the genre slightly less, so I think I did my job. And if wasn't for that pesky pandemic, Christoph would have attended his first ever ska show in 2020. The Slackers. Not a bad first ska experience.

This book would have never been published were it not for author Jeff Burk. I reached out to him in 2018 since he was the only person I knew in the publishing industry that didn't hate ska. I asked if he knew anyone that would take an interest in my ska book idea. He pointed me in the direction of CLASH, failing to mention their hatred of the music, not that it mattered, apparently.

Clemente Ruiz helped me extraordinarily with the "Land of Ska" chapter. Not only was he a wealth of information about East LA's ska scene, but he connected me some fine folks in Mexico so that I could accurately report on their scene. And my good friend Alex Rosario, his presence on that trip to Oaxaca was a highlight of my 2019. He translated the interviews in Mexico and back at home during the transcription process. We had a blast together in Mexico.

I also need to thank Steve Shafer, former Moon Records workhorse. He read an early draft of the book and gave me a solid couple hours of super helpful feedback over the phone. He also connected me to several key interviews I needed. He was always willing to help, even if it was to respond to my countless emails, prying him for even more information.

And of course, thank you to Skankin' Pickle for making me a ska fan for life. The book only happened because your music changed me. I genuinely feel bad for people that never got to see Pickle live in concert. Life changing experience.

ABOUT THE AUTHOR

Picture by Amy Bee

Aaron Carnes is a music journalist based out of Sacramento, California. His work has appeared in *Playboy, Salon, Bandcamp Daily, Sierra Club, Noisey* and *Sun Magazine.* He's also the music editor at *Good Times Santa Cruz* weekly newspaper, where he tries to sneak in ska content whenever his boss isn't looking.

Aaron has been listening to ska since the early '90s. He used to play drums in a ska band. Now he just plays ska on his car stereo. When he's not defending ska, he enjoys backpacking with his wife Amy Bee, and talking about music from every existing genre.

Though ska will always be his favorite.

ALSO BY CLASH BOOKS

TRAGEDY QUEENS: STORIES INSPIRED BY LANA DEL REY & SYLVIA PLATH

Edited by Leza Cantoral

GIRL LIKE A BOMB

Autumn Christian

99 POEMS TO CURE WHATEVER'S WRONG WITH YOU OR CREATE THE PROBLEMS YOU NEED

Sam Pink

THIS BOOK IS BROUGHT TO YOU BY MY STUDENT LOANS

Megan J. Kaleita

THE NEW YORKER HATES MY CARTOONS

Kyle Owens

TRY NOT TO THINK BAD THOUGHTS

Art by Matthew Revert

LIFE OF THE PARTY

Tea Hacic-Vlahovic

THE ELVIS MACHINE

Kim Vodicka

DARRYL

Jackie Ess

CPSIA information can be obtained
at www.ICGtesting.com
Printed in the USA
BVHW081039290421
606129BV00004B/210

9 781944 866785